DOCTRINES
OF
SALVATION

Sermons and Writings of
JOSEPH FIELDING SMITH

Compiled by
BRUCE R. McCONKIE

VOLUME III

D0906013

BOOKCRAFT
SALT LAKE CITY, UTAH

Copyright
Bookcraft
1956

PREFACE

This third volume in the *Doctrines of Salvation* series gives pointed consideration to many of the most fascinating and little understood principles of the gospel.

In it President Joseph Fielding Smith points out the signs of the times, analyzes the prophecies relative to the Second Coming of our Lord, sets forth the events which will precede and attend that glorious day, and describes the conditions destined to prevail during the millennial era.

In addition he tells how priesthood and keys operate, explains the apostolic position, and reveals how the President of the Church is chosen and set apart. Light is thrown also on *Book of Mormon* geography, patriarchal blessings, world governments, the great apostasy, and many more vital subjects.

Paying tribute to him on the 80th anniversary of his birth (July 19, 1956), his associates in the Council of the Twelve published a message of love, greeting, and affection which included the following:

"President Joseph Fielding Smith has inherited in rich measure the dauntless courage and the unswerving devotion to duty which have characterized the lives of his noble ancestors. For more than forty-six years as a member of the Council of the Twelve he has been a fearless defender of the faith and an untiring preacher of the gospel of repentance. In his vigorous denunciation of the theories of men which would negate the truths of the restored gospel, he has often drawn the criticisms of some of the exponents of the theories he has assailed, but seldom has he failed to win the admiration and respect of his severest critics because of his scholarship and the consistency of his course, which is as undeviating as the stars of heaven. No one ever has had occasion to question where he stood on any controversial issue.

"... *In his profound gospel writings and in his
theological dissertations, he has given to his associates
and to the Church a rich legacy which will immortalize
his name among the faithful.*"[1]

The standard works excepted, probably more copies
of his books on gospel subjects have been sold than of
any other man in our dispensation. Total copies sold now
run to several hundred thousand.

Certainly none in our day has spoken or written with
greater plainness, or more spiritual insight, or with
greater ability to give living meaning to the mysteries
of the kingdom than has he.

This third volume of *Doctrines of Salvation*, containing as it does many doctrinal explanations not found
elsewhere in Latter-day Saint literature, warrants the
attentive consideration of gospel students everywhere.

As with previous volumes, I am grateful to many
people for help and counsel. Chief credit goes to President Smith, himself, for the great doctrinal contribution
of the work itself. Again also I am grateful to Elder
Oscar W. McConkie, my father, and to Elder Milton
R. Hunter of the First Council of Seventy, both of whom
have given much counsel and many helpful suggestions.
And again also Elder Joseph Fielding Smith, Jr., set the
type and made many valued suggestions; and Sister
Velma Harvey, my very able secretary, typed the host
of documents involved and gave painstaking attention
to proofreading and other details.

                                        —Bruce R. McConkie

Salt Lake City, Utah
July 19, 1956

---
[1]*Era*, vol. 59, p. 495.

CONTENTS

CHAPTER 12. A VOICE FROM CUMORAH

CHAPTER 13. ISRAEL: GOD'S COVENANT RACE

CHAPTER 14. THE APOSTATE WORLD

CHAPTER 15. APOSTASY FROM LATTER-DAY KINGDOM

CHAPTER 16. KINGDOMS OF THIS WORLD

CHAPTER 17. EXODUS OF MODERN ISRAEL

CHAPTER 18. MORMON PIONEERS AND COLONIZATION

VOLUME I CONTAINS THE FOLLOWING CHAPTERS:

VOLUME II CONTAINS THE FOLLOWING CHAPTERS:

Chapter 1

SIGNS PRECEDING SECOND COMING

WHEN WILL CHRIST COME?

SECOND COMING WILL BE TOMORROW. I was asked, not long ago, if I could tell when the Lord would come. I answered, Yes; and I answer, Yes, now. I know when he will come. He will come *tomorrow*. We have his word for it. Let me read it:

"Behold, *now it is called today until the coming of the Son of Man*, and verily it is a day of sacrifice, and a day for the tithing of my people; for he that is tithed shall not be burned at his coming." (Now there is a discourse sufficient on tithing.) "For *after today cometh the burning*—this is speaking after the manner of the Lord—for verily I say, *tomorrow all the proud and they that do wickedly shall be as stubble;* and I will burn them up, for I am the Lord of Hosts; and I will not spare any that remain in Babylon."[1]

So the Lord is coming, I say, *tomorrow*. Then let us be prepared. Elder Orson F. Whitney used to write about the *Saturday Evening of Time*. We are living in the Saturday Evening of Time. This is the 6th day now drawing to its close. When the Lord says it is today until his coming, that, I think, is what he has in mind, for *he shall come in the morning of the Sabbath, or seventh day* of the earth's temporal existence, to inaugurate the millennial reign and to take his rightful place as King of kings and Lord of lords, to rule and reign upon the earth, as it is his right.[2]

Satan has usurped power and authority from the beginning, and men have followed him, but his day is

---

[1] *D. & C.* 64:23-24; Mal. 3:2; 4:1. [2] *D. & C.* 77:12.

drawing to its close, and the day is dawning for Israel,
for Zion, for the universal establishment of truth, when
the earth shall be cleansed of all impurity, all wickedness,
for *when Christ comes that which is wicked cannot
remain.*[3]

DAY OF THE LORD IS NEAR.   I believe that *the
coming of the Son of God is not far away,* how far I do
not know, but I do know that it is over 100 years nearer
than it was when Elijah the prophet came to the Prophet
Joseph Smith and Oliver Cowdery in the Kirtland
Temple on the 3rd day of April, 1836. Elijah's words
point to the fact that we are that much nearer. And this
ancient prophet declared that by the restoration of those
keys we should know that *the great and dreadful day of
the Lord is near, even at our doors.*[4]

The world is rapidly coming to its end, that is, *the
end of the days of wickedness.*[5] *When it is fully ripe in
iniquity the Lord will come* in the clouds of heaven to take
vengeance on the ungodly, for his wrath is kindled
against them.[6] Do not think that he delayeth his coming.
Many of the signs of his coming have been given, so we
may, if we will, know that the day is even now at our
doors.[7]

SOME NOW LIVING MAY SEE SECOND COMING.   The
day of the coming of the Lord is near. I do not know
when. I am not looking, however, upon the coming of
the Son of Man as I looked once upon the day when men
would speak from city to city and throughout the land
without the aid of wires, and would be heard—as something that may come in some far distant time—because
*I sincerely believe it will come in the very day when some
of us who are here today* [April 5, 1936] *will be living
upon the face of the earth.* That day is close at hand.

[3]Conf. Rep., Apr., 1935, p. 98; *D. & C.*
   1:4-16.
[4]Conf. Rep., Apr., 1951, p. 58; *D. & C.*
   110:13-16.
[5]Jos. Smith 1:4.
[6]2 Thess. 1:7-9; *D. & C.* 29:17.
[7]*Era.* vol. 34, p. 644.

It behooves us as Latter-day Saints to set our houses in order, to keep the commandments of God, to turn from evil to righteousness, if it is necessary, and serve the Lord in humility and faith and prayer.[8]

CHRIST WILL COME IN DAY OF WICKEDNESS. *When we become ripe in iniquity, then the Lord will come.* I get annoyed sometimes at some of our elders who when speaking say the Lord will come when we all become righteous enough to receive him. *The Lord is not going to wait for us to get righteous.* When he gets ready to come, he is going to come—*when the cup of iniquity is full*—and if we are not righteous then, it will be just too bad for us, for we will be classed among the ungodly, and we will be as stubble to be swept off the face of the earth, for the Lord says wickedness shall not stand.[9]

Do not think the Lord delays his coming, for *he will come at the appointed time,* not the time which I have heard some preach when the earth becomes righteous enough to receive him. I have heard some men in positions and places of trust in the Church preach this, men who are supposed to be acquainted with the word of the Lord, but they failed to comprehend the scriptures. *Christ will come in the day of wickedness,* when the earth is ripe in iniquity and prepared for the cleansing, and as the cleanser and purifier he will come, and all the wicked will be as stubble and will be consumed.[10]

GOSPEL WARNING PRECEDES SECOND COMING

WARNING VOICE ALWAYS PRECEDES JUDGMENTS. Would it not be an extraordinarily strange thing if the Lord should come and begin his reign of peace—take vengeance on the wicked, cleanse the earth from sin—and not send *messengers to prepare the way before him?*

[8]Conf. Rep., Apr., 1936, pp. 75-76.
[9]*Church News,* May 4, 1935, p. 8.
[10]*Church News,* Nov. 29, 1941, p. 4; Isa. 65:17-25; Mal. 4; *D. & C.* 101:11-31; 133:63-74.

Should we expect the Lord to come to judge the world without first giving it warning and preparing the means of escape for all who will repent?

Noah was sent to the world to warn it of the flood. If the people had hearkened, they would have escaped.[11] Moses was sent to lead Israel into the promised land to fulfil the promises made to Abraham.[12] John the Baptist was sent to prepare the way for the coming of Christ.[13] In each instance the call came through the opening of the heavens. Isaiah, Jeremiah, and other prophets were sent to warn Israel and Judah before the scattering and captivity came upon them.[14] Had they given heed a different page of history would have been written. They had their chance to hear; they were warned and had the means of escape which they rejected.

GOSPEL WITNESS PRECEDES SECOND COMING. The Lord promised to have the same interest in humanity preceding his second coming. Said he: *"And this gospel of the kingdom shall be preached in all the world for a witness unto all nations; and then shall the end come."*[15] Again: "And he shall send his angels with a great sound of a trumpet, and they shall gather together his elect from the four winds, from one end of heaven to the other."[16]

John on Patmos saw in vision in the *last days* an "angel fly in the midst of heaven, having the *everlasting gospel* to preach unto them that dwell on the earth, and to every nation, and kindred, and tongue and people."[17]

Joseph Smith declared that Moroni—an ancient prophet on this continent, and now resurrected—in partial fulfilment of this promise, taught him the gospel, giving him instruction in relation to the restoration of things preceding the coming of Christ.[18] And the Lord

[11]Moses 8:22-29.
[12]2 Ne. 3:9-10; Moses 1:25-26; Abra. 2:8-11; Gen. 15:7-21.
[13]1 Ne. 10:7-10; Isa. 40:3; Matt. 3:1-10; Mark 1:2-8; Luke 3:2-17.
[14]Isa. 28:1-8; 29:1-10; 30:1-17; Jer. 2; 4; 5; 6; 7; 8; 9; 15.
[15]Matt. 24:14; Jos. Smith 1:31.
[16]Matt. 24:31.
[17]Rev. 14:6.
[18]Jos. Smith 2:29-54.

said: "For behold, the Lord God hath sent forth the angel crying through the midst of heaven, saying: Prepare ye the way of the Lord, and make his paths straight, for the hour of his coming is nigh."[19]

Accepting this as true, Latter-day Saints believe that communication has been established with the heavens in modern times, and now *the gospel of the kingdom is sent out as a witness to the world before Christ shall come.*[20]

APOSTATE CHRISTIANITY CARRIES NO WARNING OF SECOND COMING. It is well understood that the teachings of the so-called Christian churches have been declared in all the world for many hundreds of years. In all lands churches have been organized and ministers have proclaimed their teachings. *There is nothing peculiar about their message in relation to the present age* —nothing distinctive which would mark any one or all of them as having the special declaration of the gospel of the kingdom which was promised as a witness in the latter days.

The implication in these words of our Lord—that "this gospel of the kingdom shall be preached in all the world for a witness unto all nations; and *then* shall the end come"[21]—the implication is that in the *last days* the Lord would give as a *sign* to all nations the sending *anew* of the message of the gospel of the kingdom and that it would be *different* from the teachings then being taught and received among the nations. *Otherwise how could it be distinguished and accepted as a sign of his second coming?*

Moreover, when this declaration of the gospel of the kingdom should reach all nations, *then should the end come,* or in other words, the time for the appearance of our Lord. *The preaching of the many doctrines of the*

---

[19]*D. & C.* 133:17.   [21]Matt. 24:14.
[20]*Church News,* June 6, 1931, p. 8;
    D. & C. 133:36-52.

various denominations was carried to all nations many long years ago, but the end did not come with this universal declaration.

RESTORED GOSPEL WARNS THE WORLD. Joseph Smith and his associates were taught by heavenly messengers and by revelation that the burden of this message was upon them. They were instructed that the Church of Jesus Christ of Latter-day Saints was duly appointed to send forth ambassadors for Christ with the special message of this gospel of the kingdom to all nations. The Lord said in this connection: "And the voice of warning shall be unto all people, by the mouths of my disciples, whom I have chosen in these last days. And they shall go forth and none shall stay them, for I the Lord have commanded them."[22]

The Latter-day Saints may be considered strange and peculiar in believing that they have been called upon to fulfil this ancient scripture, but it is with full confidence that the Lord has spoken that they are diligently sending missionaries into all parts of the earth. Moreover, *when all nations have heard this message, as it has been revealed in these last days, then may we look forth for the coming of our Lord and Savior Jesus Christ,* for at that day all nations will have been warned by the messengers who were sent unto them according to the Lord's promise.[23]

MODERN INVENTIONS AID IN RAISING WARNING VOICE. This work of preaching the gospel to the nations has not yet been finished. The missionaries of the Church are now going out with this message, but the Lord has said he would cut short his work in righteousness,[24] moreover that he would hasten it in its time.[25] By means of modern invention and discovery we can readily see how this may be accomplished, and the hearts of the people of the earth be reached by radio, through the press, and

[22]*D. & C.* 1:4-5.   [24]*D. & C.* 52:11; 84:96-97; 109:59.
[23]*Church News,* Nov. 7, 1931, p. 6.   [25]*D. & C.* 88:73.

by communication such as the nations of the earth did not have in former times. I do not know how long it will be before this mission shall be accomplished and these words of our Lord and Savior Jesus Christ shall be fulfilled, but that he will work *speedily*, that he will accomplish his purposes within the time that he has set, I fully believe, and his promises shall not fail.[26]

DISASTERS FOLLOW REJECTION OF GOSPEL WARNING. From time to time, someone filled with hatred of the truth, in the blind desire to destroy the work of the Lord, appeals to the nations to cast out the elders of Israel who are carrying this message of salvation unto all who will believe, and warning others that they may be left without excuse.

It would be a sorry day for any nation, where the gospel is being preached, should it conclude to drive the elders of the Church from its borders and deny them the right to preach the gospel among the people. *The elders insure peace unto the nations,* so long as they will hear the message of salvation and will protect and defend the truth. When the time comes that the nations will cast the elders out and no longer receive their testimony, but "bow to Satan's thrall," as we heard in the anthem this afternoon, woe be unto them.

We read in the word of the Lord that *after* the testimony of the elders will come wrath and indignation upon the people. For after their testimony will come the testimony of earthquakes that shall cause suffering and sorrow, and men shall fall upon the ground for fear. There shall come also the testimony of thunderings, and the voice of lightnings, and the voice of tempests, and the voice of the waves of the sea heaving themselves beyond their bounds. All things shall be in commotion, and men's hearts shall fail them because of fear that shall come upon the people. These things shall *follow* the testimony of the elders of the Church of Jesus Christ of

[26]*Church News,* Jan. 7, 1933, p. 5.

Latter-day Saints, when the people of the world reject them and drive them from their borders.[27]

GOSPEL ACCEPTANCE BEFORE SECOND COMING

"TIMES OF GENTILES" TO BE FULFILLED. We go unto them with a message of peace, of truth, of eternal salvation, calling upon them to repent of their sins and enter into the true fold, where they may receive rest. When they will not do this, but to the contrary, will listen to the unrighteous and condemn the truth, then God will withdraw the gospel from among them. *In that day the times of the Gentiles will be fulfilled and the gospel will be carried to the Jews.*[28] For, this gospel must be preached to them as well as to the Gentile nations; and a remnant of the Jews will gather—as they are gathering since the dedication of their land for their return—in Palestine, and as a remnant of Ephraim and his fellows are now gathering to the land of Zion.

JEWS TO BE CONVERTED AT SECOND COMING. The Jews in due time will be established in their own land, and the Lord will come, according to his promise, unto his people in the hour of their distress and will deliver them from their enemies. Then will they look upon him and discover his wounds and shall say: "What are these wounds in thine hands?" And he shall answer them: "Those with which I was wounded in the house of my friends." Then will they fall down and worship him as their Redeemer—the Son of God.[29] *After that they will be cleansed of their sins and shall receive the gospel.*[30]

And the nations that seek to destroy Jerusalem in that day will the Lord destroy, for he shall be King over all the earth, and righteousness shall prevail among the people.[31] Zion shall be established on this continent; Jerusalem will be re-established on the old continent, and

---

[27]D. & C. 88:86-95.
[28]D. & C. 45:21-30; Rom. 11:25; Luke 21:24; *Inspired Version*, Luke 21:25, 32.
[29]Zech. 12:8-14; 13:6; *D. & C.* 45:47-53.
[30]D. & C. 133:35.
[31]Zech. 14.

wickedness will depart from the earth, for when Christ comes and the righteous with him, the wicked will be as stubble and will be consumed.[32]

Therefore, I desire to bear my testimony unto all people and say unto those who raise their hands against this work, See that you do it not, for this is the work of God. He has established it, and when you reject it, you reject him, and after the testimony of the elders will come the testimony of trouble and distress as the prophets have predicted.[33]

JEWS TO BEGIN TO BELIEVE BEFORE SECOND COMING. Not many of the Jews, I take it from my reading of the scriptures, will believe in Christ before he comes. The *Book of Mormon* tells us that they shall *begin* to believe in him.[34] They are now *beginning* to believe in him. The Jews today look upon Christ as a great Rabbi. They have accepted him as one of their great teachers; they have said that, "He is Jew of Jew, the greatest Rabbi of them all," as one has stated it. When the gospel was restored in 1830, if a Jew had mentioned the name of Christ in one of the synagogues, he would have been rebuked. Had a rabbi referred to him, the congregation would have arisen and left the building. And so, we see the sentiment has changed. Now I state this on Jewish authority that they are beginning to believe in Christ, and some of them are accepting the gospel.

But in the main they will gather to Jerusalem in their unbelief; the gospel will be preached to them; some of them will believe. Not all of the Gentiles have believed when the gospel has been proclaimed to them, but the great body of the Jews who are there assembled will not receive Christ as their Redeemer until he comes himself and makes himself manifest unto them.[35]

[32]D. & C. 133:63-74.
[33]Conf. Rep., Apr., 1911, pp. 124-126.

[34]2 Ne. 30:7-18; 1 Ne. 10:11-14; 22:11-12; 2 Ne. 6:10-18; 9:1-2; 10:5-9; 25:16-18; 3 Ne. 20:29-46; Morm. 5:14.
[35]*Gen. & Hist. Mag.*, vol. 14, pp. 4-5.

WHERE LORD WILL FIND FAITH AT HIS COMING.
I can testify that when the Lord will come, he will find
faith upon the earth.[36] That faith, however, which he will
find, shall be *limited to a very small portion of the inhabitants of the earth.* He will not find faith in the nations
abroad to any noticeable extent; he will not find faith
among the peoples of the earth who have not received
the gospel as it has been restored. But there will be faith
among those of the house of Israel who have been gathered out from the nations and who have repented of
their sins and received the message that came through
the Prophet Joseph Smith.[37]

JOSEPH SMITH: MESSENGER BEFORE THE LORD

MESSENGER TO PREPARE WAY FOR SECOND
COMING. One of the quotations given to Joseph Smith
by Moroni, September 21, 1823, was the following:
"Behold, *I will send my messenger, and he shall prepare
the way before me: and the Lord, whom ye seek, shall
suddenly come to his temple,* even the messenger of the
covenant, whom ye delight in: behold, he shall come, saith
the Lord of hosts."[38]

In quoting the words of Malachi to Joseph Smith the
Angel Moroni also said that these words were shortly to
be fulfilled: *"But who may abide the day of his [Christ's]
coming? and who shall stand when he appeareth? for he
is like a refiner's fire, and like fullers' soap:* And he shall
sit as a *refiner* and *purifier* of silver: and he shall *purify*
the sons of Levi, and purge them as gold and silver, that
they may offer unto the Lord an offering in righteousness.
Then shall the offering of Judah and Jerusalem be pleasant unto the Lord, as in the days of old, and as in former
years.

"And *I [Christ] will come near to you to judgment;*

36Luke 18:8.   38*Church News*, Sept. 12, 1931, p. 2;
37Conf. Rep., Oct., 1916, p. 68;   Mal. 3:1; Jos. Smith 2:36.
   D. & C. 1:17-21.

and I will be a swift witness against the sorcerers, and against the adulterers, and against false swearers, and against those that oppress the hireling in his wages, the widow, and the fatherless, and that turn aside the stranger from his right, and fear not me, saith the Lord of hosts."[39]

SECOND COMING A DAY OF VENGEANCE AND JUDGMENT. In believing that this has reference to the second coming of Christ the Latter-day Saints stand in a peculiar position among all people, for it is the general belief that this had fulfilment in the first coming of Christ. If we investigate the matter, however, it is made very clear that in the days of the ministry of the Redeemer of the world, he did not come in *judgment* and to *purify* in the crucible so that all dross should be *destroyed*. In that day he was abused and persecuted and denied by men. The widow and the fatherless were not given justice against those who oppressed them. Sorcerers and adulterers were not punished, and all men were able to abide that day.

But, when Christ comes the second time it will be in the clouds of heaven, and it shall be *the day of vengeance against the ungodly,* when those who have loved wickedness and have been guilty of transgression and rebellion against the laws of God will be destroyed. All during the ministry of Christ wickedness ruled and seemed to prevail, but when he comes in the clouds of glory as it is declared in this message of Malachi to the world, and which was said by Moroni to be near at hand, then Christ will appear as the *refiner* and *purifier* of both man and beast and all that pertains to this earth, for the earth itself shall undergo a change and receive its former *paradisiacal glory.*[40]

JOSEPH SMITH PREPARED WAY FOR RETURN OF LORD. *Joseph Smith was sent to prepare the way for this second coming, by the proclamation of the fulness of the*

---

[39]Mal. 3:2-5; Jos. Smith 2:36.   [40]D. & C. 101:23-31; Isa. 65:17-25.

gospel and the granting to all men the means of escape
from iniquity and transgression. The fulfilment of this
prophecy by Malachi is even now at our doors, and before
many years have passed away Christ shall come as the
refiner and purifier of this earth which today is suffering
in the throes of lawlessness and transgression.

When that day comes, then all that is evil shall be
removed, and the words of the Lord shall be fulfilled
wherein he has said: "I have trodden the winepress alone:
and of the people there was none with me: for I will
tread them in mine anger, and trample them in my fury;
and their blood shall be sprinkled upon my garments, and
I will stain all my raiment. For the day of vengeance
is in mine heart, and the year of my redeemed is come."[41]

In this day messengers of the Lord have been sent.
John the Baptist came to Joseph Smith and Oliver Cowdery and gave them his priesthood, *thus preparing the
way for the coming of the Lord.*[42] Moreover, *the Lord
has come suddenly to his temple* and in it ministered to
Joseph Smith and Oliver Cowdery, April 3, 1836. In
that temple *Joseph and Oliver received authority for the
purging of the sons of Levi, and for the gathering of the
Jews* so that eventually their offerings may be *pleasant*
before the Lord, when they return to their land and are
forgiven for their transgressions.[43]

LORD HAS "SUDDENLY COME TO HIS TEMPLE."
Malachi said the Lord would suddenly come to his
temple.[44] In 1830 our Savior said he would come suddenly to his temple.[45] That coming was for a definite
purpose: To restore keys; to purge the sons of Levi; to
prepare for the offering of Judah when the Jews will be
cleansed of their iniquity; and to be as a refiner and purifier, bringing salvation to all men who will obey his voice.

It is true that many even of the Latter-day Saints

[41]*Church News*, Sept. 19, 1931, p. 6;
    Isa. 63:3-4; D. & C. 133:50-51, 63-
    64.
[42]D. & C. 13; Jos. Smith 2:68-72.
[43]*Church News*, Sept. 12, 1931, p. 2;
    D. & C. 110:1-16.
[44]Mal. 3:1.
[45]D. & C. 36:8.

are looking forth to that coming of our Lord. Let us stop
and reflect a moment. Has the Lord not come already
suddenly to his temple to bring about these glorious
purposes? *Christ appeared suddenly in this temple.* Then
he sent Moses with the keys for the gathering of Israel.
*Since Moses established Aaron and the Levites in their
priesthood, do not these keys also confer the power in
this dispensation for the purging of Levi and Judah that
they may offer an offering in righteousness?*

Do not the keys held by Elias confer all that was
held by Abraham? Do not the keys held by Elijah grant
to the Church all the power of sealing authority? Is it
not a fact that either in this temple, or in some other consecrated spot, all the keys of all the prophets since the
world began have now been revealed and restored to
earth for the *complete consummation of the work of the
Lord? Is not the great and dreadful day of the Lord very
near our doors? What else by way of authority for the
salvation of man is to be revealed? Is not the fulness of
the gospel here?*[46]

COMING OF CHRIST AT ADAM-ONDI-AHMAN. Dan-
iel speaks of the coming of Christ, and that day is near
at hand. There will be a great gathering in the Valley
of Adam-ondi-Ahman; there will be a great council held.
The Ancient of Days, who is Adam, will sit. The judgment—not the final judgment—will be held, where *the
righteous who have held keys will make their reports and
deliver up their keys and ministry.* Christ will come, and
Adam will make his report. *At this council Christ will
be received and acknowledged as the rightful ruler of
the earth.* Satan will be replaced.[47] Following this event
every government in the world, including the United
States, will have to become part of the government of

---

[46]*Era,* vol. 39, p. 208; Mal. 3:1-5;
  D. & C. 110:1-16.

[47]Dan. 7:9-14, 21-27; 12:1-3; *D. & C.*
  27:11; 78:15-16; 107:53-57; 116;
  117:8, 11; Joseph Fielding Smith,
  *Teachings of the Prophet Joseph
  Smith,* pp. 122, 158.

God.[48] Then righteous rule will be established. The earth will be cleansed; the wicked will be destroyed; and the reign of peace will be ushered in.[49]

Now we are looking forward to that time. We are hoping for it; we are praying for it. *The righteous will rejoice when he comes,* because then peace will come to the earth, righteousness to the people, and that same spirit of peace and joy and happiness which prevailed upon this continent for 200 years among the Nephites shall again be established among the people and eventually shall become universal, and Christ shall reign as Lord of lords and King of kings for 1,000 years. We are looking forward to that time.[50]

THE LAST DAYS

WHAT IS MEANT BY THE LAST DAYS. The Lord has declared, by his own voice and by revelation to his servants, the prophets, that we are living in the *last days.*[51] When we speak of the last days, we do not mean that this is the end of the earth, that it shall cease presently to exist. We mean that we are living in *that period of time known as the dispensation of the fulness of times,* in which the Father has promised to gather all things together in Christ, both which are in heaven and which are on earth.[52] We mean we are living in the day when unrighteousness shall cease, when wickedness shall no longer be found on the face of the earth, when this earth shall be turned over, according to the promise the Lord made to Daniel the Prophet, to the saints of the Most High, who shall possess it forever and ever.[53]

PERILOUS NATURE OF LAST DAYS. We are living in a critical period of the world's history. Great events

---

[48]D. & C. 87:6.
[49]Pers. Corresp.
[50]Church News, Feb. 6, 1932, p. 8.
[51]D. & C. 1:4; 20:1; 27:6; 39:11; 63:58;
  84:2, 117; 86:4; 112:30; 115:4;
  132:7.

[52]Eph. 1:9-10; D. & C. 27:12-13.
[53]Millennial Star, vol. 93, p. 241; Dan.
  7:22, 26-27.

are before us. The Lord in his mercy, and with justice
and judgment, is going to cut short his work in righteousness.[54] The decrees have gone forth, and it behooves us
as members of the Church to be united and to serve him
and keep all his commandments.[55]

We are living in a day of trouble, of tribulation,
when men's hearts are failing them. The Lord pointed
out this day while in his ministry and admonished by
prophecy those living now to watch and pray, that they
might not be led astray, that they might not be found
unprepared, should they be so fortunate as to be here
at the great day of his coming.[56]

We are living in perilous times, in a day when *the
mission of the Church is* perhaps *more pronounced,* and
our message to the world more clearly defined, than ever
before. As a people we stand as witnesses for Christ
in a day when the world has turned from him, when they
are teaching the doctrines of men and discarding the
fundamental truths of the Christian faith.[57]

HARVEST OF THE WHEAT: BURNING OF THE TARES.
The parable the Lord taught of the wheat and the tares
had reference to the *last days.* According to the story a
sower planted good seed in his field, but while he slept
the enemy came and sowed tares in the field. When the
blades began to show, the servants desired to go and
pluck up the tares, but the Lord commanded them to let
both the wheat and the tares grow up together until the
harvest was ripe, lest they root up the tender wheat while
destroying the tares. Then at the end of the harvest,
they were to go forth and gather the wheat and bind
the tares to be burned. In the explanation of this parable,
the Lord said to his disciples that *"the harvest is the end
of the world; and the reapers are the angels."*[58]

The tares and the wheat are growing together and

---

[54]*D. & C.* 52:11; 84:97.
[55]Conf. Rep., Oct., 1919, p. 146.
[56]Conf. Rep., Apr., 1931, p. 68; Luke
21:25-26.

[57]Conf. Rep., Apr., 1924, p. 40.
[58]*Church News,* Aug. 2, 1941, p. 2;
Matt. 13:24-30, 36-43; *D. & C.* 86:1-
11.

have been growing in the same field for all these years, but the day is near at hand when the wheat will be garnered, and the tares likewise will be gathered to be burned, and there will come a separation, the righteous from the wicked. And it behooves each one of us to keep the commandments of the Lord, to repent of our sins, to turn unto righteousness, if there is need of repentance in our hearts.[59]

IMMINENT SEPARATION OF RIGHTEOUS AND WICKED. The tares are being bound in bundles to be burned. The wheat is being garnered into barns, and *the day of separation is near at hand. Even the Church shall be cleansed, and those who are of the world, who are numbered among the members of the Church, will be cast out,* and will find their place among those who are unworthy, where there shall be wailing and gnashing of teeth.[60]

Build up and strengthen the members of the Church in faith in God; goodness knows we need it. There are so many influences at work to divide us asunder, right among the members of the Church, and *there is going to come, one of these days in the near future, a separation of the wheat from the tares, and we are either wheat or tares.* We are going to be on one side or the other.[61]

The time will come, just as sure as we live, that *there will be a separation between the righteous and the unrighteous.*[62] *Those who will not keep the law of the Lord will deny the faith, for he will withdraw his Spirit from them if they do not repent,* after laboring with them and doing all that is possible to keep them in the line of duty. He will withdraw his Spirit from them and they will be left unto themselves. They must take one side or the other, for this separation must surely come.[63]

[59]Conf. Rep., Apr., 1918, pp. 156-157.
[60]Conf. Rep., Oct., 1922, p. 75; D. & C. 121:23-26.
[61]Rel. Soc. Mag., vol. 18, p. 688.
[62]D. & C. 63:54.
[63]Conf. Rep., Apr., 1911, p. 87.

ANGELS NOW REAPING THE EARTH. "Verily I say unto you, ye are clean, but not all; and there is none else with whom I am well pleased." That was said of the Church over 100 years ago. The Lord is not pleased with us today, for we are not clean, all of us. "For all flesh is corrupted before me; and the powers of darkness prevail upon the earth, among the children of men, in the presence of all the hosts of heaven—Which causeth silence to reign, and all eternity is pained, and *the angels are waiting the great command to reap down the earth, to gather the tares that they may be burned;* and, behold, the enemy is combined."[64]

That revelation was given January 2, 1831, and in that day the Lord said that all flesh was corrupt before him. What did he say about all flesh in the days of Noah?[65] *Do you think the world has improved?* If you do, you have not read very carefully these scriptures. So the angels were waiting, 100 years ago, to go forth to bind the tares and reap down the earth.

President Wilford Woodruff declared by revelation, after the dedication of the Salt Lake Temple, that the angels spoken of here, who were waiting to go forth to bind the tares and to reap down the earth, had been loosed and sent on their mission.[66]

You will remember in the parable of the tares the Lord said to his servants that they were not to disturb the tares, lest in rooting them up they would root up the wheat also, because the blade was tender. Let both, he said, remain until the harvest is fully ripe. Then he tells us that that harvest was to come at the end of the world.[67]

As far back as 1893 the prophet of the Lord, President Wilford Woodruff, declared that the angels had been sent out to bind the tares and to prepare the earth

---

[64]*D. & C.* 38:10-12.
[65]Moses 8:28-30; Gen. 6:11-13.
[66]G. Homer Durham, *Discourses of Wilford Woodruff,* pp. 251-252.
[67]Matt. 13:24-30, 36-43; *D. & C.* 86:1-11.

for the burning; and yet the burning is not to come until
the earth is ripe in iniquity.[68]

REBELLIOUS TO BE CUT OFF AT SECOND COMING.
The 22nd and 23rd verses of the 3rd chapter of Acts
have reference to Christ and are yet to be fulfilled. They
are as follows: "For Moses truly said unto the fathers,
A prophet shall the Lord your God raise up unto you of
your brethren, like unto me; him shall ye hear in all things
whatsoever he shall say unto you. And it shall come to
pass, that every soul, which will not hear that prophet,
shall be destroyed from among the people."[69]

This is in keeping with the expression in the first
section of the *Doctrine and Covenants* that "the day
cometh that they who will not hear the voice of the Lord,
neither the voice of his servants, neither give heed to the
words of the prophets and apostles, shall be cut off from
among the people."[70]

This prophet of whom Moses spoke is Christ, and
when he sees fit to speak and to give commandments unto
the people, with the power and force with which it shall
be given at some future time, not only will the members
of the Church be removed who refuse to hear, but his
judgments shall go forth upon the nations and upon the
ungodly among them, who shall perish, and *that day is
near at hand.*[71]

---

[68]*Church News*, May 8, 1937, p. 5.   [70]*D. & C.* 1:14.
[69]Jos. Smith 2:40; 3 Ne. 20:23.   [71]*Gen. & Hist. Mag.*, vol. 14, p. 5.

CHAPTER 2

SIGNS OF THE TIMES

TURMOIL AND CALAMITIES OF LAST DAYS

PROPHETS FORETOLD LATTER-DAY CALAMITIES. *The distress and perplexity, bloodshed and terror, selfish ambition of despotic rulers, such as the world has never before seen, all indicate that the great and dreadful day of the Lord is very near, even at our doors.* We have been warned by the prophets from the beginning of time. They have declared, by revelation from the Lord, that *in this present day, confusion, bloodshed, misery, plague, famine, earthquake, and other calamities, would cover the face of the earth.*[1] The Lord told his disciples of these dreadful scenes and said men's hearts would fail them because of these things coming upon the earth.[2] . . .

It is very evident from what we see daily in the papers that we are living in perilous times. The present condition of the world should not, however, cause us any great surprise, for we have been amply informed that these days are at hand. Only the unbelieving and rebellious against the teachings of our Lord and his prophets have failed to comprehend these momentous events. . . .

ENOCH SAW TRIBULATIONS OF LAST DAYS. Enoch saw our day; in fact, the Lord revealed to him the history of mankind from the beginning to the end of time. He was anxious to know when the day would come wherein

---

[1] D. & C. 1; 2; 29; 43; 45; 58:4-12; 63:32-37, 49-54; 64:23-25; 86; 87; 88:86-116; 97:15-28; 101:22-38; 110; 112:23-26; 133; Matt. 24; Mark 13; Luke 21; 1 Thess. 4:13-18; 5:1-10; 2 Thess. 1:7-12; 2:1-12; 2 Pet. 3:1- 14; Jude 1:14-19; Rev. 7; 8; 9; 10; 11; 17; 18; 19; Isa. 63; 64; 65; 66; Ezek. 37; 38; 39; Dan. 11; 12; Joel 1; 2; 3; Zeph. 1; 2; 3; Hag. 2; Zech. 12; 13; 14; Mal. 3; 4; Moses 7:60-67; Jos. Smith 1.

[2] Luke 21:25-26.

this earth should be cleansed from all the iniquity upon its face and have rest. The Lord answered him:

"As I live, even so will I come in the *last days, in the days of wickedness and vengeance,* to fulfil the oath which I have made unto you concerning the children of Noah; And the day shall come that the earth shall rest, but before that day the heavens shall be darkened, and a veil of darkness shall cover the earth; and the heavens shall shake, and also the earth; and *great tribulations shall be among the children of men, but my people will I preserve.*"[3]

WORLD AS CORRUPT AS IN NOAH'S DAY. Our Savior promised that the days preceding his second coming will be typical of the days of the flood. A glance at the 6th chapter of Genesis will reveal the conditions of the world in the days of Noah and the flood and the reason for the cleansing by water.[4] This comparison is not to be taken figuratively, but literally, as it is given. The world today is corrupt and filled with violence as it was at that earlier day, for now, as then, all flesh has corrupted its way upon the earth. The Lord promised that he would never again destroy the entire world with a flood of water, but he did promise to cleanse it the second time with *sword* and with *fire.*

We may safely say that today *the anger of the Lord is kindled against this generation for its wickedness, and the earth again groans under the weight of iniquity which is practiced upon its face.* The Almighty has not forgotten his promise made to Enoch, and the day is soon at hand when the earth again will be cleansed of all iniquity and shall rest for a thousand years.[5]

LORD SENDS WARS AND TURMOIL IN LAST DAYS. It is very displeasing to some self-righteous souls to have anyone speak of these things and say that *punishment, by war, pestilence, famine and the disturbance of the ele-*

---

[3]Moses 7:60-61.   [5]Moses 7:28-67.
[4]Moses 7; 8.

ments, is coming upon mankind by decree of a just God,
because of the transgressions of his holy laws. Nevertheless this happens to be the case, for the Lord has declared
it. His anger is kindled against the abominations and
sins of the world.[6]

The evidence that *the great and dreadful day of the
Lord is near*, as declared by Malachi and Moroni,[7] is seen
in the many signs of the times. In discoursing upon the
scene which should precede his coming, the Savior said
that there should be *"wars and rumours of wars,"* for "nation shall rise against nation, and kingdom against kingdom: and there shall be *famines*, and *pestilences*, and
earthquakes, in divers places." Moreover there were to
be many "great *signs* and *wonders;* insomuch that, if it
were possible, they shall deceive the very elect." When
we see the fig tree putting forth its leaves we know that
summer is nigh.[8] This comparison the Lord made to the
signs of his second coming.

DISCOVERIES, INVENTIONS, LEARNING: SIGNS OF
THE TIMES. All will admit that we are living in a most
wonderful age, the greatest in many respects this world
has ever seen. There are great signs and wonders in the
earth, such as were never given to man before. The great
discoveries, inventions, the pouring out of *learning,*
theory and principle both true and false, by which many
are deceived, are signs and wonders which are given us
and which we should heed.[9] The *airplane* swiftly winging
its way through the heavens; the *radio* bringing to us the
voices of men from all parts of the earth; the great *engi-
neering and mechanical undertakings* which bring the
many conveniences to man; the building of skyscrapers
and the harnessing of *electricity* and making it work in
its various forms; the great *medical discoveries* and surgi-

---

[6]*Church News,* Aug. 2, 1941, p. 1;
  D. & C. 43:17-35; 63:32-35; 88:86-
  94.
[7]Mal. 4:5-6; Jos. Smith 2:36-39;
  D. & C. 2; 110:13-16.
[8]Matt. 24:6-7, 24, 32-33.
[9]Dan. 12:4; 2 Thess. 2:7-12; 2 Tim.
  2:16; 3:1-7.

cal skill with the thousand and one other great wonders, have all been given through the will and power of God.

There is trouble in the earth among the elements as well as among mankind.[10] The hearts of men in the nations are failing them. Earthquakes are extremely frequent and "in divers places." In these and numerous other ways we see the fig tree putting forth its leaves, and we have had the warning. Yet many, if not most, of the inhabitants of the world fail to see anything significant in all of this, and they say that things are going on as they have been doing from the beginning.[11]

BLINDNESS OF PEOPLE IN LAST DAYS. One of the great signs is the *lack of faith in God* and the rapid departure from the fundamentals of the Christian doctrines by the people of the earth, fulfilling the prediction of the Lord that when he comes he will scarcely find faith on the earth.[12]

One of the marked signs of the last days is the *blindness of the people;* we are told they would have eyes and see not, and ears but hear not, and hearts but understand not. If in the days of Jesus this was true of the Jews and surrounding nations, it is doubly so now in relation to the nations with which we are acquainted.[13]

All of these signs and wonders with the commotion in the earth, Moroni told Joseph Smith, were about to come upon the world, and to impress the youthful Prophet with the significance of these events the angel quoted the words of the prophets who many centuries ago wrote of these things.[14]

STRIKES AND LABOR TROUBLES: SIGNS OF THE TIMES. Today the whole world is in the slough of wickedness. Bitterness and hate have entered the hearts of the mighty; their hearts are failing them, and fear has

---

10*D. & C.* 43:22-26; 88:88-91.
11 Pet. 3:3-14.
12*Church News,* Sept. 26, 1931, p. 7; Luke 18:1-8.
13*Gen. & Hist. Mag.,* vol. 31, p. 71; Isa. 6:9-12; John 12:37-41.
14*Church News,* Sept. 26, 1931, p. 7; Jos. Smith 2:35-50.

overtaken them. Surely the word of the Lord is true:
"The whole world groaneth under sin and darkness even
now."[15] In our own fair land, said by the Lord to be
choice above all other lands, *dissatisfaction, distress,* and
turmoil reign. *Strikes* have for many months crippled
industry. *Capital and labor are at cross purposes. Property is being wantonly and maliciously destroyed. Force*
is being used to accomplish selfish ends. Legislation is
advocated to help to reach such ends. Discontent and
hatred are born of such conditions.

In the midst of all this turmoil and destruction the
Latter-day Saints should dwell in peace and safety. This
they may do if they will be honest with themselves, with
their fellowmen, and with their God.[16]

RESPONSIBILITY FOR WORLD-WIDE DEPRESSION.
One of the brethren yesterday stated that practically
every speaker up to that time had said something about
the *depression.* I suppose I will not be out of place if I
too say something about it. I would like to place the
blame for it where it belongs. It is so easy for mankind
to blame somebody else for their own mistakes, and so
easy for us, because of our human nature, to take credit
when the thing that is accomplished is something that
pleases and benefits. But we never want to shoulder a
responsibility for our mistakes that do not please, and so
we endeavor to place that kind of responsibility
somewhere else and on others.

When the children of Israel came out of Egypt, they
were led by Moses as he was directed of the Lord. Constantly they murmured against him, when they found
themselves confronting difficulties, and wanted to go
back to Egypt to their tasks and to their tribulation.[17]

Now, brethren and sisters, let us shoulder our own
responsibilities and not endeavor to place them somewhere else. The responsibility for this depression is part-

---

[15] *D. & C.* 84:49-53. [17] Ex. 16; 17; Num. 11:31-35.
[16] *Era,* vol. 40, p. 377.

ly mine; it is partly yours. It is the fault of the farmer, of the merchant, of the educator, the business man, the professional man—in fact, men in all walks of life. That is where the responsibility belongs. And why? Because of a *failure to heed the commandments of God.*

I say it is partly mine. It is mine insofar as I may have failed to heed the commandments. It is mine wherein I may have failed to follow the counsels that have been given from this pulpit for many years. It is your fault because you too, perhaps, have failed to heed those counsels. It is the fault of the whole world, because they have refused to hear the word of God, to heed the warnings that have come from him, not only through ancient prophets and apostles but in the words that have been declared from time to time by modern prophets.

ECONOMIC DEPRESSION: A SIGN OF THE TIMES. The world today is full of selfishness, greed, the desire to possess. For many years we have been living extravagantly. Our *wants* have been supplied—not our needs alone, but our wants—and we have wanted much. Most of us have been able to obtain them, and now a time comes when we find ourselves somewhat curtailed, hedged around about, not having so many privileges, and our desires are not so fully granted, and so we begin to complain. But *we should get rid of our selfishness and greed, our desire to possess that which is beyond the needs and blessings which are really ours.*

It is time for men to humble themselves, to repent and seek the Lord. I think the general theme of this conference has been that of repentance. I think it is most timely. I have been crying repentance up and down through the stakes of Zion for years. I think it is needed.

Depression has come because we have forsaken God. Now, I am not speaking of the Latter-day Saints when I say that. I make this saying have general application. The people of this nation, and the people of other nations, have forsaken the Lord. We have violated his laws. We have failed to hearken to his promises. We have not considered that we were under obligation to keep his commandments, and the laws of the land as well as the laws of God are not respected. The Sabbath day has become a day of pleasure, a day of boisterous conduct, a day in which the worship of God has departed, and the worship of pleasure has taken its place. I am sorry to say that many of the Latter-day Saints are guilty of this. We should repent.[18]

WHY LATTER-DAY CALAMITIES COVER EARTH

REBELLION AGAINST GOD: A SIGN OF THE TIMES. In this land, as well as in other lands, men have forgotten God. They are not worshiping him with all their might, mind, and strength. They are not worshiping him at all. I am speaking now of the general run of mankind. Instead of keeping his commandments they are violating them. More people disregard the commandments than keep them.

This *rebellion against God*—for that is what it is—is not confined to those who do not profess religion or even to belief in the Lord Jesus Christ, for the evil has crept within the borders of the Church itself, and there are many who call themselves Latter-day Saints who are guilty of these offenses.

In the opening prayer Brother Parker Robison prayed that this nation, of which we form a part, might, through repentance, escape the judgments that are predicted, and which will follow in case there is not repentance. Let me read the word of the Lord concerning this land, as it is contained in the second chapter of the Book of Ether:

"And he [the Lord] had sworn in his wrath unto the brother of Jared, that whoso should possess this land of promise, from that time henceforth and forever, should serve him, the true and only God, or they should be

---

[18]Conf. Rep., Oct., 1932, pp. 88-89.

swept off when the fulness of his wrath should come upon them. And now, we can behold the decrees of God concerning this land, that it is a land of promise; and whatsoever nation shall possess it shall serve God, or they shall be swept off when the fulness of his wrath shall come upon them. And the fulness of his wrath cometh upon them when they are ripened in iniquity." Then we are informed that the God of this land is Jesus Christ.[19]

WICKEDNESS BRINGS STRIKES, WAR, DISTRESS. I fear for the United States, and I fear for other nations. *The trouble that we read about in Spain, today, is the result of accumulated wickedness coming down through ages. Peoples are not destroyed in righteousness, but in wickedness, and the Lord has decreed that the wicked shall slay the wicked, and in that land that is taking place today.*[20] Similar things will take place in other lands; and this country, in which we live, shall not escape, unless men turn again to the worship of God and accept Jesus Christ. They have discarded him, and they have ridiculed his commandments.

The Lord said, "Why call ye me, Lord, Lord, and do not the things which I say?"[21] Again he said, "If thou lovest me thou shalt serve me and keep all my commandments."[22]

Are we serving the Lord? Are we keeping his commandments? Or are we following the trend of the times and the evils of the times? This land in which we live is full of trouble. Other lands are filled with trouble, contention and strife. *The strikes that are taking place, the commotion, the distress, the troubles we see on every side, are the result of wickedness.* They do not come from righteousness. These things do not come because the people are loving the Lord, but because they have

---

[19]Ether 2:8-12.
[20]D. & C. 63:33.
[21]Luke 6:46.
[22]D. & C. 42:29.

forsaken him, and because the time has come for the harvest and *reaping* of the earth.[23]

DISOBEDIENCE BRINGS EARTHQUAKES AND DUST STORMS. Our attention has been called during the last few weeks to a number of conditions prevailing in our own land, and in other lands, of a very evil nature. In a far off part of the world there has been a terrible *earthquake*—thousands of people have lost their lives. In our own land during the past few months, in a season when the land is usually covered with snow, in some of our middle states the people have been troubled with *dust storms*.

We have had a touch of it in our own land here. The *whirlwinds* have raised the surface of the earth in clouds of dust and carried it off to deposit it somewhere else, and in this way there has been great destruction. It has caused considerable commotion, in addition to the distress, and some alarm among those who have taken particular notice. Our scientists fear that unless something is done to protect the land, this country in many places, now fruitful, may eventually become barren and unproductive.

There are *reasons* for these unfavorable conditions. Now what I am about to say will not be considered scientific and perhaps will be ridiculed by those who consider themselves to be scientific, but I do not care a thing about that. I want to say to you, my brethren and sisters, that the hand of the Lord is in this. It is not all because men have left the ground in such condition that the wind can disturb its surface, but *it is because men violate the commandments of God and refuse to hearken unto his word;* and these things are in fulfilment of the predictions that have been made by the prophets of old and also the prophets in our own time. . . .

PLAGUES, VIOLENCE, DEPRESSION FOLLOW DISOBEDIENCE. *It is not the will of the Lord that there should*

[23]*Church News,* May 8, 1937, p. 5.

come upon the people disaster, trouble, calamity, and depression (as we have got into the habit of speaking of some of our troubles), *but because man himself will violate the commandments of God and will not walk in righteousness, the Lord permits all of these evils to come upon him.* In the beginning, the Lord blessed the earth for men's sake.[24] It was his intention that men, if they would only keep the commandments of the Lord, should have the good things of the earth and live in peace and happiness in the spirit of righteousness. . . .

The Lord has made the declaration in our own day that it was his good pleasure to give to men *the fulness of the earth,* and the Lord is pleased to have them use it, and he would pour out upon them his blessings in abundance if they would only hearken and be obedient to the laws which he has given them for their guidance.[25] But, men are rebellious; they are not willing to live in that law and profit thereby; they are not willing to receive the good things of the earth as the Lord would give to them in abundance; but in their narrow-mindedness, shortsightedness, and in their greed and selfishness, they think they know better than the Lord does. And so, they pursue another course, and the result is that the blessings of the Lord are withdrawn, and in the place thereof come *calamity, destruction, plagues,* and *violence.* Men have themselves to blame.[26]

POOR HEALTH, AFFLICTION FOLLOW DISOBEDIENCE. We sometimes wonder why we have *affliction.* We wonder why we do not have the best of *health.*[27] From this which I have read,[28] we may very properly infer that *affliction sometimes comes upon us because we ourselves are not faithful in the performance of duty and in keeping the commandments of the Lord.*[29]

What a pity it is that people will pay little heed to

---

[24]Moses 2:11-12; Gen. 1:11-12.
[25]D. & C. 59:5-20.
[26]*Church News,* May 4, 1935, p. 3.

[27]D. & C. 89:18-21; Ex. 16:26; Deut. 7:12-15; 28:58-63.
[28]D. & C. 93:40-43.
[29]*Rel. Soc. Mag.,* vol. 18, p. 683.

sacred counsels, and in their madness and love of the things of the world take the hard road and have to receive punishment when there is a means of escape. When these calamities come, what right have the people of Zion to expect protection! And, if the righteous among them are called upon to suffer, *the sin will be at the door of the rebellious who have not hearkened to this counsel.*[30]

WITHDRAWAL OF SPIRIT BRINGS CALAMITIES. Now, that was a calamity which came upon the world, when the Lord decreed that he would withhold his spirit from the inhabitants of the earth.[31] He had no reference to the Holy Ghost, because they never had the gift of the Holy Ghost, but he had reference to the light of truth, or Spirit of Christ, which would lead them to the truth, if they would heed it. This spirit he was withdrawing from them because of their wickedness, and the withdrawal of his spirit would bring upon them these calamities—the pestilences, the plagues, and all the rest of it that is mentioned here, including bloodshed, and war.

JOSEPH SMITH WARNS OF CALAMITIES TO COME. The Prophet Joseph Smith instructed his brethren and informed them of the calamities that were to come. He warned the world of its wickedness, and he told these good men of the Council of the Twelve, who were associated with him, that *because of the wickedness of the world and its corruption, destruction would come upon it.*[32] Some of these brethren say that as he told them of these things he wept as our Savior wept when he looked upon Jerusalem.[33]

President Wilford Woodruff, speaking of this testimony and this warning to the world which the Prophet had seen in vision of things which were coming upon the earth, said: "I heard the Prophet Joseph Smith bear his

---

[30]*Church News,* Aug. 2, 1941, p. 2.   [33]Luke 19:41-44.
[31]*D. & C.* 63:32-33.
[32]Joseph Fielding Smith, *Teachings of the Prophet Joseph Smith,* pp. 47-49, 87, 161-163, 252-253.

testimony to these events that would transpire in the
earth," and after predicting that they were now at our
doors, President Woodruff said also: "We cannot draw
a veil over the events that await this generation. No man
that is inspired by the Spirit and power of God can close
his ears, his eyes, or his lips, to these things." I think
we have no right to close our ears, and we have no right
to be silent and shut our eyes against the warnings that
the Lord has given and placed before us which we are
commanded to declare to the nations of the earth. . . .

I heard President Wilford Woodruff, in this stand,
this same place where I stand, bear witness as he had
done in other places, in 1893, and up to the time of his
death, that the angels who had been waiting to go forth
to reap down the earth had now been sent upon that
mission, and they were in the earth. Therefore, he said
we may look for calamities, for destruction, for plague
and bloodshed.[34] . . .

WICKEDNESS IS INCREASING IN WORLD. Let me
call your attention to the fact that *this world is not growing better*. If I may be pardoned for the expression: We
need not "kid" ourselves into thinking that this world is
growing better. If so, then the prophecies have failed.[35]
This world today is full of wickedness. That *wickedness
is increasing*. True, there are many righteous people
scattered throughout the earth, and it is our duty to search
them out and give unto them the gospel of Jesus Christ
and bring them out of Babylon. The Lord has said to
them: "Go ye out from Babylon," which is the
world.[36] . . .

If you think the world is getting better, just observe
and witness the vulgarity and the near-approach to in-
decency that we find published in some pictorial magazines and so frequently on the screen. Think of the
corruption and the debasing conditions due to the indul-

---

[34]G. Homer Durham, *Discourses of*   [35]*D. & C.* 38:11-12; 2 Ne. 28:15-23.
Wilford Woodruff, pp. 229-231.   [36]*D. & C.* 133:5; Rev. 18:4; Isa. 48:20.

gence in liquor and tobacco and other narcotics and drugs. Think of the immorality which is so prevalent throughout the country.

We are made aware of the evils which existed in our army camps by the reports in the paper, the magazines, and from the lips of our own boys who have returned. Now pressure is brought upon us to bring to pass the compulsion of our youth at the tender years when they are most impressionable, and force them into military camps where they will have no protection, or very little, from the vices which are so prevalent in army camps. I want to say to you, my brethren and sisters, for one, I am opposed to it![37]

WORLD CONDITIONS WILL GET WORSE. We hear occasionally somebody make the statement that things are as bad as they could be, that they could not be worse. I want to tell you they could be worse, a great deal worse. If I read the signs of the times, *we have not suffered yet as much as we are going to suffer, unless we repent.*

From this stand men have prophesied in the name of the Lord for many decades. President Brigham Young, President John Taylor, President Wilford Woodruff, and others of our leading brethren and presidents of the Church, have raised the warning voice. They have called attention to these present conditions. The Lord has also prophesied of these things, and they have been mentioned by ancient seers and prophets. We have had ample warning. We have been told of the calamities that are coming. We have been taught how we might avoid them, how we might be protected, if we would only hear the counsels that come to us, heed the testimony of truth. If we fail, we cannot escape. . . .

Do not think that we have reached a condition where things could not be worse. *Unless there is repentance they will be worse.* And so I cry repentance to this

[37]Conf. Rep., Apr., 1946, pp. 155-158.

people, to the Latter-day Saints, to the people of this nation, and to the nations of the earth everywhere.[38]

HOW TO ESCAPE CALAMITIES

How Zion May Escape the Lord's Scourge. "Nevertheless, Zion shall escape *if* she observe to do all things whatsoever I have commanded her. But if she observe not to do whatsoever I have commanded her, I will visit her according to all her works, with *sore affliction,* with *pestilence,* with *plague,* with *sword,* with *vengeance,* with *devouring fire.* Nevertheless, let it be read this once to her ears, that I, the Lord, have accepted of her offering; and *if she sin no more none of these things shall come upon her.*"[39]

This way of escape, insuring the protection of the Lord, is a very simple one. Unfortunately, many of the people of Zion have refused to take advantage of this promise.[40]

As I observe conditions among the people I cannot see how we are going to escape when the judgments are to pass over the nations, which are promised in this revelation and in others which I cannot take time to read. Because of our disobedience and our failure to keep the commandments of the Lord, the *righteous,* as in times past, *may be called upon to suffer with the unrighteous among us.*[41]

Are the Saints Keeping the Commandments? So I rejoiced in having the voice of warning raised. Are we keeping the Sabbath day holy, as Latter-day Saints, when the picture shows are filled every Sunday afternoon and evening, and that, too, in communities of Latter-day Saints; when the pleasure resorts are crowded on the Sabbath day; when we turn our attention to Sunday pleasure rather than to the worship of God? Do we have

---

[38]Conf. Rep., Oct., 1932, pp. 90-92.
[39]D. & C. 97:25-26.
[40]*Millennial Star,* vol. 103, pp. 612-622.
[41]Smith, *op. cit.,* pp. 162-163.

a claim upon his blessings, and are we entitled to have
the angels of destruction pass us by, according to the
promise that is given here,⁴² *if* we will keep the commandments of God? Are we doing it?

Are we guilty of finding fault with those who preside over us? Are we willing to listen to the counsels that
they give to us, and receive the voice of God as it comes
through the one who stands to represent him as his
mouthpiece upon the face of the earth? How many of
us are willing to do that? We stood upon our feet here
this morning and sang, "We Thank Thee, O God, for a
Prophet," and yet there are some among us who criticize
him, who find fault with him. When he speaks by the
power of the inspiration of Almighty God, we are ready
to condemn him, as we have done in times past.

Do you think, under these conditions, that we are
prepared to escape from these penalties here enumerated
in this revelation, given on the 2nd day of August in
the year 1833, a month after our people had been driven
from their homes for violating the commandments which
they solemnly had promised they would keep?

REPENTANCE NEEDED TO ESCAPE CALAMITIES. I
want to raise the warning voice, and I am doing it among
the stakes of Zion, as you happen to know. I want to cry
repentance. Are we keeping ourselves clean and pure
and unspotted from the sins of the world, and are we
entitled to receive the blessings?

I want to tell you the judgments have gone forth and
they are going forth. All these *strikes* that are taking
place, this *commotion,* this *unrest,* this *dissatisfaction,* this
desire on the part of people to overthrow governments—
and that is going to come, for hasn't the Lord said that
he will make an *end* of all nations? Is it not so recorded
in these revelations?⁴³ And so it must be. The angels of
destruction have gone forth upon their mission. . . .

⁴²D. & C. 86:5-7.   ⁴³D. & C. 87:6.

The judgments of the Almighty are being poured out, and they shall continue, for the Prophet of God has said it. *We shall not escape, unless we repent,* turn to the Lord, honor our priesthood, and our membership in this Church, and be true and faithful to our covenants."

SAINTS MAY ESCAPE PLAGUES BY OBEDIENCE. Now, my brethren and sisters, in this time of peace—I do not know how long it will last—in this day of prosperity, let us be humble and remember the Lord and keep his commandments and feel that the dangers before us are far greater than they are in the days of trial and tribulation. Do not think for a moment that the days of trial are over. They are not. *If we keep the commandments of the Lord, we shall prosper, we shall be blessed;* the plagues, the calamities that have been promised will be poured out upon the peoples of the earth, and we shall escape them, yea, they shall pass us by.

But remember the Lord says if we fail to keep his word, if we walk in the ways of the world, they will not pass us by, but we shall be visited with floods and with fire, with sword and with plague and destruction. *We may escape these things through faithfulness.* Israel of old might have escaped through faithfulness, but they refused to keep the commandments of the Lord and they were not saved.[45] Therefore I plead with you: Pay your tithing,[46] keep the Word of Wisdom,[47] pray unto the Lord, honor him in all things by keeping his commandments, that his blessings may be poured out and that we may receive them in abundance,[48] and in humility we may walk before him and be entitled not only to the blessings that come to us in this mortal life, but to the blessings of eternal life, the greatest gift of God.[49]

SAINTS CAN ESCAPE SCOURGES IF RIGHTEOUS. We have the means of escape through obedience to the gospel

44Conf. Rep., Apr., 1937, pp. 60-62.   47D. & C. 89:18-21.
45Deut. 28; 29; 30.   48D. & C. 59:7-24.
46Mal. 3:7-12.   49Conf. Rep., Apr., 1929, p. 56.

of Jesus Christ. Will we escape? When I see, even among the Latter-day Saints the violation of the laws of the Lord, I fear and I tremble. I have been crying repentance among the stakes of Zion for 30 years, calling upon the people to turn to the Lord, keep his commandments, observe the Sabbath day, pay their honest tithing, do everything the Lord has commanded them to do, to live by every word that proceedeth forth from the mouth of God.

By doing this we shall escape the calamities.

I am going to repeat what I have said before, for which I have been severely criticized from certain quarters, that even in this country we have no grounds by which we may escape, no sure foundation upon which we can stand, and by which we may escape from the calamities and destruction and the plagues and the pestilences, and even the devouring fire by sword and by war, *unless we repent* and we keep the commandments of the Lord, for it is written here in these revelations.

So I cry repentance to the Latter-day Saints, and I cry repentance to the people of the United States, as well as to the people of all the earth.[50]

How to Better World Conditions. The Lord intends that men shall be happy; that is his purpose. But men refuse to be happy and make themselves miserable, because they think their ways are better than God's ways, and because of selfishness, greed, and the wickedness that is in their hearts; and that is the trouble with us today. The leaders of our nation are struggling and trying to do something to better conditions. I can tell you in a few words just how it can be done, and *it is not going to be done by legislation—it is not going to be done by pouring money out upon the people.*

Temporary relief is not going to better the situation, because we will still be struggling and fighting and contending with *crime*, with *disease*, with *plagues*, and with

[50]Conf. Rep., Oct., 1940, p. 117.

pestilence, with the *whirlwinds,* and with the *dust storms,* and with the *earthquakes* and everything else coming upon the face of the earth, according to the predictions of the prophets—all because men will not heed the warning voice.

When we quit loving money and get the love of gold out of our hearts and the greed and selfishness, and learn to love the Lord, our God, with all our hearts, and our neighbor as ourselves, and get on our knees and learn to pray and repent of our sins, we will have prosperity, we will have peace, we will have contentment. *But the people will not repent no matter what warning is made, no matter how much their attention is called to these things; the people will not repent because their hearts are set upon evil, and destruction awaits them.*[51]

WORLD CONDITIONS PROVE APOSTASY OF CHRISTIANITY. I am very sorry that the greater portion of the earth at this time should be in turmoil, that the great nations abroad should be at war and in such deadly conflict [1916]. Nevertheless, I realize that these are judgments that have come upon these nations, who have departed from the gospel of the Lord and have not repented of their sins, and will not hearken to the message of the elders of Israel. These judgments now being poured out on the nations have been predicted by the prophets and they are coming because of the iniquities that exist in the earth.

If the people were of one mind, if they were of one heart, if they were living the gospel of our Lord, as he has instructed us to live it, then such conditions could not possibly prevail. The Lord has declared that unless we are one we are not his,[52] and where his gospel has taken hold of the people there cannot be such bitterness of feeling, contention and bloodshed, as we find over the greater portion of the earth today. *The present condition of the world is an incontrovertible evidence that the power and*

---

[51]*Church News,* May 4, 1935, p. 6.   [52]*D. & C.* 38:27.

*purity of the gospel is not to be found in their churches
and that they are not in fellowship with the Lord.*[53]

WHY THE RIGHTEOUS DIE IN WAR. Why do the
righteous have to suffer, and why does the Lord take
some of our good boys away when he brings judgment
upon the people?

The Lord says he pours his *blessings* upon the just
and the unjust.[54] Again he said it must needs be that
offenses come, but woe be to them by whom they come.[55]
*All through the ages some of the righteous have had to
suffer because of the acts of the unrighteous, but they
will get their reward.*[56] Many of those who are taken in
these days of battle are called because they are needed
for work on the other side. They are not to be condemned
because they are taken away when judgments are being
poured out, for no condemnation can be laid at their
doors. Evidently there is a need for them on the other
side.[57]

[53]Conf. Rep., Oct., 1916, p. 68.   [56]Dan. 11:35.
[54]Matt. 5:45.   [57]Pers. Corresp.
[55]Matt. 18:7; Luke 17:1.

CHAPTER 3

WAR AND THE SECOND COMING

CHRIST DECREED WARS FOR LAST DAYS

WAR AND DESOLATION TO PRECEDE SECOND COMING. In that great revelation on war, the Lord has told us that beginning with the rebellion of South Carolina great destructions would come, and they would continue to be poured out upon the earth until the time should come when the decrees of God would be fully consummated, finished, and he would make an *end of all nations*.[1] I look for that to be fulfilled, and Christ will come to reign; his kingdom will be established on earth as in heaven, as he has taught us to pray: "Our Father which art in heaven, Hallowed be thy name. Thy kingdom come. Thy will be done in earth, as it is in heaven."[2] I pray for that time to come.

I plead with the Latter-day Saints to stand firm and faithful in the discharge of every duty, keeping the commandments of the Lord, honoring the priesthood, that we may stand when the Lord comes—whether we be living or dead, it matters not—to be partakers of this glory. Remember, when this time comes, this earth is to be cleansed of its unrighteousness, and the wicked shall be as stubble and shall pass away.[3]

LORD DESTROYED WICKED IN FLOOD OF NOAH. God said unto Noah: "The end of all flesh is come before me, for the earth is filled with violence, and behold *I will destroy all flesh from off the earth*."[4] It should be remembered that the Lord said *he* would do it!

---

[1]*D. & C.* 87:1-8.
[2]Matt. 6:9-10; *D. & C.* 65:1-6; Rev. 11:15; Dan. 7:9-10, 13-14, 18, 27.
[3]Conf. Rep., Apr., 1935, p. 99; Mal. 4.
[4]Moses 8:30; Gen. 6:13.

So the Lord commanded Noah to build an ark into which he was to take his family and the animals of the earth to preserve seed after the flood, and all flesh that was not in the ark perished *according to the Lord's decree*. Of course this story is not believed by the wise and the great among the children of men, any more than was Noah's story in his day.

LORD KILLED INHABITANTS OF SODOM AND GOMORRAH. Then after this new start men again became carnal, sensual, and devilish upon the earth, and drastic punishment had to be meted out to some of the earth's inhabitants once more *according to the Lord's decree*. In the days of Abraham there were two cities known as Sodom and Gomorrah in which wickedness was without measure, and the Lord said to Abraham that *he* was going to *destroy these cities*.

Abraham pleaded with the Lord to spare them, which the Lord promised to do if 10 righteous souls could be found therein. Since this could not be done *"the Lord rained upon Sodom and upon Gomorrah brimstone and fire from the Lord out of heaven," and these cities with all their inhabitants were destroyed*.[5] And again the Lord said *he* did it! But the self-righteous and the wise of this present day say this is not a true record, for a merciful God would not do such a thing even if the people were wicked.

LORD COMMANDED ISRAEL TO DESTROY AMORITES. About this time the Lord promised to give to Abraham for an everlasting inheritance all of this land where Sodom and Gomorrah were and all of the land from "the river of Egypt unto the great river, the river Euphrates," but Abraham was told that his posterity could not possess the land for 400 years, because *"the iniquity of the Amorites is not yet full."*[6] When the time came and the wickedness of the Amorites was full, *the Lord com-*

---
[5]Gen. 19:1-29.   [6]Gen. 15:13-21.

*manded Israel to take their armies and cleanse the land
of this wickedness* and take possession of the inheritance
which had been promised their father Abraham.[7]

ISRAEL AND JUDAH CURSED FOR INIQUITY. And
thus, down through the ages, we discover, if we are willing to believe what is written in the scriptures, that
*judgments and destructions had to be poured out upon
the wicked because they would not repent.* Even the
kingdoms of Israel and Judah were destroyed and the
people scattered because of the anger of the Lord which
was kindled against them for their transgressions.[8] At
least this is the case if we are willing to believe the word
of the Lord given through his prophets.

JAREDITES DESTROYED FOR REJECTING CHRIST. Not
only were these punishments meted out to the inhabitants
of the so-called old world, but destructions awaited the
inhabitants of this western world for the same cause.
Through their prophets they were constantly reminded
that this land is "choice above all other lands, which the
Lord God had preserved for a righteous people." And
he, the Lord, had "sworn in his wrath unto the brother
of Jared, that whoso should possess this land of promise,
from that time henceforth and forever, should serve him,
the true and only God, or they should be swept off when
the *fulness of his wrath should come upon them.*"[9] When
these people refused to worship the true and living God,
then his wrath came upon them—if we are willing to
believe the record—and they were swept off.[10]

LORD DESTROYED NEPHITES AND LAMANITES FOR
INIQUITY. Then another people came to possess the land
under all the blessings of protection and guidance of the
Lord. These same promises and warnings were made to
the second group of inhabitants, and the prophets who
were raised up among them constantly warned them of

[7]Deut. 20:17.   [9]Ether 2:7-8.
[8]Deut. 28.   [10] Ether 14; 15.

these promises the Lord had made.[11] But these people also fell from grace, and the wrath of the Almighty came upon them. So wicked had they become at the time of the crucifixion of our Lord that *it became necessary for him to destroy many of their cities by earthquake, flood, fire, and other forms of destruction.*

Yes, it is true, the same meek and lowly Nazarene, who came into the world and offered himself a sacrifice for sin because of the great love his Father and he had for the human family—he "who is infinite and eternal, from everlasting to everlasting the same unchangeable God,"[12] who loves little children and suffered them to come unto him—found himself under the necessity of meting out punishment to the inhabitants of this choice land and that too in a most drastic fashion. Hearken to his words which he uttered after his resurrection:

"Wo, wo, wo unto this people; wo unto the inhabitants of the *whole earth* except they shall repent; for the devil laugheth, and his angels rejoice, because of the slain of the fair sons and daughters of my people; and *it is because of their iniquity and abomination that they are fallen!* Behold that great city Zarahemla *have I burned with fire, and the inhabitants thereof.* And behold, that great city Moroni *have I caused to be sunk in the depths of the sea, and the inhabitants thereof to be drowned.* And behold, that great city Moronihah *have I covered with earth, and the inhabitants thereof, to hide their iniquities and their abominations from before my face,* that the blood of the prophets and the saints shall not come any more unto me against them."[13]

The Lord also sent destructions upon the cities of Gilgal, Onihah, Mocum, Jerusalem, Gadiandi, Gadiomnah, Jacob, Gimgimno, Jacobugath, Laman, Josh, Gad, Kishkumen and others.[14]

---

[11] 2 Ne. 10:9-19.
[12] D. & C. 20:17.
[13] 3 Ne. 9:2-5.
[14] 3 Ne. 9:6-14.

DESTRUCTION AWAITS WICKED OF OUR DAY. But, says the self-righteous modernist, such things could not be, for God is "a God of Love," and the Savior "a man of peace," and the God I worship does not "decree death upon farmers, factory hands," and "women and children, regardless of who has sinned!"

We who live in the present day should take heed and profit by the experiences of those who have gone before and not fall into their grievous errors. We should remember that the same warnings have been given to us and "to all the inhabitants of the earth," that *destruction awaits this age unless they refrain from wickedness and abominations.* Let us not forget that the Lord said that it should be in this day as it was in the days of Noah.[15]

We should remember also that he is still a "God of wrath" as well as a "God of love," and that he has promised to pour out his wrath upon the ungodly, and "take vengeance upon the wicked" who will not repent. Not only did the ancient prophets predict that such should be the case in these latter days, but the Lord has spoken it in our own dispensation.[16]

WICKED TO SLAY WICKED UNTIL THE LORD COMES. The Lord says *he has decreed wars.*[17] Why? Because of the hatred in the hearts of men, because of the wickedness in the hearts of men, because they will not repent. Here is another passage: "And it shall come to pass, because of the wickedness of the world, that *I will take vengeance upon the wicked,* for they will not repent; for the cup of mine indignation is full; for behold, my blood shall not cleanse them if they hear me not."[18]

These things the Lord said through his Prophet in warnings that have come to the people of this nation and other lands. The Lord says the wicked will not repent,

---

[15]Matt. 24:37-41.
[16]*Gen. & Hist. Mag.*, vol. 31, pp. 66-
   69; D. & C. 1:8-16; 2; 29:9-21;
   63:32-35; 86:5-7; 87; 133:41-74.
[17]D. & C. 63:32-35.
[18]D. & C. 29:17.

and *because they will not repent he has decreed wars to come upon them,* and *the wicked shall slay the wicked,*[19] *and thus the earth will be cleansed,* as we read in the 24th chapter of Isaiah, *until there shall be few men left.*

I know that what I am saying is not pleasing to some people, and that I will be criticized for it, but I do not care about that; it is the word of the Lord, and I want to warn the Latter-day Saints. I am going to read another passage of scripture: "For behold, and lo, *vengeance cometh speedily upon the ungodly as the whirlwind; and who shall escape it? The Lord's scourge shall pass over by night and by day, and the report thereof shall vex all people; yea, it shall not be stayed until the Lord come.*"[20]

No Peace on Earth Until Christ Comes. I read from another revelation just a moment ago where the Lord said that the time was coming when *peace* would be taken from the earth,[21] and I declare to you that *it has been taken from the earth;* and I say now—no, I don't say it, the Lord says it—"*it shall not return until the Lord comes.*"

So, let them cry peace; let them seek for peace; *they will not find it until Christ comes,* who is the Prince of Peace, to take his place where he rightfully belongs as King of kings, ruling and reigning upon the face of the earth. *There will be no peace in this land or any other land, but there will be plague, trial, and suffering from this time forth until Christ comes. The only escape is by repentance on the part of the people, and they will not repent.*

Will Saints Escape Latter-day Perils? What about the Latter-day Saints? In one passage that I have read it says that the saints will hardly escape.[22] Well, *I do not think they are going to escape.* I will tell you

---

[19] D. & C. 63:33.
[20] D. & C. 97:22-23.
[21] D. & C. 1:35.

[22] D. & C. 63:34; 112:23-26; 1 Pet. 4:17-18.

why: "For the indignation of the Lord is kindled against their abominations and all their wicked works." (That *is the people of the earth.*) "*Nevertheless, Zion shall* escape if she observe to do all things whatsoever I have commanded her. But *if she observe not to do whatsoever I have commanded her, I will visit her according to all her works, with sore affliction,* with *pestilence,* with *plague,* with *sword,* with *vengeance,* with *devouring fire.* Nevertheless, let it be read this once to her ears, that I, the Lord, have accepted of her offering; and if she sin no more none of these things shall come upon her."[23]

That was said over 120 years ago—in 1833. The Lord made the promise to the Latter-day Saints that *if they would keep his commandments, they should escape* when these destructions like a whirlwind should come suddenly—when all these trials and sufferings should come upon the people of the earth, the Latter-day Saints might escape if they would keep his commandments.

SAINTS MUST REPENT TO ESCAPE PLAGUES. *We are not keeping his commandments.* Some of the Latter-day Saints are to the best of their ability, but many of them are not. We are covenant-breakers; we violate the Sabbath day, we will not keep it holy; we do not keep our bodies clean; I do not believe we pray—a large part of us, I mean. As far as the fast day is concerned, we have forgotten it. We are not half as good as we think we are. *We need repentance, and we need to be told to repent.* We need to have our attention called to these conditions that we might repent and turn to the Lord with full purpose of heart lest these destructions come upon us.

We do not pay our tithing—some of us pay tithing, which is one-tenth of that which we receive, and some of us pay donations and call it tithing; some of us do not pay at all.[24]

DESTRUCTION OF WICKED AN ACT OF MERCY. Some people think it is not like God to take *vengeance*

---

[23]*D. & C.* 97:24-27.   [24]*Church News,* May 4, 1935, p. 6.

upon people, because he is a merciful God. The fact is
*he takes vengeance upon the ungodly because he is mer-
ciful.* He is merciful to them in removing them and shows
consideration for all *others* who keep his commandments.
It was for this very reason that he destroyed Sodom and
Gomorrah, and cleansed Palestine when Israel entered
the land, and destroyed so many Nephite cities at the
time of his crucifixion. It was the meek and lowly Nazarene who did all of these things, because in his mercy
and justice he had to cleanse the earth for the benefit
of the sinful as well as for the righteous who remained.[25]

WARS ATTENDING SECOND COMING

BATTLES OF ARMAGEDDON AND GOG AND MAGOG.
*Before the coming of Christ, the great war, sometimes
called Armageddon,*[26] *will take place* as spoken of by
Ezekiel, chapters 38 and 39. *Another war of Gog and
Magog will be after the millennium.*[27]

"TIME" OF FINAL WAR NOT REVEALED. During the
past two years the question has constantly arisen and
been discussed in priesthood classes, Sunday Schools,
and in private conversations—"Is this great war (World
War II) which has cast its evil shadow over a large portion of the world, and which threatens to engulf all the
rest of mankind, the great last war to precede the second
coming of our Lord, as predicted by the prophets?"

We may answer this question by saying we truly
hope that it is; but the Lord very definitely informed his
disciples that not even the angels in heaven knew the day
nor the hour when he should make his appearance, but
his Father only.[28] Therefore, unless the Lord sees fit to
reveal to us the information, we do not know when or
where this great conflict will end. Let us hope and pray
that it may be the last struggle before permanent peace

[25]*Church News,* Nov. 29, 1941, p. 3.   [27]Joseph Fielding Smith, *Teachings of
[26]Rev. 16:15-21.   the Prophet Joseph Smith,* p. 280.
                                                   [28]Matt. 24:36; Jos. Smith 1:40.

and righteousness shall be sent down from heaven and Christ come to take his rightful place as King of kings upon the earth.[29]

FINAL WAR TO MAKE "A FULL END OF ALL NA-TIONS." In regard to the wars (World War II) now raging on the earth, I am sure the prophets have spoken of them. The Lord told Joseph Smith that the war between the States, commencing with the rebellion of South Carolina, was the *beginning of the end. At that time peace was taken from the earth,* and the prediction was made that beginning at that place, eventually war would be *poured out* upon all nations, bringing *misery, death, mourning, famine, plague, earthquake, vivid lightnings,* and so forth, causing the inhabitants of the earth to be made "to feel the wrath, and indignation, and chastening hand of an Almighty God, *until the consumption decreed hath made a full end of all nations."*[30] It appears that now this is in course of fulfilment. . . .

SIEGE OF JERUSALEM TO END FINAL WAR. Ezekiel has given us in the 38th and 39th chapters much in detail in relation to *the great battle which shall precede the coming of the Son of Man to reign.* Joel and Daniel also prophesied of these great events, which may even now be on the way to complete consummation.[31]

One thing we are given by these prophets definitely to understand is that *the great last conflict before Christ shall come will end at the siege of Jerusalem.* So said Ezekiel and Daniel, and the Lord declared to Joel: "For, behold, in those days, and in that time, when I shall bring again the captivity of Judah and Jerusalem [i.e. the return from captivity], *I will also gather all nations, and will bring them down into the valley of Jehoshaphat,* and will plead with them there for my people and for my heritage Israel, whom they have scattered among the nations, and parted my land."[32]

[29]*Millennial Star,* vol. 103, p. 610.
[30]*D. & C.* 87:6.
[31]Joel 2; 3; Dan. 8; 11; 12.
[32]Joel 3:1-2.

At this time, prophesied Joel, will the Lord judge the heathen: "Put ye in the sickle, for the harvest is ripe: come, get you down; for the press is full, the fats overflow; for their wickedness is great. *Multitudes, multitudes in the valley of decision: for the day of the Lord is near in the valley of decision.*"[33]

So we are given to understand that *when the armies gather in Palestine will be the time when the Lord shall come in judgment* and to make the eventful decision which will confound the enemies of his people and establish them in their ancient land forever.

CHRIST TO COME IN MIDST OF FINAL BATTLE. Zechariah is another prophet who has plainly spoken of these great events. According to his predictions *the nations will gather and lay siege to Jerusalem.* Part of the city will fall, with dire consequences to its inhabitants, when a great earthquake will come, the Mount of Olives will cleave in twain, and the persecuted people will flee into this valley for safety. At that particular time will the Savior come as their Deliverer and show them his hands and his feet. They will look upon him and ask him where he received his wounds, and he will tell them they were received in the house of his friends—he is Jesus Christ, their Redeemer. Then will they fall to the ground and mourn, every family apart, because their ancestors persecuted their King and the children have followed in the footsteps of the fathers.

At that time shall come the redemption of the Jews. Jerusalem shall then be rebuilt and the promises that it shall become a holy city will be fulfilled. The punishment which shall come upon those who lay siege to this land will be their destruction. The prophets have portrayed this in much detail with all its horrors.[34] These events are confirmed in the revelations to the Prophet Joseph Smith,

[33]Joel 3:13-14.   [34]Zech. 11; 12; 13; 14; Ezek. 38; 39; Zeph. 3.

as found in the *Doctrine and Covenants*, particularly
sections 29, 45, and 133.

ELDERS TO WARN OF FINAL WARS. Much more
could be written in detail regarding these conflicts, but
what is written will suffice. It is, of course, a gloomy
picture; but is it not the duty of the elders of Israel to
speak of these things with a warning voice? Shall we
close our eyes and our ears and seal our understandings
simply because some things are unpleasant to the ear and
to the eye? Shall we refuse to raise a warning voice when
danger approaches, when trouble is near, when destruction is at our door? Such a course would be cowardly
if we know the truth. We cannot cry "all is well" when
danger lurks on every side. We must not lull the people
to sleep in a false security. President Woodruff declared
that "no man that is inspired by the Spirit and power of
God can close his ears, his eyes, or his lips to these
things!"[35]

PEACE TAKEN FROM EARTH

NO PEACE AGAIN UNTIL CHRIST COMES. *Peace has
been taken from the earth, and it will not return until
Christ comes to bring it.* When that day arrives, he has
promised to "send forth his angels, and they shall gather
out of his kingdom all things that offend, and them which
do iniquity," but when that day comes, he further says,
"then shall the righteous shine forth as the sun in the
kingdom of their Father."[36]

One year after the organization of the Church peace
could not have been taken from the earth, in justice, but
the Lord said the time would speedily come.[37] That time
has come. *Peace has departed from the world. The devil
has power over his own dominion.* This is made manifest
in the actions of men, in the distress among the nations,

---

[35]*Church News*, Aug. 2, 1941, p. 3.   [37]*D. & C.* 1:35.
[36]*Era*, vol. 40, p. 377; Matt. 13:41-43,
    49-50; *D. & C.* 63:54.

in the troubles that we see in all lands, including this land which was dedicated to liberty.

There is no peace. Men's hearts are failing them. Greed has the uppermost place in the hearts of men. Evil is made manifest on every side, and people are combining for their own selfish interests. Because of this I was glad to hear the warning voice raised by our beloved President and by his counselors, yesterday, and by others of the brethren who have spoken; for I think this should be *a time of warning*, not only to the Latter-day Saints, but to all the world. *We owe it to the world to raise a voice of warning, and especially to the members of the Church.*[38]

No World Peace Because of Wickedness. We do not need to be worrying about the times and the seasons when Christ shall come, but we do need to watch and pray and be ready. Paul, by prophecy, declares that in the day when these calamities shall come, the people would be saying, "peace and safety," in other words, would be seeking for safety, and seeking for peace, and during these very times would come destruction upon them.[39]

What is the matter with the nations today? They are frightened, aren't they? Each nation is contending and contesting with other nations—trying to enter into agreements in regard to armaments, trying to curtail other nations, and trying to build up themselves—and at the same time asking for peace conferences and conventions, and world courts and leagues of nations, and everything else, in order that they might establish peace in the earth, *which they cannot do because they will not get down to the fundamental principles upon which peace is based.*

As long as they have in their hearts selfishness and greed, and the desire for power and for wealth, and for

[38]Conf. Rep., Apr., 1937, p. 59.   [39]1 Thess. 5:1-7.

all of the other things that belong to *this world*, and
forget the things of the kingdom of God, there will be
no peace, and there will be no contentment. There will
be quarreling and contention, strife and war, and in
the midst of all their labor, trouble will come which they
could avoid, and that very easily, by repentance, getting
contrite spirits and broken hearts, and loving their
neighbors; but this they will not do.

Isn't it the height of absurdity to think that nations
calling themselves Christians, worshiping presumably the
same God, will stand ready to spring at each other's
throats? In a revelation given to the Church, the Lord
said, "If ye are not one ye are not mine,"[40] and in speaking to his disciples, when he was upon the earth, he said,
"Why call ye me, Lord, Lord, and do not the things which
I say?"[41]

FEAR IS BASIS FOR MODERN SEARCH FOR PEACE.
The nations of the earth today are crying for peace. But
why? Is it because in their hearts is found the love of
God? No! But because of *fear*—fear of their fellows.
Unrighteousness, the desire to possess, the spirit of greed
and to take advantage of others, has brought to pass a
condition of unrest. These, together with the wickedness
which is in the hearts of the people, have brought a condition of trouble and woe among the nations, so that they
fear and tremble, not because one nation believes or
thinks that the Lord is blessing other peoples more than
he is blessing it, but because the nations know what is
in their *own* hearts; and they fear that the same thing
is in the hearts of their neighbors; and in that they are
justified, for that spirit of envy and strife is everywhere
in the world.[42]

PEACE LOST BECAUSE GOSPEL REJECTED. Today
we find this world torn asunder, wickedness prevailing in

[40]D. & C. 38:27.
[41]Church News, May 4, 1935, p. 6;
    Luke 6:46.
[42]Church News, Feb. 6, 1932, p. 5.

the hearts of the people, distress among the nations, bloodshed such as the world has never seen before. I am going to be bold enough to say that *all of this could have been avoided;* it would have been unnecessary *if the inhabitants of the world had hearkened to the voice of the elders of Israel who are sent to them with this message of salvation,* and which they refused to receive.

FUTILITY OF INSINCERE PRAYERS FOR PEACE. Furthermore, we cry for peace; we are called upon to pray for peace, and we are praying for peace. I have never had very much confidence in the proclamation or the request that was made asking the people of this country to pray for peace, for the very good reason that it was not *sincere.* We cannot pray to the Lord and say: "Listen to our cause; bring victory to us; do what we want you to do; *but don't ask us to do what you want us to do.*"

We have heard from quite a number of those who have spoken in this conference of the wickedness that prevails throughout the world, the wickedness among the boys who have gone into the armed forces of the country, the wickedness of the people who are not in those forces. We all know those things are true, that immorality is rampant, that drunkenness and the filthy use of tobacco are weakening the constitutions of those who go out to fight, and these evils are also among those not in the armed forces. The world is full of evil.[48]

WHAT OF THE FUTURE? *Trouble in the earth will continue; there will be distress, calamity, and perplexity among the nations.*

We need not look for peace in the immediate future because peace will not come. Nevertheless, we may look forward with rejoicing; we need not be downcast, but in the spirit of faith and hope, and in the fear of the Lord, we should look to the future with feelings of joy, of humility, and of worship, with the desire in our hearts,

---

[48]Conf. Rep., Oct., 1944, pp. 144-145.

stronger if possible than ever, of serving the Lord and keeping his commandments, for the day of his coming draws near.[44]

WATCH AND BE READY

LORD WILL COME AS A THIEF IN NIGHT. *"Watch therefore: for ye know not what hour your Lord doth come.* But know this, that if the goodman of the house had known in what watch the thief would come, he would have watched, and would not have suffered his house to be broken up. Therefore *be ye also ready: for in such an hour as ye think not the Son of man cometh."*[45]

So I say to you, my brethren and sisters, and to all who may hear my voice, we are living in the dispensation of the fulness of times. In the year 1836 one of the ancient prophets stood before Joseph Smith and Oliver Cowdery and conferred upon them certain keys that had been promised to be revealed before the second coming of Christ. After he had given authority unto these two young men, he said unto them: "By this ye may know that the great and dreadful day of the Lord is near, even at the doors."[46] That was in 1836, 120 years ago; 120 years have passed. We are that much nearer the opening of that door and the coming of Christ.

I know that there are many, and even some among the Latter-day Saints, who are saying just as the Lord said they would say, "The Lord delayeth his coming."[47] One man said: "It is impossible for Jesus Christ to come inside of three or four hundred years." But I say unto you, Watch.

I do not know when he is going to come. No man knows. Even the angels of heaven are in the dark in regard to that great truth.[48] But this I know, that *the signs that have been pointed out are here.* The earth is full of calamity, of trouble. The hearts of men are failing

---

[44]*Church News,* Jan. 7, 1933, p. 5.   [47]*D. & C.* 45:26; 2 Pet. 3:3-14.
[45]Matt. 24:42-44.   [48]Matt. 24:36-37.
[46]*D. & C.* 110:16.

them. We see the signs as we see the fig tree putting forth her leaves; and knowing this time is near, it behooves me and it behooves you, and all men upon the face of the earth, to *pay heed to the words of Christ, to his apostles and watch,* for we know not the day nor the hour. But I tell you this, it shall come as a thief in the night, when *many of us will not be ready for it.*[49]

RESTORED GOSPEL PREPARES MEN FOR SECOND COMING. The Lord restored the fulness of the gospel for the salvation of mankind, *if men would only hearken and obey his voice and the voice of his servants.* His Church has again been established in the world, and the Master sent forth his servants to all parts of the earth proclaiming *the day of repentance and salvation.* These servants have gone forth crying as did the great prophet and forerunner of our Lord in his former coming, "Repent ye: for the kingdom of heaven is at hand."[50]

They were promised that they should go forth with power and authority, "And the voice of warning shall be unto all people, by the mouths of my disciples, whom I have chosen in these last days. And they shall go forth and none shall stay them, for I the Lord have commanded them. . . . Wherefore, fear and tremble, O ye people, for what I the Lord have decreed in them shall be fulfilled."[51] With this commission the servants of the Lord have gone forth with the message of salvation, and where they could not go they have sent the word, so that it has been proclaimed virtually in all parts of the earth.[52]

NEED TO TEACH CHILDREN IN THESE PERILOUS TIMES. There never was a time in the history of the Church when we have been surrounded by so many evils, temptations, and conditions that allure and entice the children of Zion from paths of righteousness as we find today. It behooves each one of us to be on the alert, and

---

[49]*Millennial Star,* vol. 93, pp. 250-251.
[50]Matt. 3:2.
[51]*D. & C.* 1:4-7.
[52]*Millennial Star,* vol. 103, pp. 611-612.

constantly keep in mind the fact that we belong to the Church, that the Lord has given unto us the fulness of the gospel with all its promises, and that it depends upon our faithfulness and our obedience and integrity to these principles of truth and to the Church whether or not we reap the blessings.

The Lord, in an early day, had to rebuke some of the leading elders of the Church, because conditions were not as they ought to be in their homes. I wonder if most of us would not receive a like rebuke if the Lord should speak again in like manner. In the 93rd section of the *Doctrine and Covenants,* the Lord says, "But I have commanded you to *bring up your children in light and truth.*"[53] All through these revelations we find this instruction that the parents are to bring up their children, to teach them in light and truth.

In another section, 68, the Lord says that if parents do not teach their children so that they will understand the principle of baptism, and teach them to pray, and to have faith in the principles of the gospel, when they reach the age of accountability (eight years) that he will hold those parents responsible, and if their children, through lack of training, should grow up in ignorance of the truth and deny the faith, that he will require an accounting at the hands of their parents. So you see we all have a very grave responsibility.[54]

---

[53]*D. & C.* 93:40.
[54]*Rel. Soc. Mag.,* vol. 18, p. 183;
    D. & C. 68:25-31.

CHAPTER 4

THE MILLENNIUM AND NEW JERUSALEM

LIFE ON THE PARADISIACAL EARTH

MILLENNIAL CLEANSING NOW AT OUR DOORS. This is the word of the Lord: *"All flesh is corrupted before me."*[1] Now, the world has not improved since the Lord uttered those words in 1831. This earth is groaning today under the violence of corruption and sin. Wickedness is in the hearts of the children of men; and so it will continue according to the revelations of the Lord *until* that day when Christ shall come in the clouds of heaven, as he said, in red apparel, coming in the spirit of vengeance to take vengeance on the ungodly, and to cleanse the earth from sin.[2] *We speak of the time when the earth shall be cleansed from sin as the millennium.* We look forward to it; the prophets have spoken of it.[3]

In our own day messengers have come from the presence of the Lord declaring that it is even now at our doors,[4] and yet many, even among the Latter-day Saints, go about their affairs as though this coming of the Lord Jesus Christ and the ushering in of this reign of peace had been indefinitely postponed for many generations. I say to you that *it is at our doors.* I say this with all confidence because the Lord has said it. His messengers have said it as they have come from his presence bearing witness of him.

ARE SAINTS PREPARED FOR MILLENNIUM? We have been warned and forewarned of the great and dreadful

---

[1]*D. & C.* 38:11.
[2]*D. & C.* 133:46-51; Isa. 63:1-6.
[3]Isa. 2; 4; 11; 65:17-25; Micah 4:1-7;
  2 Pet. 3:4-14 *D. & C.* 29:9-29;
  43:17 - 34; 45:11 - 60; 63:49 - 54;
  101:23-37.

[4]*D. & C.* 110:13-16.

day of the Lord which is now even at our doors. Is it not time for us to take notice? Should not the members of the Church of Jesus Christ of Latter-day Saints be sober-minded, have the spirit of humility, and faith, and prayer in their hearts, endeavoring to know the purposes of the Lord and to stand before him in righteousness and thus be prepared should that day come while we are living? Is it not a *fatal mistake* for us to feel that this day is yet a long time off, that it is not to come in our generation, and therefore, we may in safety receive the spirit of the world, and seek after the things the world delights in, its follies and its wickedness? The Lord expects better things of us. He expects us to keep his commandments, and watch and pray and stand, as he has declared, in holy places and be not moved.

These are perilous times. This is a day when we are in grave danger—danger because of the teachings of men, danger because of the lack of faith in the hearts of men, because the philosophies of the world have a tendency to undermine the fundamental things of the gospel of Jesus Christ. These are things we must contend against. There is a spirit of indifference in the world toward religion today. People are not worshiping in spirit and truth, but the Lord expects us, members of the Church of Jesus Christ of Latter-day Saints, to worship in spirit and truth, to walk in righteousness, and to stand in this liberty which will make us free, spoken of in these revelations.[5]

EARTH TO BE RENEWED WHEN MILLENNIUM COMES. Latter-day Saints believe that the day is near, even at the doors, when Christ shall make his appearance as the rightful ruler of the earth. When that time comes, *the whole earth and all things which remain upon its face shall be changed, and "the earth will be renewed and receive its paradisiacal glory."*[6] That means that the earth

---

[5]*Church News,* Jan. 7, 1933, p. 7;   [6]Tenth Article of Faith.
    D. & C. 88:86-87.

shall be brought back to a similar condition which prevailed when peace and righteousness ruled and before death entered with its awful stain of evil and destruction.

When that day comes wickedness must cease and every unclean creature shall be swept from the earth for they will not be able to endure the changed conditions.[7]

All *"element shall melt with fervent heat; and all things shall become new, that my knowledge and glory may dwell upon all the earth. And in that day the enmity of man, and enmity of the beasts, yea, the enmity of all flesh, shall cease from before my face."*[8]

Why shall it cease? Because all things upon the face of the earth that are corruptible shall be removed, whether they are men or beasts, they who have wickedness in their hearts cannot stay—they shall be as stubble —they shall be consumed and pass away.[9] And so the earth shall be *cleansed* that the knowledge of the Lord shall cover the face of the earth.[10]

PARADISIACAL STATUS OF ALL LIFE DURING MILLENNIUM. "And in that day whatsoever any man shall ask, it shall be given unto him. And in that day Satan shall not have power to tempt any man. And there shall be no sorrow because there is no death. In that day an infant shall not die until he is old; and his life shall be as the age of a tree; And when he dies he shall not sleep, that is to say in the earth, but shall be changed in the twinkling of an eye, and shall be caught up, and his rest shall be glorious."[11] That will be a glorious day. It is not a day to be dreaded by those who are righteous, but it is a day, *a dreadful day, unto the wicked,* as you can see from these scriptures, and many more to which I might refer,[12] for *all who will not put themselves in harmony with the gospel of Jesus Christ and with his ever-*

---

[7]*Church News,* May 14, 1932, p. 6; D. & C. 101:24.
[8]D. & C. 101:25-26; 2 Pet. 3:10-14; Isa. 11:6-9; 65:25.
[9]Mal. 4; D. & C. 29:9; 64:23-24; 101:24; 133:64.
[10]Isa. 11:9; Jer. 31:34; Hab. 2:14.
[11]D. & C. 101:27-31; Isa. 65:17-25.
[12]Mal. 4; D. & C. 29:9-11; 133:41-74.

lasting truth, and have in their hearts peace, shall be consumed.

It shall be in that day that the lion shall lie down with the lamb and eat straw as the ox, and all fear, hatred, and enmity shall depart from the earth because *all things having hate in their hearts shall pass away;* and there shall come a change, *a change over men, a change over the beasts* of the field, and upon *all* things living upon the face of the earth.

According to this word I have read there shall be harmony, and love, and peace, and righteousness because Satan is bound that he cannot tempt any man, and that will be the condition that shall be upon the earth for 1,000 years. Not only that, but men shall live *free from sin* and *free from the ravages of disease* and *death* until they reach the age of 100 years. Infants shall not die, they shall live until they have filled the measure of their mortal creation. In fact, mortality shall be reduced to a minimum.[13]

TEMPLE WORK BY MORTALS DURING MILLENNIUM. However, there shall be *mortality* upon the face of the earth during the thousand years, because of the great work that is to be accomplished of salvation for the dead. During that thousand years of peace the great work of the Lord shall be in the temples, and into those temples the people shall go to labor for those who have passed beyond and who are waiting to have these ordinances which pertain to their salvation performed for them by those who still dwell in mortality upon the earth. And so there shall be mortal men, but they shall live from the time of birth until they are 100 years old and shall then be changed suddenly.

Men will have power over disease, and their bodies will become vigorous and strong, for it will be a *new creation* of all things when Christ shall come.

---

[13]*D. & C.* 63:49-52.

RESURRECTION OF RIGHTEOUS AT BEGINNING OF MILLENNIUM. Again, when the Lord comes, not only is this change going to come to the earth and to those who remain upon the earth, to the fish of the sea, to the fowl of the air, and the beasts upon the earth, but the graves are to be opened, and the *righteous dead,* they who have kept the commandments of the Lord, are going to come forth; they shall receive their resurrection no matter when they have lived.[14]

All those who have died in Christ shall come forth from the dead at his coming and shall dwell upon the earth as Christ shall be upon the earth during this millennium. They shall not *remain* here *all* the time during the thousand years, but they will mingle with those who are still here in mortal life.[15] These resurrected saints and the Savior himself, shall come to give instruction and guidance; to reveal unto us the things we ought to know; to give us information concerning the work in the temples of the Lord so we may do the work which is essential to the salvation of worthy men.

It matters not so far as we are concerned whether we die before that day comes or are living on the earth, for if we die in righteousness we shall be raised in the resurrection of the just, and shall be caught up to meet Christ in the clouds of glory when he comes to take possession of the earth, as King of kings and Lord of lords. This is the gospel of Jesus Christ. It is declared in the revelations of the Lord which are found in the *Bible* and the *Doctrine and Covenants.*

WICKED REMAIN IN SPIRIT PRISON DURING MILLENNIUM. However, if we have not kept the commandments of the Lord, if we have been unjust, and lovers of sin and our hearts have been set upon evil, then we shall die and shall not live again until the thousand years

---

[14]*D. & C.* 76:50-80; 88:96-99; Rev. 20:4-6.

[15]Joseph Fielding Smith, *Teachings of the Prophet Joseph Smith,* pp. 268-269.

are ended.[16] *It is decreed that the unrighteous shall have to spend their time during this thousand years in the prison house prepared for them where they can repent and cleanse themselves through the things which they shall suffer.*

John, in his great vision, saw the rest of the dead and they lived not again until the thousand years were ended.[17] That is a calamity—it is a dreadful thing to contemplate, for there shall be a great host of men swept off the face of the earth because of their wickedness. The bodies of these will have to remain in the grave and their spirits in the spirit house to be taught repentance and faith in God while the thousand years of peace are progressing upon the earth.

I wish, my good brethren and sisters, that we would read these revelations, that we would make ourselves more familiar with that which they contain, for there shall be *a judgment when Christ comes.*[18] We are informed that the books shall be opened, the dead shall be judged out of the things which are written in the books and among the books will be the *book of life.* We shall see its pages; *we shall see ourselves just as we are.* And we are to understand with a righteous understanding that the judgments which are meted out to us are just and true, whether we come into the kingdom of God, to receive these glorious blessings, or whether we are banished into the realm of the dead.[19]

GOSPEL AND CHURCH IN MILLENNIUM

MARRIAGE SUPPER OF LAMB IS AT SECOND COMING. "And a voice came out of the throne, saying, Praise our God, all ye his servants, and ye that fear him, both small and great. And I heard as it were the voice of a great multitude, and as the voice of many waters, and as the voice of mighty thunderings, saying, Alleluia: for the

---

[16]*D. & C.* 76:81-88, 98-112; 88:100-102.
[17]Rev. 20:5.

[18]Matt. 25:31-46.
[19]*Church News,* Jan. 7, 1933, p. 7; Rev. 20:11-15; 2 Ne. 9:10-16, 46.

Lord God omnipotent reigneth. Let us be glad and rejoice, and give honour to him: for *the marriage of the Lamb is come, and his wife hath made herself ready.* And to her was granted that she should be arrayed in fine linen, clean and white: for *the fine linen is the righteousness of saints.* And he saith unto me, Write, *Blessed are they which are called unto the marriage supper of the Lamb.* And he saith unto me, These are the true sayings of God."[20]

This prophecy of the *marriage of the Lamb* is a figure of speech, having reference to the second coming of our Savior and the *feast,* or *supper,* that the righteous shall receive at his coming. When teaching the Jews, and more especially his disciples, the Savior spoke of the *Bridegroom* when referring to himself.[21]

RIGHTEOUS SAINTS ARE BRIDE OF LAMB. In Revelation, chapter 21, the comparison is made to a marriage of the Lamb with the city New Jerusalem: "And I John saw the holy city, new Jerusalem, coming down from God out of heaven, prepared as *a bride adorned for her husband.* And I heard a great voice out of heaven saying, Behold, the tabernacle of God is with men, and *he will dwell with them,* and they shall be his people, and God *himself shall be with them, and be their God. . . .*

"And there came unto me one of the seven angels which had the seven vials full of the seven last plagues, and talked with me, saying, Come hither, I will shew thee *the bride, the Lamb's wife.* And he carried me away in the spirit to a great and high mountain, and shewed me that great city, the holy Jerusalem, descending out of heaven from God, Having the glory of God: and her light was like unto a stone most precious, even like a jasper stone, clear as crystal."[22]

In the *Doctrine and Covenants* we find the following: "That thy *church* may come forth out of the wilder-

---

[20]Rev. 19:5-9.
[21]Matt. 9:15; 25:1-13; *D. & C.* 33:17; 65:3; 88:92; 133:10, 19.
[22]Rev. 21:2-3, 9-11.

ness of darkness, and shine forth fair as the moon, clear as the sun, and terrible as an army with banners; And be *adorned as a bride* for that day when thou shalt unveil the heavens, and cause the mountains to flow down at thy presence, and the valleys to be exalted, the rough places made smooth; that thy glory may fill the earth."[23]

The vision of John and the revelation to Joseph Smith both have reference to the same event, the second coming of our Lord in his power and glory, to receive his Church or kingdom, the *New Jerusalem being the capital city of the Church,* and there is no difference in the meaning whether reference is to the Church or the New Jerusalem, for the righteous will have inheritance in the New Jerusalem. Therefore *the bride of the Lamb is the organization of the righteous who have inheritance in the holy city.*[24]

TELESTIAL WICKEDNESS BRINGS MILLENNIAL DESTRUCTION. When the reign of Jesus Christ comes during the millennium, *only those who have lived the telestial law will be removed.* The earth will be cleansed of all its corruption and wickedness. Those who have lived *virtuous lives,* who have been *honest* in their dealings with their fellow man and have *endeavored to do good* to the best of their understanding, shall remain.

To Malachi it was revealed that, "All the *proud,* yea, and all that do *wickedly,* shall be stubble: and the day that cometh shall *burn* them up, saith the Lord of hosts, that it shall leave them neither root nor branch."[25] Isaiah also declared that because the people had broken the everlasting covenant and defiled the earth, "therefore the inhabitants of the earth are *burned,* and *few men left.*"[26]

In this dispensation the Lord revealed the following: "And prepare for the revelation which is to come, when the veil of the covering of my temple, in my tabernacle,

---

[23]D. & C. 109:73-74.   [25]Mal. 4:1.
[24]*Era,* vol. 57, p. 304.   [26]Isa. 24:6.

which hideth the earth, shall be taken off, and all flesh shall see me together. And *every corruptible thing*, both of man, or of the beasts of the field, or of the fowls of the heavens, or of the fish of the sea, that dwells upon all the face of the earth, *shall be consumed;* And also that of element shall melt with fervent heat; and all things shall become new, that my knowledge and glory may dwell upon all the earth."[27]

So we learn that *all corruptible things*, whether men or beasts or element, shall be consumed; but *all that does not come under this awful edict shall remain.* Therefore, the *honest* and *upright* of all nations, kindreds, and beliefs, who have kept the *terrestrial* or *celestial law*, will remain. Under these conditions, people will enter the great reign of Jesus Christ carrying with them their beliefs and religious doctrines. Their agency will not be taken from them.

VARIOUS CHURCHES FOUND DURING MILLENNIUM. On this subject President Brigham Young has said: *"In the millennium men will have the privilege of their own belief,* but they will not have the privilege of treating the name and character of Deity as they have done heretofore. No, but every knee shall bow and every tongue confess to the glory of God the Father that Jesus is the Christ."[28]

The Prophet Joseph Smith has said: *"There will be wicked men on the earth during the thousand years. The heathen nations who will not come up to worship will be visited with the judgments of God, and must eventually be destroyed from the earth."*[29]

The saying that there will be *wicked* men on the earth during the millennium has been misunderstood by many, because the Lord declared that the wicked shall not stand, but shall be consumed.[30] In using this term

[27]*D. & C.* 101:23-25.
[28]*Discourses of Brigham Young*, 1925 ed., pp. 182-183; 1943 ed., p. 119.
[29]Smith, *op. cit.*, pp. 268-269; Zech. 14:16-21.
[30]*D. & C.* 5:18-19; 29:9-10; 101:23-25.

wicked it should be interpreted in the language of the Lord as recorded in the *Doctrine and Covenants,* section 84, verses 49-53. Here the Lord speaks of those who have not received the gospel as being *wicked* as they are still under the bondage of sin, having not been baptized. *The inhabitants of the terrestrial order will remain on the earth during the millennium, and this class is without the gospel ordinances.*

The Lord said through Isaiah, speaking of the millennium: "For, behold, I create new heavens and a new earth: and the former shall not be remembered, nor come into mind. But be ye glad and rejoice for ever in that which I create: for, behold, I create Jerusalem a rejoicing, and her people a joy. And I will rejoice in Jerusalem, and joy in my people: and the voice of weeping shall be no more heard in her, nor the voice of crying. There shall be no more thence an infant of days, nor an old man that hath not filled his days: for the child shall die an hundred years old; but the *sinner* being an hundred years old shall be *accursed*."[31]

SPREAD OF GOSPEL DURING MILLENNIUM. The gospel will be taught far more intensely and with greater power during the millennium, *until all the inhabitants of the earth shall embrace it.* Satan shall be bound so that he cannot tempt any man. Should any man refuse to repent and accept the gospel under those conditions then he would be *accursed.* Through the revelations given to the prophets, we learn that during the reign of Jesus Christ for a thousand years *eventually all people will embrace the truth.*

Isaiah prophesied of the millennium as follows: "The wolf also shall dwell with the lamb, and the leopard shall lie down with the kid; and the calf and the young lion and the fatling together; and a little child shall lead them. And the cow and the bear shall feed; their young ones shall lie down together: and the lion shall eat straw

---

[31]Isa. 65:17-20; *D. & C.* 101:28-31.

like the ox. And the sucking child shall play on the hole of the asp, and the weaned child shall put his hand on the cockatrice' den. They shall not hurt nor destroy in all my holy mountain: *for the earth shall be full of the knowledge of the Lord, as the waters cover the sea.*"[32]

This chapter in Isaiah, Moroni quoted to the Prophet Joseph Smith and said to him it was about to be fulfilled.[33] *If the knowledge of the Lord covers the earth as the waters do the sea, then it must be universally received.* Moreover, the promise of the Lord through Jeremiah is that it will no longer be necessary for anyone to teach his neighbor, "saying, Know the Lord: for they shall all know me, from the least of them unto the greatest of them, saith the Lord."[34]

DECEASED CHILDREN TO CHOOSE MATES IN MILLENNIUM. We have people coming to us all the time just as fearful as they can be that a child of theirs who has died will lose the blessings of the kingdom of God unless that child is sealed to someone who is dead. They do not know the wishes of their child who died too young to think of marriage, but they want to go straight to the temple and have a sealing performed. Such a thing as this is unnecessary and in my judgment wrong.

The Lord has said through his servants that during the millennium those who have passed beyond and have attained the resurrection will reveal in person to those who are still in mortality all the information which is required to complete the work of these who have passed from this life. Then the dead will have the privilege of making known the things they desire and are entitled to receive. In this way no soul will be neglected and the work of the Lord will be perfected.

It is the duty of parents who have children who have died and who were old enough to be endowed, to go to the temple and perform this endowment for them. When

---

[32]Isa. 11:6-9; 65:25; Hab. 2:14.
[33]Jos. Smith 2:40.
[34]*Era,* vol. 58, pp. 142, 176; Jer. 31:34.

you have done this, you may let the matter of further
work rest, except the sealing of these children to their
parents, until the proper time comes.[35]

FINAL CELESTIAL DESTINY OF EARTH. The righteous dead are to come forth from their graves, and there
will be a mingling of mortals and immortals upon the
earth. Christ and the resurrected saints who hold the
priesthood shall teach the people, so there can be no mis-
understandings and mistakes. For 1,000 years shall this
happy time of peace prevail and *in due time all the inhabitants of the earth shall be brought into the fold of
the Church.*

When the thousand years are ended, Satan shall
be loosed for a little season and *wickedness shall return
to the earth.* Satan shall gather his forces and in anger
attempt a vain effort to wrest the earth from Christ.
Michael, the great prince, the archangel, who once graced
the earth and was known as Adam, the father of the
human family, shall fight the battles of the just and shall
overcome. The last resurrection shall take place, and
the rest of the dead, who had no place in the millennial
reign shall be brought forth to the *final judgment.* All
men shall be judged according to their works.[36]

Then the end shall come and the earth shall pass
away in *death,* but to be raised in the *resurrection* by
which it shall be made a *celestial body* and the fit abode
of celestial beings who shall dwell in the presence of God
the Father and his Son Jesus Christ forever as priests
and kings unto the Most High.[37]

TWO MILLENNIAL WORLD CAPITALS

ZION: THE LAND OF JOSEPH. There are many references in the *Bible* to *Zion,* a land or place separate and
distinct from *Jerusalem.* Two such passages are found

---

[35]*Gen. & Hist. Mag.,* vol. 21, p. 154.
[36]*D. & C.* 88:86-116; 1 Cor. 15:24-28;
    Rev. 20.
[37]*Church News,* Aug. 19, 1933, p. 4;
    D. & C. 88:16-28.

in the 2nd chapter of Isaiah and the 4th chapter of Micah.[38] It would be foolish to say that these references to Zion were to the hill in Jerusalem where David dwelt. Through modern revelation the Lord has made it known that the *American continent is Zion*. It is to be on this land that the city Zion, the New Jerusalem, shall be built. These predictions are clearly stated in the *Book of Mormon* and are in perfect accord with the writings of the *Bible*.[39]

This western continent is known as the *land of Joseph* and is also designated as the *land of Zion*. The holy city which is to be built upon this land is sometimes called the *City of Zion*. We should keep in mind that these terms (City of Zion, and New Jerusalem) have reference to the same sanctified place from whence shall go forth the law, with the word of the Lord from Jerusalem. Enoch's city was also called *Zion*, which means by interpretation, the *pure in heart*.[40]

JUDAH GATHERS TO JERUSALEM, EPHRAIM TO ZION. "And it shall come to pass in the *last days*, that the mountain of *the Lord's house shall be established in the top of the mountains*, and shall be exalted above the hills; and all nations shall flow unto it. And many people shall go and say, Come ye, and let us go up to the mountain of the Lord, to the house of the God of Jacob; and he will teach us of his ways, and we will walk in his paths: for *out of Zion shall go forth the law*, and *the word of the Lord from Jerusalem*."[41]

The statement is very clear that two separate cities, or centers, are mentioned by Isaiah. In modern revelation this is confirmed, and we are informed just where *the city of Zion—which is the New Jerusalem—*shall be built.

In order to get a proper understanding of this question, it is necessary to explain the fact that *Palestine is*

[38]Isa. 2:2-5; Micah 4:1-7; 2 Ne. 12:2-5.
[39]*Era*, vol. 26, p. 960; 3 Ne. 20:22; 21:20-29; Ether 13:2-11.
[40]*Era*. vol. 33, pp. 467-468; Moses 7:17-21, 68-69.
[41]Isa. 2:2-3.

to be the gathering place of the tribe of Judah and "the children of Israel his companions," after their long dispersion as predicted by the prophets. America is the land of Zion. It was given to Joseph, son of Jacob, and his descendants to be an everlasting inheritance. The children of *Ephraim* (son of Joseph) and "all the house of Israel his companions," *will be gathered to Zion,* or America.[42]

In the blessing given by Jacob to his son Joseph the inheritance of America is foreshadowed and predicted in the following words: "Joseph is a fruitful bough, even a fruitful bough by a well; whose branches run over the wall: . . . The blessings of thy father have prevailed above the blessings of my progenitors *unto the utmost bound of the everlasting hills:* they shall be on the head of Joseph, and on the crown of the head of him that was separate from his brethren."[43]

Because of his faithfulness and integrity, Joseph received greater blessings than the progenitors of Jacob and was rewarded with the land of Zion. His brothers, with malicious intent, separated him and cast him out from among them. The Lord, in rewarding him, separated him from his brothers—the other tribes of Israel— and gave him an inheritance in a land that is choice above all other lands, which, we have learned from the *Book of Mormon* and modern revelation, is America.

Two Holy Cities: Zion and Jerusalem. In this great day of gathering, the Lord has commanded that those of the house of Israel who are scattered among the Gentiles should flee unto Zion, and those who are of the house of Judah should flee unto Jerusalem, "unto the mountains of the Lord's house," which is their gathering place.[44]

In each land a holy city shall be built which shall be the capital from whence the law and the word of the

---

[42]Ezek. 37:15-28.   [44]D. & C. 133:12-13.
[43]Gen. 49:22-25.

Lord shall go forth to all peoples. The Savior said to the Nephites: "Behold, this people will I establish in *this land,* unto the fulfilling of the covenant which I made with your father Jacob; and *it shall be a New Jerusalem.* And the powers of heaven shall be in the midst of this people; yea, even I will be in the midst of you."[45]

Moroni, writing of the Jaredites, has said: "Behold, Ether saw the days of Christ, and he spake concerning *a New Jerusalem upon this land.* And he spake also concerning the house of Israel, and the Jerusalem from whence Lehi should come—after it should be destroyed it should be built up again, a holy city unto the Lord; wherefore, it could not be a new Jerusalem for it had been in a time of old; but it should be built up again, and become *a holy city of the Lord;* and it should be built unto the house of Israel."[46]

TWO HOLY CITIES: JERUSALEM AND NEW JERUSALEM. We are informed in the revelation given to Joseph Smith the Prophet, that *the city of Zion and the New Jerusalem is one and the same.* In a number of revelations the Lord speaks of the New Jerusalem which is to be built.[47] For instance, we read: "And *it shall be called the New Jerusalem,* a land of peace, a city of refuge, a place of safety for the saints of the Most High God; And the glory of the Lord shall be there, and the terror of the Lord also shall be there, insomuch that the wicked will not come unto it, and *it shall be called Zion.*"[48]

Also: "Yea, the word of the Lord concerning his church, established in the last days for the restoration of his people, as he has spoken by the mouth of his prophets, and for the gathering of his saints to stand upon Mount Zion, *which shall be the city of New Jerusalem.*"[49]

Jerusalem of old, after the Jews have been cleansed and sanctified from all their sin, shall become *a holy city*

⁴⁵3 Ne. 20:22.
⁴⁶Ether 13:2-5.
⁴⁷D. & C. 28:9; 42:9.

⁴⁸D. & C. 45:66-67; 57:2; 58:7.
⁴⁹D. & C. 84:2-5.

where the Lord shall dwell and from whence he shall send forth *his word* unto all people. Likewise, on this continent, the city of Zion, New Jerusalem, shall be built, and *from it the law of God shall also go forth.* There will be no conflict, for *each city shall be headquarters for the Redeemer of the world,* and *from each he shall send forth his proclamations as occasion may require.* Jerusalem shall be the gathering place of Judah and his fellows of the house of Israel, and Zion shall be the gathering place of Ephraim and his fellows, upon whose heads shall be conferred "the richer blessings."[50]

Zion and Jerusalem Separate Cities. Many prophecies in the *Bible* refer to Jerusalem and to Zion as *separate* places. It is evident that these references do not apply to the hill Zion which is a part of the city of Jerusalem. Among these predictions we cite the following:

"O *Zion,* that bringest good tidings, get thee up into the high mountain; O *Jerusalem,* that bringest good tidings, lift up thy voice with strength; lift it up, be not afraid; say unto the cities of Judah, Behold your God!"[51]

"The Lord also shall roar out of *Zion,* and utter his voice from *Jerusalem;* . . . So shall ye know that I am the Lord your God dwelling in *Zion,* my holy mountain: *then shall Jerusalem be holy,* and there shall no strangers pass through her any more."[52]

In Isaiah, Zion and Jerusalem are called *cities: "Thy holy cities are a wilderness, Zion is a wilderness, Jerusalem a desolation."*[53] Isaiah and other prophets also predict that headquarters for Zion in the last days should be established in the mountains, and people from all nations should say: "Come ye, and let us go up to the mountain of the Lord, to the house of the God of Jacob; and he will teach us of his ways, and we will walk in his paths: for *out of Zion shall go forth the law, and the word of the Lord from Jerusalem."*[54]

[50]*Era,* vol. 22, pp. 814-816; *D. & C.* 133:26-35.
[51]Isa. 40:9.
[52]Joel 3:16-17.
[53]Isa. 64:10.
[54]Isa. 2:3.

ZION AND JERUSALEM: TWO WORLD CAPITALS.
When Joseph Smith translated the *Book of Mormon*, he
learned that America is the land of Zion which was given
to Joseph and his children and that on this land the *City
Zion*, or *New Jerusalem*, is to be built. He also learned
that *Jerusalem in Palestine is to be rebuilt and become a
holy city*.[55] These *two cities*, one in the land of Zion and
one in Palestine, are to become *capitals for the kingdom
of God during the millennium*.

In the meantime, while the work of preparation is
going on and Israel is being gathered, many people are
coming to the land of Zion saying: "Come ye, and let us
go up to the mountain of the Lord, to the house of the
God of Jacob." The Latter-day Saints are fulfilling this
prediction, since they are being gathered from all parts
of the earth and are coming to the house of the Lord in
these valleys of the mountains. Here they are being
taught in the ways of the Lord through the restoration
of the gospel and by receiving blessings in the temples
now erected. Morever, *before many years have passed
away, the Lord will command the building of the City
Zion, and Jerusalem in Palestine will in due time be
cleansed and become a holy city* and the habitation of the
Jews *after* they are cleansed and are willing to accept
Jesus Christ as their Redeemer.[56]

TEMPLES IN ZION AND JERUSALEM. "And righteousness will I send down out of heaven; and truth will
I send forth out of the earth, to bear testimony of mine
Only Begotten; his resurrection from the dead; yea, and
also the resurrection of all men; and righteousness and
truth will I cause to sweep the earth as with a flood, to
gather out mine elect from the four quarters of the earth,
unto a place which I shall prepare, *an Holy City*, that
my people may gird their loins, and be looking forth for

[55]3 Ne. 20:22; 21:20-29; Ether 13:1- [56]*Church News*, Nov. 21, 1931, p. 6.
12.

the time of my coming; for there shall be my tabernacle, and *it shall be called Zion, a New Jerusalem.*

"And the Lord said unto Enoch: Then shalt thou and all thy city meet them there, and we will receive them into our bosom, and they shall see us; and we will fall upon their necks, and they shall fall upon our necks, and we will kiss each other; *And there shall be mine abode, and it shall be Zion,* which shall come forth out of all the creations which I have made; and for the space of a thousand years the earth shall rest."[57]

When Christ comes in fulfilment of this promise, *there will be on the earth two great cities made holy with holy sanctuaries, or temples.*[58] One will be the city of Jerusalem in the land of Judah, which shall be rebuilt; the other the city Zion, or the New Jerusalem, in the land of Joseph.[59]

LAND OF ZION

NORTH AND SOUTH AMERICA COMPRISE LAND OF ZION. Members of the "Reorganized" Church inform us that Zion does not include Utah, but is limited to Jackson County, Missouri, and the regions round about, Nauvoo being one of the "corner stones"; and they say that when the saints came westward, they left the borders of Zion. Moreover, they claim that since temples were to be built in Zion and Jerusalem, all the temples we may build in Utah or the West are not recognized of the Lord on this ground alone, if no other.

We accept the fact that the *center place* where the City New Jerusalem is to be built, is in Jackson County, Missouri. It was never the intention to substitute Utah or any other place for Jackson County. But we do hold that Zion, when reference is made to the land, is as broad as America, both North and South—*all of it is Zion.* If Zion is limited in its scope to the country surrounding

---

[57]Moses 7:62-64.   [59]*Era,* vol. 33, p. 468.
[58]Ezek. 37:28; *D. & C.* 133:12-13, 30-35.

Jackson County, it is indeed too bad that Nephi did not
know that fact. What a glorious thing it would have been
had there been a few "Reorganites" in his day to inform
him of it. Then he and his people would not have fallen
into the error of building temples—like unto Solomon's
at Jerusalem—away off down in Central or South America,[60] but they could have placed one in Jackson County,
or the regions round about. It was really an unfortunate
occurrence.

ZION: A LAND CHOICE ABOVE ALL OTHER LANDS.
But to be serious. The *Book of Mormon* informs us that
the whole of America, both North and South, is *a choice
land above all other lands, in other words—Zion.* The
Lord told the Jaredites that he would lead them to a land
"which is choice above all the lands of the earth."[61] We
understand that they landed in Central America where
their kingdom existed the greater part of their residence
in America.

When the Lord began to lead the family of Lehi
to this land, he said to them: "And inasmuch as ye shall
keep my commandments, ye shall prosper, and shall be
led to *a land of promise;* yea, even a land which I have
prepared for you; yea, *a land which is choice above all
other lands.*"[62] It is generally understood that they
landed in South America, and that their nations, the
Nephites and Lamanites, dwelt in South and Central
America during the greater part of their sojourn here.
At any rate, the time of their civilization was principally
spent in the south and not in the region now comprising
the United States. This proves beyond the possibility of
doubt that the choice land was South as well as North
America, and while the City New Jerusalem, which the
Book of Mormon tells us is to be built on this land that
is choice above all other lands, will be in Jackson County,

60 2 Ne. 5:16.
61 Ether 1:42.
62 1 Ne. 2:20.

nevertheless, if one accepts the *Book of Mormon, one must accept the whole hemisphere as the land of Zion.*

At the April conference of the Church, held at Nauvoo in 1844, the Prophet Joseph Smith declared that the whole of America was Zion.[63]

GARDEN OF EDEN AND CITY ZION SAME PLACE. In accord with the revelations given to the Prophet Joseph Smith, we teach that *the Garden of Eden was on the American continent located where the City Zion, or the New Jerusalem, will be built.*[64] When Adam and Eve were driven out of the Garden, they eventually dwelt at a place called *Adam-ondi-Ahman,* situated in what is now Daviess County, Missouri.[65] Three years before the death of Adam he called the righteous of his posterity at this place and blessed them,[66] and it is at this place where Adam, or Michael, will sit as we read in the 7th chapter of Daniel.[67]

LANDS OF ZION AND JERUSALEM TO UNITE. We are committed to the fact that Adam dwelt on this American continent. But when Adam dwelt here, it was not the American continent, nor was it the Western Hemisphere, for all the land was in *one place,* and all the water was in one place. There was no Atlantic Ocean separating the hemispheres. "And God said, let the waters under the heaven be gathered together unto *one place,* and let the dry land appear: and it was so. And God called the dry land Earth; and the gathering together of the waters called he Seas: and God saw that it was good."[68]

If all the water was in *one place,* then naturally all the land was in one place; therefore, the shape of the earth, as to the water and the land surface, was not as we find it today. Then we read in Genesis that there came a time when the earth was divided.[69] There are

---

[63]*Origin of the "Reorganized" Church,* pp. 96-97; Smith, *op. cit.,* p. 362.
[64]*D. & C.* 57:1-3; 84:1-3.
[65]Smith, *op. cit.,* pp. 122, 158-159.
[66]*D. & C.* 107:53-57.
[67]Dan. 7:9-14, 21-22, 26-27.
[68]Gen. 1:9-10.
[69]Gen. 10:25.

some people who believe that this simply means that the land surface was divided among the various tribes, but this is not the meaning; *it was an actual dividing of the surface of the earth,* and it was broken up as we find it now.

The Lord revealed to the Prophet Joseph Smith that *when he comes, as a part of the great restoration, this land surface will be brought back to its original form.* When that time comes, the land of Zion (Western Hemisphere) and the land of Jerusalem "shall be turned back into their own place, and the earth shall be like as it was in the days before it was divided."[70] John saw this day when "every island fled away, and the mountains were not found."[71]

BUILDING THE NEW JERUSALEM

EARLY SPECULATION AS TO SITE OF NEW JERUSALEM. When it was made known that the New Jerusalem was to be built in America, the saints began to wonder where the city would be. Hiram Page, one of the witnesses of the *Book of Mormon,* secured a "peep stone" by means of which he claimed to receive revelation for the Church. Among the things he attempted to make known was where this city was to be built. Considerable commotion naturally prevailed, and even Oliver Cowdery was deceived into accepting what Hiram Page had given. The Prophet Joseph Smith had some difficulty in correcting this evil and composing the minds of the members of the Church.

Good came out of this incident, however, for the Lord made it known that there was but one at a time who was empowered with the gift of receiving revelation for the Church, and this was to be a law by which the Church was to be governed. In this same revelation the Lord corrected the false teaching of Hiram Page and informed the Church that the site for the New Jerusalem had not been revealed, but when it was revealed it would be "on the borders of the Lamanites."[72] Oliver Cowdery was appointed to go on a mission to the Lamanites and, later, Parley P. Pratt and Ziba Peterson were called to accompany him. In this way the gospel message was taken into Jackson County, Missouri.

SAINTS TO INHERIT ZION IN TIME AND ETERNITY. Early in 1831, the headquarters of the Church were transferred from Fayette, New York, to Kirtland, Ohio, where the Lord said he would give to the Church his law, and where they should be endowed with power from on high.[73] The Lord also promised to reveal to the saints the place of their inheritance: "And this shall be my covenant with you, ye shall have it for *the land of your inheritance,* and for the *inheritance of your children forever,* while the earth shall stand, and *ye shall possess it again in eternity,* no more to pass away."[74]

When the members of the Church gathered to Kirtland, the Lord gave them his law. He also gave instruction for the purpose of preparing them for their inheritance. He called upon the elders to go forth declaring his word "into the regions westward," and to build up his Church, "Until the time shall come when it shall be revealed unto you from on high, when the city of the New Jerusalem shall be prepared, that ye may be gathered in one, that ye may be my people and I will be your God."[75] The Bishop of the Church was instructed in relation to the property of the saints; the care of the storehouse, in looking after the wants of the poor and needy; and also in laying up funds for the purchase of lands and the building up of the New Jerusalem, the site of which was soon to be revealed.[76]

SITE OF NEW JERUSALEM REVEALED. Early in June, 1831, a conference was held in Kirtland. At the close

[72]D. & C. 28:1-16.   [75]D. & C. 42:8-9.
[73]D. & C. 38:32.   [76]D. & C. 42:10, 30-42.
[74]D. & C. 38:20,

of this conference, June 7th, the Lord said: "I, the Lord, will make known unto you what I will that ye shall do from this time until the next conference, which shall be held in Missouri, upon the land which I will consecrate unto my people, which are a remnant of Jacob, and those who are heirs according to the covenant. . . . And thus, even as I have said, if ye are faithful ye shall assemble yourselves together to rejoice upon *the land of Missouri, which is the land of your inheritance,* which is now the land of your enemies. But, behold, *I, the Lord, will hasten the city in its time,* and will crown the faithful with joy and with rejoicing."[77]

Obedient to this commandment the elders journeyed forth two by two and in due time arrived in Jackson County, Missouri. There, in answer to their earnest prayer, the Lord revealed the site of the New Jerusalem and the place for the building of his temple, or holy sanctuary, which had been seen by Enoch and also by Ether, as being established in the last days.

In making this site known the Lord said: "Hearken, O ye elders of my church, saith the Lord your God, who have assembled yourselves together, according to my commandments, in this land, which is the land of Missouri, which is the land which I have appointed and consecrated for the gathering of the saints. Wherefore, *this is the land of promise, and the place for the city of Zion.*"[78] The place for the building of the temple was then pointed out. August 2, 1831, the land was dedicated by Sidney Rigdon as a possession and inheritance for the saints, and the following day the Prophet Joseph Smith dedicated the site for the temple on a spot a short distance west of the court house in Independence.

BUILDING OF NEW JERUSALEM DEFERRED. That the New Jerusalem, or City Zion, was to be built at once and the temple erected also, naturally was the thought of the assembled brethren. The Lord had previously

[77]*D. & C.* 52:2, 42-43.   [78]*D. & C.* 57:1-2.

given them a commandment respecting their duties and
had instructed them in relation to his law to be observed
in Zion. He indicated, also, that the city was not to be
built at that time. "Ye cannot behold with your natural
eyes, for the present time, the design of your God concerning those things which shall come *hereafter*, and the
glory which shall follow after much tribulation. For *after
much tribulation come the blessings*. Wherefore the day
cometh that ye shall be crowned with much glory; *the
hour is not yet, but is nigh at hand*."[79]

It is true that the Lord would have blessed the saints
and would have commenced the establishment of the
Holy City at that time had they hearkened faithfully to
his commandments, but from these words of the Lord
it is plain to see that *the glory of Zion was future*,
although in the spiritual sense near at hand.

In other revelations it was made plain that the elders
would have to be endowed with power from on high and
go forth to declare the gospel to the nations and "push
the people together from the ends of the earth," *before*
Zion could be built.[80] So the Lord in the very beginning
instructed the saints that the building of the New Jerusalem and its sacred temple would be deferred until many
other things were accomplished, and they had passed
through much tribulation.

CITY OF ZION AND TEMPLE YET TO BE BUILT.
Nearly 100 years have passed since the site of Zion was
dedicated and the spot for the temple was chosen, and
some of the members of the Church seem to be fearful
lest the word of the Lord shall fail. Others have tried
to convince themselves that the original plan has been
changed and that the Lord does not require at our hands
this mighty work which has been predicted by the prophets of ancient times. *We have not been released from this
responsibility, nor shall we be*. The word of the Lord
will not fail.

---

[79]*D. & C.* 58:3-4.   [80]*D. & C.* 58:44-58.

If we look back and examine his word carefully, we will discover that nothing has failed of all that he has predicted, neither shall one jot or tittle pass away unfulfilled. It is true that the Lord commanded the saints to build to his name a temple in Zion. This they attempted to do, but were prevented by their enemies, so the Lord did not require the work at their hands *at that time*.[81] The release from the building of the temple did not, however, cancel the responsibility of building the City and the House of the Lord, *at some future time. When the Lord gets ready for it to be accomplished, he will command his people, and the work will be done.*[82]

---

[81]*D. & C.* 124:49-54.   [82]*Era,* vol. 33, pp. 468-469.

CHAPTER 5

PRIESTHOOD: GOD'S ETERNAL POWER

ETERNAL NATURE OF PRIESTHOOD

AUTHORITY: A UNIVERSAL PRINCIPLE. *Authority is an eternal principle operative throughout the universe.* To the "utmost bounds" of space all things are governed by law emanating from the Lord our God. On Kolob and other giant governing stars and in the tiny electron, infinitesimally small and of which all things are composed, *divine authority is manifest in the form of immutable law.* All space is filled with matter and that matter is *controlled and directed* by an All-Wise and Omniscient Creator.[1]

PRIESTHOOD: ITS NATURE AND PURPOSE. Priesthood is divine authority which is conferred upon men that they may officiate in the ordinances of the gospel. In other words, *priesthood is a part of God's own power,* which he bestows upon his chosen servants that they may act in his name in proclaiming the gospel and officiating in all the ordinances thereof. All such official acts performed by these duly authorized servants are recognized by the Author of our salvation.[2]

Man cannot act legally in the name of the Lord unless he is vested with the priesthood, which is divine authority. No man has the power or the right to take this honor to himself. Unless he is called of God, as was Aaron,[3] he has no authority to officiate in any of the ordinances of the gospel; should he do so his act is not valid or recognized in the heavens. The Lord has said

[1]*Era,* vol. 31, p. 256; D. & C. 88:36-45; Abra. 3:1-28.
[2]*Millennial Star,* vol. 90, p. 305; D. & C. 1:38.
[3]Heb. 5:4; Ps. 105:26; Ex. 28; 29; Lev. 8; D. & C. 27:8.

his house is a house of order, and he has given the commandment that no man shall come unto the Father but by his divine law which is established in the heavens.[4]

All men who assume authority, but who have not been properly called, will have to answer for their acts in the day of judgment. Nothing that they perform in the name of the Lord is valid, for it lacks the stamp of divine authority. To deceive and lead others to believe that unauthorized acts are valid when performed in the name of the Lord is a grievous sin in the sight of God[5]

LEGAL ADMINISTRATORS ESSENTIAL TO SALVATION. The question of priesthood or divine authority is vital, since it concerns the salvation of each of us. It is impossible for a man to enter the kingdom of God without complying with the laws of that kingdom. Only authorized officers may properly officiate in rites and ceremonies of the kingdom. No man has the right to assume the authority and officiate without being ordained to the ministry. To do so is an unauthorized and illegal act.[6]

ANTIQUITY OF MELCHIZEDEK PRIESTHOOD

PRIESTHOOD IN PRE-EXISTENCE. In regard to the holding of the priesthood in pre-existence, I will say that there was an organization there just as well as an organization here, and men there held authority. *Men chosen to positions of trust in the spirit world held priesthood.*[7]

ADAM HELD KEYS AND PRIESTHOOD. To Adam, after he was driven from the Garden of Eden, the plan of salvation was revealed, and upon him the *fulness* of the priesthood was conferred. As Michael, the prince, *he holds the keys of all the dispensations,* which appointment he received under Jesus Christ, "Who hath appointed Michael your prince, and established his feet, and set him upon high, and given unto him the *keys of*

---

[4]*D. & C.* 132:8-12.
[5]*Church News,* Aug. 22, 1931, p. 2; *D. & C.* 63:60-62.
[6]*Millennial Star,* vol. 90, p. 305.

[7]Pers. Corresp.; Alma 13:3-9; Joseph Fielding Smith, *Teachings of the Prophet Joseph Smith,* pp. 157, 167, 365.

salvation under the counsel and direction of the Holy One, who is without beginning of days or end of life."[8]

Adam received the holy priesthood and was commanded by the Lord to teach his children the principles of the gospel. Moreover, Adam was baptized for the remission of his sins, for the same principles by which men are saved now were the principles by which men were saved in the beginning. In that day as many as repented and were baptized received the gift of the Holy Ghost by the laying on of hands. Adam made all these things known to his sons and daughters.[9]

PRIESTHOOD FROM NOAH TO ABRAHAM. As time went on men departed from the truth, and the priesthood was withdrawn. All flesh became corrupt, and the Lord said: "The end of all flesh is come before me, for the earth is filled with violence."[10] So the flood was sent and the earth was cleansed from its wickedness. The Lord then appointed Noah and his sons to stand at the head of the human family. Noah, too, received the holy priesthood and taught his children the gospel.

However, after a few hundred years had passed men became corrupt and refused to follow the teachings of their fathers. Again there was an apostasy. During this time there was one man in the city of Ur, among the few that remained faithful to the Lord, who sought after righteousness. . . . The Lord answered Abraham's prayer, and he received the priesthood under the hands of Melchizedek, king of Salem, who is called king of peace. Melchizedek was a great high priest, and so faithful was he that the Church in his day called the *Priesthood after the Order of the Son of God* by his name, or the *Melchizedek Priesthood*.[11]

Many Christian teachers have been greatly puzzled because of the reference in the Book of Hebrews to Mel-

---

[8]*Church News*, Aug. 11, 1945, p. 1; D. & C. 78:16.
[9]Moses 5:11-15, 57-59; 6:1-9, 50-68; D. & C. 20:17-28.
[10]Moses 8:13-30.
[11]D. & C. 84:6-17; 107:1-4; Abra. 1:1-4; Alma 13:14-19; *Inspired Version*, Gen. 14:26-36.

chizedek.[12] *Bible* commentators have scratched their heads and reached false conclusions trying to solve the mystery. It was not Melchizedek who was without father and without mother and without beginning of days or end of life, but it was the priesthood which he held. The proper reading of this scripture is as follows:

"For this Melchizedek was ordained a priest after the order of the Son of God, which *order* was without father, without mother, without descent, having neither beginning of days, nor end of life. *And all those who are ordained unto this priesthood are made like unto the Son of God, abiding a priest continually.*"[13]

HISTORICAL DEVELOPMENT OF PRIESTHOOD OF-FICES. *Down through time there has been a gradual development in the offices in the priesthood.* Adam held the Melchizedek Priesthood, with all of its keys and authorities, and today stands in his place as Michael, the Archangel, with presiding authority over all the earth. Next comes Noah, who also was the father of all living in his day after the flood. He too held the fulness of the priesthood. Yet from Adam to Moses the order of priesthood was that of the *Patriarchal order. These men were high priests and patriarchs.*[14]

PRIESTHOOD IN ANCIENT ISRAEL

HIGHER PRIESTHOOD LOST BY REBELLION. When Israel came out of Egypt, it was the intention of the Lord to organize the men of *all* the tribes into a royal priesthood,[15] conferring upon them all the gifts and privileges of the higher or Melchizedek Priesthood, which holds the keys of the fulness of the gospel and "holdeth the key of the mysteries of the kingdom, even the key of the knowledge of God." Because of rebellion and unwillingness to hearken to the commandments given by Moses,

[12]Heb. 7:1-4.
[13]*Millennial Star*, vol. 90, pp. 305-306; *Inspired Version*. Heb. 7:3.
[14]*Era*, vol. 38, pp. 209-212.
[15]Ex. 19:5-6; 1 Pet. 2:5, 9.

these great privileges and blessings were denied them,
although Moses did all in his power to teach and sanctify
them.

"But they hardened their hearts and could not endure his [God's] presence; therefore, the Lord in his
wrath, for his anger was kindled against them, swore
that they should not enter into his rest while in the wilderness, which rest is the fulness of his glory. Therefore,
he took Moses out of their midst, and the Holy Priesthood also; And the lesser priesthood continued, which
priesthood holdeth the key of the ministering of angels
and the preparatory gospel; Which gospel is the gospel
of repentance and of baptism, and the remission of sins,
and the law of carnal commandments, which the Lord in
his wrath caused to continue with the house of Aaron
among the children of Israel until John, whom God raised
up, being filled with the Holy Ghost from his mother's
womb."[16]

If Israel had remained faithful, they would have had
all the blessings and privileges of the Melchizedek Priesthood, but instead they were confined to the scope of the
blessings of the Aaronic Priesthood and also became
subject to the measures of the Law of Moses, which contained many temporal laws, some of which were severe
and drastic in their nature.[17] This condition continued
until the resurrection of Jesus Christ, when this carnal
law was fulfilled and was replaced by the fulness of the
gospel.[18] The Aaronic Priesthood did not lose the right
to the ministering of angels in the days of restoration
when Jesus Christ came to fulfil the law, and this power
continues in the Church today, which is fully attested in
the words of John.[19]

PROPHETS HELD MELCHIZEDEK PRIESTHOOD.
When the Lord took Moses out of Israel, he took the

---

[16]D. & C. 84:18-27.
[17]Mosiah 13:27-31.
[18]Gal. 3:19-24; 3 Ne. 9:15-22; 12:18;
   15:1-10.

[19]Era, vol. 57, pp. 622-623; D. & C.
   13.

higher priesthood also and left Israel with the lesser
priesthood which holds the keys to the temporal salvation
of mankind—the temporal gospel—that which deals with
repentance and baptism particularly, but does not have to
do with the higher ordinances which have been revealed
in the dispensation in which we live.

Therefore, in Israel, the common people, the people
generally, did not exercise the functions of priesthood in
its fulness, but were confined in their labors and ministra-
tions very largely to the Aaronic Priesthood. The withdrawal of the higher priesthood was from the people as
a body, but the Lord still left among them men holding
the Melchizedek Priesthood, with power to officiate in
all its ordinances, so far as he determined that these ordinances should be granted unto the people. Therefore
Samuel, Isaiah, Jeremiah, Daniel, Ezekiel, Elijah, and
others of the prophets held the Melchizedek Priesthood,
and their prophesying and their instructions to the people
were directed by the Spirit of the Lord and made potent
by virtue of that priesthood which was not made manifest generally among the people of Israel during all
these years.[20]

We may presume, with good reason, that never was
there a time when there was not at least one man in Israel
who held this higher priesthood (receiving it by special
dispensation) and who was authorized to officiate in the
ordinances, but this power and authority was withdrawn
from among the people and they were denied the privilege
of the ordinances which pertain to the fulness of glory,
or the entering into the rest of the Lord.

ISRAEL GIVEN AARONIC PRIESTHOOD. We see that
the power of the holy priesthood, which we call the *Melchizedek Priesthood,* was denied to the tribes of Israel,
and they were denied the higher ordinances which today
may be received in the temples; they had to be content

[20]*Gen. & Hist. Mag.,* vol. 13, pp. 55-
56; Smith, *op. cit.,* p. 181.

with the lesser blessings and the carnal law. At that time, also, the Lord declared that he would not continue the order which had existed, that of ordaining the firstborn of each of the families in Israel, but would substitute the males of one of the tribes of Israel to be the priests for the people, and would limit them in their jurisdiction to the duties of offering sacrifice, and the ordinance of baptism, and other duties which would come under the direction of the carnal law.

The Lord called Aaron, the brother of Moses, and Aaron's sons, and they were ordained and set apart to preside in this lesser priesthood, which has come to be known as the *Aaronic Priesthood*. Then the Lord called the males of the tribe of Levi, to which Aaron belonged, all those who were between the ages of 30 and 50 years, to assist Aaron and his sons in the priestly office.[21]

LEVITES HELD AARONIC PRIESTHOOD. The Aaronic Priesthood is divided into the *Aaronic* and the *Levitical*, yet it is but *one* priesthood. This is merely a matter of designating certain duties *within* the priesthood. The sons of Aaron, who *presided* in the Aaronic order, were spoken of as holding the *Aaronic Priesthood;* and the sons of Levi, who were not sons of Aaron, were spoken of as the *Levites. They held the Aaronic Priesthood* but served under, or in a lesser capacity, than the sons of Aaron.[22]

PRIESTHOOD IN ISRAEL WHEN CHRIST CAME. The authority of the priesthood was manifest in the days of the Savior's coming. By virtue of the priesthood held by Zacharias, the father of John the Baptist, the angel appeared to him. Simeon, the prophet, blessed the infant Jesus, and the scriptures say that Simeon was filled with the Holy Ghost. So there were a few still remaining who had faith and the power of the priesthood.[23]

[21]*Church News,* Aug. 11, 1945, p. 6;   [22]*D. & C.* 107:1, 13-14.
    Num. 3:5-51; 4:1-49; 8:10-19.   [23]Luke 1:5-80; *D. & C.* 84:26-27.

MELCHIZEDEK PRIESTHOOD ONLY AMONG NE-
PHITES. The Nephites did not officiate under the
authority of the Aaronic Priesthood. They were not
descendants of Aaron, and there were no Levites among
them. There is no evidence in the *Book of Mormon* that
they held the Aaronic Priesthood until after the ministry
of the resurrected Lord among them, but the *Book of
Mormon* tells us definitely, in many places, that the priesthood which they held and under which they officiated
was the Priesthood after the *holy order*, the order of the
Son of God. This higher priesthood can officiate in every
ordinance of the gospel, and Jacob and Joseph, for instance, were consecrated priests and teachers after this
order.[24]

PRIESTHOOD AND THE LINEAGE OF ABRAHAM. Jacob
may have had many daughters for all we know, and their
children would be entitled to the blessings of the gospel,
the same as the children of Keturah, wife of Abraham,
or the children of Ishmael. Remember that the priesthood
was not confined *solely* to the descendants of Jacob.
Moses got his priesthood from Jethro who was not a
descendant of Jacob, but was a descendant of Abraham.
The blessings of Abraham are to be given to the Gentiles
who repent and receive the gospel, and by adoption they
become of the seed of Abraham.[25]

RESTORATION OF AARONIC PRIESTHOOD

NO MODERN AUTHORITY WITHOUT RESTORATION.
Following the apostasy from the doctrine and practices
of the Church of Jesus Christ of former-day saints, it
became necessary that there be an opening of the heavens,
and for the Lord to speak again, and by his own mouth
and the mouth of his ancient disciples again to restore
the truth which had been lost. In the apostasy, the
authority to act in the name of the Lord had been taken

---

[24] 2 Ne. 6:2; Mosiah 29:42; Alma 6:8;   [25] Pers. Corresp.; Abra. 2:9-11; D. & C.
13:1-20; Moro. 3:1-4.   84:6-16; Gen. 25:1-34.

away from the earth, and as John saw in his revelation, the priesthood was taken back to God while the Church of Jesus Christ had been driven into the wilderness.[26]

There was but one way for that priesthood to be restored to men on the earth—by an opening of the heavens. This was done, and John the Baptist came first with the keys of the Aaronic Priesthood,[27] then came Peter, James, and John with the keys of the Melchizedek Priesthood, which authorities were given to Joseph Smith and Oliver Cowdery.[28]

It is a false notion which prevails today that men may *assume* the authority to speak and officiate in the name of the Lord Jesus Christ when they have not been divinely called. The commission given by our Lord to his disciples nearly two thousand years ago does not authorize any man today to officiate in the ordinances of the gospel or to preach and expound the scriptures by divine authority.[29] The *Bible* does not and cannot give to any man this right to exercise the functions of the priesthood. This can only come, as in days of old, by authority from the Son of God or his properly constituted representatives.[30]

WHY JOHN WAS CHOSEN TO RESTORE AARONIC ORDER. There are several very significant matters connected with the conferring of the Aaronic Priesthood upon Joseph Smith and Oliver Cowdery, which may briefly be discussed.

1. The reason John the Baptist was sent from the heavens to confer the Priesthood of Aaron is that there was no one among mortals with the keys of that authority. Had there been, then there would have been no necessity for a restoration of this authority, and John would not have been sent.

2. It was John the Baptist who held the *presidency*

---

[26]Rev. 12:1-17.   [29]Matt. 28:16-20; Mark 16:14-18.
[27]D. & C. 13.   [30]*Church News*, Dec. 13, 1950, p. 15.
[28]D. & C. 27:12; 128:20.

of this priesthood in the days of his ministry as the fore-runner of Jesus Christ. As a Levite, and his authority coming to him by divine right of descent, he was the rightful *presiding priest of the Aaronic order in Israel.* This authority had come to him by lineage, and the Lord has made it known that John "was baptized while he was yet in his childhood, and was ordained by the angel of God at the time he was eight days old unto this power, to overthrow the kingdom of the Jews, and to make straight the way of the Lord before the face of his people, to prepare them for the coming of the Lord, in whose hands is given all power."[31]

Had the Church of God been in existence with the Jews in that day, instead of the Jews being in a dreadful state of apostasy, then John the Baptist would have taken his proper place as the presiding priest of the Aaronic order. But they recognized him not and failed to understand his authority, even as they failed to comprehend the authority of our Lord. The authority of John was that which was conferred upon Aaron and which came down by right of lineage to Eleazar and his posterity after him;[32] but the Jews failed to recognize John and rejected him. By right of his authority John laid the foundation for the overthrow of their kingdom, or power, which was based on a false foundation. Had they accepted John then also would they have accepted Christ, the Lord, their rightful King and the great High Priest of their salvation.

There is perfect order in the kingdom of God, and he recognizes the authority of his servants. It was for this reason John, who acted under the direction of Peter, James, and John, came to Joseph Smith and Oliver Cowdery and restored the Aaronic Priesthood, which John held in the dispensation of the meridian of time, and which became lost in the great apostasy because of

---

[31]D. & C. 84:28.   [32]Ex. 28:1, 40-43; 29:4-9; Num. 3:1-4.

the paganizing and corrupting of the Church of Jesus Christ.

WHY PROPHET GAINED PRIESTHOOD BEFORE BAPTISM. 3. Another thing very significant in the coming of John is the fact that he, who was at the time a resurrected personage, conferred upon Joseph Smith and Oliver Cowdery the priesthood and then required of them that they baptize each other. In the natural order of things, men are baptized before the priesthood is conferred upon them. In this case the order was reversed.

We may conclude quite safely that with the limited knowledge which they had at that time, these two inexperienced young men, had they been guilty of perpetrating a fraud, would not have thought of this. It is most likely that they would have made the claim that the angel first baptized them and then gave them the priesthood. Had they made such a statement as this it would have been fatal to their story. It is an important fact, shown by direct acts and by implication in all the scriptures, that God has done for men all that men can *not* do for themselves to secure salvation, but he expects men to do all for themselves that is in their power.

MAN MUST DO ALL HE CAN FOR OWN SALVATION. In accordance with this principle, it is contrary to the order of heaven, instituted before the foundation of the earth, for holy messengers who have passed through the resurrection, or messengers who belong to the heavenly sphere, to come to earth and perform work for men which they can do for themselves. Based on this law—for it is an eternal law—Jesus Christ came into the world and died for all, thus redeeming the world from the effects of Adam's fall and giving to all men the resurrection, irrespective of belief or unbelief in him, or of righteousness or wickedness.

All men were under the curse and unable to free themselves, and Christ came and offered himself as the infinite atonement and satisfied the law. Moreover, the shedding of his blood redeemed all men, who will repent and accept his truth, from their individual sins, but none else, for he has said: "For, behold, the Lord your Redeemer suffered death in the flesh; wherefore he suffered the pain of all men, that all men might repent and come unto him. And he hath risen again from the dead, that he might bring all men unto him, on conditions of repentance."[33]

It is a most serious error to believe that Jesus did everything for men if they would but confess him with their lips, and there is nothing else for them to do. Men have work to do if they would obtain salvation. It was in harmony with this eternal law that the angel directed Cornelius to Peter,[34] and that Ananias was sent to Paul.[35] It was likewise in obedience to this law that Moroni, who understood the writings upon the Nephite plates, did not do the translating, but under the direction of the Lord gave to Joseph Smith the Urim and Thummim by which he was able to accomplish that important work by the gift and power of God.

RE-CONFERRAL OF AARONIC PRIESTHOOD. 4. After the priesthood had been given to Joseph and Oliver and at the command of the heavenly messenger, they were baptized; then by the same messenger they were instructed to lay hands upon each other and re-confer the authority the angel had given them, thus placing the ordination and baptism in the proper relationship. These details, which would have been overlooked by impostors, tell us a significant tale and bear an appealing testimony of the truthfulness of these two men.[36]

AARONIC PRIESTHOOD TO REMAIN ON EARTH. The Priesthood of Aaron, or the Levitical Priesthood, will not end when the sons of Levi make their offering in righteousness, but it will remain on the earth as long

---

[33]D. & C. 18:11-12.
[34]Acts 10.
[35]Acts 9:1-22.
[36]Church News, Sept. 2, 1933, p. 4; Jos. Smith 2:68-74.

as mortals dwell here. Before the days of Moses and
Aaron all priesthood was known as *Melchizedek*. Then
the Lord conferred a priesthood on Aaron and the Levites
that they might officiate in temporal things.

This priesthood continued in the Church which was
organized by our Redeemer until the apostasy drove the
Church into the wilderness. *As long as we have temporal things on the earth this priesthood is necessary.*
Eventually, when the earth is celestialized, I suppose all
priesthood will be of the higher order. Oliver Cowdery's
interpretation of the words of John the Baptist, on this
point, was that this priesthood *"shall remain upon earth,
that the Sons of Levi may yet offer an offering unto the
Lord in righteousness."*[37]

SONS OF AARON AND OF LEVI

LITERAL DESCENDANT OF AARON AS PRESIDING
BISHOP. There are some men in the Church who have
been blessed by patriarchs and pronounced descendants
of Levi, but they have not made any claim to the office
of bishop, for the revelation governing this situation says
literal descendant of Aaron, not of Levi. There is evidently a great host of men who are descendants of Levi
but not of Aaron.

The person spoken of in the revelations as having
the right by lineage to the bishopric is the one who is the
firstborn. By virtue of his birth he is entitled to hold "the
keys or authority of the same." This has reference only
to the one who *presides over the Aaronic Priesthood. It
has no reference whatever to bishops of wards.* Further,
such a one must be designated by the First Presidency of
the Church and receive his anointing and ordination
under their hands. The revelation comes from the Presidency, not from the patriarch, to establish a claim to the
right to preside in this office. In the absence of knowledge concerning such a descendant, any high priest,

chosen by the Presidency, may hold the office of Presiding Bishop and serve with counselors.[38]

MODERN SONS OF AARON AND LEVI. Who are the sons of Aaron and Levi today? They are, by virtue of the blessings of the Almighty, those who are ordained by those who hold the authority to officiate in the offices of the priesthood. It is written that those so ordained become the sons of Moses and of Aaron. Also: "And the sons of Moses and of Aaron shall be filled with the glory of the Lord, upon Mount Zion in the Lord's house, *whose sons are ye;* and also many whom I have called and sent forth to build up my Church."[39] So the Lord has spoken, and this was said to *those who held the Melchizedek Priesthood.*

OFFERING OF THE SONS OF LEVI. What kind of offering will the sons of Levi make to fulfil the words of Malachi and John?[40] Logically such a sacrifice as they were authorized to make in the days of their former ministry when they were first called.[41] Will such a sacrifice be offered in the temple? Evidently not in any temple as they are constructed for work of salvation and exaltation today. It should be remembered that the great temple, which is yet to be built in the City Zion, will not be one edifice, but twelve. Some of these temples will be for the lesser priesthood.[42]

When these temples are built, it is very likely that provision will be made for some ceremonies and ordinances which may be performed by the Aaronic Priesthood and a place provided where the sons of Levi may offer their offering in righteousness. This will have to be the case because *all things are to be restored.* There were ordinances performed in ancient Israel in the tabernacle when in the wilderness, and after it was established at

[38]Pers. Corresp.; *D. & C.* 68:13-21; 107:13-17.
[39]*D. & C.* 84:32-34.
[40]Mal. 3:1-4; *D. & C.* 13; 124:39; 128:24.
[41]Ezek. 43:18-27; 44:9-27.
[42]*History of the Church,* vol. 1, pp 357-359.

Shiloh in the land of Canaan, and later in the temple built by Solomon. The Lord has informed us that this was the case and has said that in those edifices ordinances for the people were performed.[43]

These temples that we now have, however, the Lord commanded to be built for the purpose of giving to the saints the blessings which belong to their exaltation, blessings which are to prepare those who receive them to "enter into his rest, . . . which rest is the fulness of his glory," and these ordinances have to be performed by authority of the Melchizedek Priesthood, which the sons of Levi did not hold.[44]

RESTORATION OF BLOOD SACRIFICES. We are living in the dispensation of the fulness of times into which all things are to be gathered, and *all things* are to be restored since the beginning. Even this earth is to be restored to the condition which prevailed before Adam's transgression.[45] Now in the nature of things, the law of sacrifice will have to be restored, or *all things* which were decreed by the Lord would not be restored. It will be necessary, therefore, for the sons of Levi, who offered the blood sacrifices anciently in Israel, to offer such a sacrifice again to round out and complete this ordinance in this dispensation. Sacrifice by the shedding of blood was instituted in the days of Adam and of necessity will have to be restored.[46]

The sacrifice of animals will be done to complete the restoration when the temple spoken of is built; at the beginning of the millennium, or in the restoration, blood sacrifices will be performed long enough to complete the fulness of the restoration in this dispensation. Afterwards sacrifice will be of some other character.[47]

[43]D. & C. 124:38-39.
[44]*Church News*, Aug. 11, 1945, p. 6; D. & C. 84:24.
[45]Acts 3:19-21; Eph. 1:10; Tenth Article of Faith; Isa. 65:17-25; D. & C. 101:22-31.
[46]Moses 5:5-8.
[47]Pers. Corresp.; Smith, *op. cit.*, p. 172; 3 Ne. 9:19-20.

RESTORATION OF MELCHIZEDEK PRIESTHOOD

"Reorganites" Deny Restoration of Melchizedek Priesthood. Was the Melchizedek Priesthood
conferred upon Joseph Smith and Oliver Cowdery by
Peter, James, and John?

In the *History of the Church*, no account is given
of the *date* when the Melchizedek Priesthood was restored. For this reason certain parties not of the Church,
who *profess* to believe in the divine mission of the martyred Seer, in order to bolster up their weak position,
have made the claim that this priesthood was not restored
by those heavenly messengers, but that it grew out of
the Aaronic Priesthood, which was restored by John the
Baptist on the 15th day of May, 1829. According to this
claim, the Prophet and Oliver Cowdery, having received
the Aaronic Priesthood, did, by virtue of that priesthood,
on the 6th day of April, 1830, ordain each other elders,
and that this eldership ordained high priests and apostles.

The actual statement, as officially published by the
so-called "Reorganized" Church, is: "In justification of
the course taken, and the principles involved on 'the
question of authority,' we have ever courted, and still
do, investigation of the rigid character of the facts in the
first organization. Here they are: Joseph Smith and
Oliver Cowdery were ordained to the lesser priesthood
by an angel; *then, by this authority and a commandment,
they, on the 6th day of April, ordained each other elders,*
and this eldership ordained high priests and apostles,
and this high priesthood ordained, by commandment, the
President of the High Priesthood—the highest office in
the church; so that the alleged *lesser ordained [sic] the
greater,* is common to both the first organization and the
Reorganization alike. The same class of facts justify
both or condemn both."[48]

---

[48]*History of the Reorganized Church
of Jesus Christ of Latter Day Saints,*
vol. 3, pp. 224-225.

ALL OFFICES ARE ONLY APPENDAGES TO PRIEST-
HOOD. While it is true that Joseph Smith and Oliver
Cowdery ordained each other elders on the 6th day of
April, 1830, and that this was the first office *in the
Church,* yet the fact remains that this was not the beginning of the Melchizedek Priesthood in the dispensation of the fulness of times. *The priesthood is greater
than the office, and all offices in the priesthood, we are
taught, are appendages to the priesthood.*[49] *For this
reason the keys of the priesthood were conferred upon
these men and not the appendages to that priesthood,
which were held by common consent in the Church after
the organization.*[50]

OURS IS THE GREAT AGE OF RESTORATION. We
learn from the scriptures that all things from the beginning must flow into this dispensation, and that in this
dispensation all things should be restored. Peter taught
this principle to the Jews;[51] and that it was understood by
Paul, we learn from his epistle to the Ephesians, 1st
chapter and 9th and 10th verses.

One of the first apostles, and a martyr to the cause,
Elder David W. Patten, has left with us his testimony.
Said he:

*"The dispensation of the fulness of times is made
up of all the dispensations that have ever been given
until this time.* Unto Adam first was given a dispensation. It is well known that God spake to him with his
own voice in the Garden and gave him the promise of the
Messiah. And unto Noah was a dispensation given, for
Jesus said, 'As it was in the days of Noe, so shall it be
also in the days of the Son of man,'[52] and as the righteous
were saved then, and the wicked destroyed, so it will
be now: And from Noah to Abraham, and from Abraham
to Moses, and from Moses to Elias, and from Elias to
John the Baptist, and from John to Jesus Christ, and from

[49]D. & C. 107:5.   [51]Acts 3:19-21.
[50]D. & C. 20:63-65; 26:2; 124:144.   [52]Luke 17:26.

Jesus Christ to Peter, James, and John. The apostles all
received in their time a dispensation by revelation
from God, *to accomplish the great scheme of restitution*
spoken of by the holy prophets since the world began,
the end of which is the dispensation of the fulness of
times, in which all things shall be fulfilled that have been
spoken of since the earth was made."[53]

The Prophet tells us that in the dispensation of the
fulness of times "that a whole and complete and perfect
union, and welding together of dispensations, and keys,
and powers, and glories should take place, and be
revealed from the days of Adam even to the present
time."[54]

RESTORATION MUST INCLUDE ALL KEYS AND
PRIESTHOOD. *If all* things are to be restored, and if the
dispensation of the fulness of times is made up of, and
is a uniting of, *all* dispensations, with their *keys* and
powers, since the days of Adam, *then those who held the
keys of these various dispensations would have to confer
them upon the head of one who stands at the head of the
last dispensation,* and the Prophet Joseph Smith is that
one. This being true, then, among other keys, it would
be necessary for Peter, James, and John, who held the
keys of the kingdom, in the dispensation of the meridian
of time, to appear to the Prophet Joseph Smith and
bestow upon him their keys and authority.

That the keys of *all dispensations* were bestowed,
we learn from the words of the Prophet, as recorded in
section 128 of the *Doctrine and Covenants,* verse 21:

"And the voice of Michael, the archangel; the voice
of Gabriel, and of Raphael, and of divers angels, from
Michael or Adam down to the present time, all declaring
their dispensation, their rights, their keys, their honors,
their majesty and glory, and the power of their priesthood; giving line upon line, precept upon precept; here a

---

[53]*Elders Journal,* July, 1838.   [54]*D. & C.* 128:18.

little, and there a little; giving us consolation by holding
forth that which is to come, confirming our hope."

And in verse 20: "The voice of Peter, James, and
John in the wilderness between Harmony, Susquehanna
county, and Colesville, Broome county, on the Susquehanna river, declaring themselves as possessing the *keys
of the kingdom*, and of the *dispensation of the fulness of
times.*"

PETER, JAMES, AND JOHN RESTORED PRIESTHOOD
AND KEYS. If, therefore, Peter, James, and John held
the keys of the dispensation of the fulness of times, it
would be necessary for them to bestow those keys upon
Joseph and Oliver, before these men could obtain them.
That they did obtain them, we know, and that the keys
of the kingdom were conferred by these heavenly
messengers, we have evidence to show.

In section 27, verses 5 to 8, of the *Doctrine and
Covenants*, the Lord declares that he shall partake of the
sacrament with Joseph Smith and Oliver Cowdery in his
kingdom, and also with John, "Which John I have sent
unto you, my servants, Joseph Smith, Jun., and Oliver
Cowdery, to ordain you unto the *first* priesthood which
you have received, that you might be called and ordained
even as Aaron."

And in verses 12 and 13: "And also with Peter, and
James, and John, *whom I have sent unto you*, by whom
I have ordained you and confirmed you to be apostles,
and especial witnesses of my name, and bear the *keys* of
your ministry and of the *same things* which I revealed
unto them; Unto whom I have committed the keys of my
kingdom, and a dispensation of the gospel for the last
times; and for the fulness of times, in the which I will
gather together in one all things, both which are in
heaven, and which are on earth."

Here the Lord declares that Joseph, the Prophet,
and Oliver Cowdery were ordained by Peter, James, and
John. In section 18, verse 9, a revelation given in June,

1829, nearly a year before the Church was organized, the Lord declares that Oliver Cowdery was called with the *same* calling as was Paul, *which was the Melchizedek Priesthood*, as an especial witness of his name. It was after this call to be special witnesses, and after the bestowal of the Melchizedek Priesthood, that the Prophet and Oliver—when the Church was organized—ordained each other elders. *The priesthood with its keys existed before the Church organization, but not the offices in the Church, which belong to the Church and are held by the consent of the same.*

OLIVER COWDERY TESTIFIES OF PRIESTHOOD RESTORATION. In regard to the ordination of Joseph Smith and Oliver Cowdery to these *two* priesthoods, we have the testimony of both, recorded outside of the *Doctrine and Covenants.* Oliver Cowdery, in the year 1848, testified at Kanesville, as follows:

"I was present with Joseph when an holy angel from heaven came down and conferred on us, or restored, the Aaronic Priesthood, and said to us, at the same time, that it should remain on earth while the earth stands. I was also present with Joseph when the higher or Melchizedek Priesthood was conferred by holy angels from on high. This priesthood we then conferred upon each other by the will and commandment of God."

From this we see that, in the case of the restoration of the higher priesthood, as well as in that of the lower, they ordained each other by commandment, after having received the keys from those who held them—Peter, James, and John.

We also have Oliver's testimony, recorded by his own hand, as early as the year 1835. The account is quite interesting, and was recorded in the patriarchal blessing book of Patriarch Joseph Smith, Sen., by Oliver, who at that time was the recorder. This is his statement:

"He [Joseph] was ministered unto by the angel, and by his direction, he obtained the records of the Nephites,

and translated by the gift and power of God. He was
ordained by the angel John, unto the lesser or Aaronic
Priesthood, in company with myself, in the town of Harmony, Susquehanna County, Pennsylvania, on Friday,
the 15th day of May, 1829; after which we repaired to
the water, even to the Susquehanna River, and were
baptized; he first administering unto me, and after, I to
him. But before baptism our souls were drawn out in
mighty prayer, to know how we might obtain the blessings of baptism and of the Holy Spirit according to the
order of God; and we diligently sought for the right of
the fathers, and the authority of the holy priesthood, and
the power to administer the same; for we desired to be
followers of righteousness, and the possessors of greater
knowledge, even the knowledge of the mysteries of the
kingdom of God. Therefore we repaired to the woods,
even as our father Joseph said we should, that is, to the
bush, and called upon the name of the Lord, and he answered us out of the heavens. And while we were in
the heavenly vision, the angel came down and bestowed
upon us this priesthood; and then, as I have said, we
repaired to the water and were baptized. *After this, we
received the high and holy priesthood;* but an account of
this will be given elsewhere, or in another place."

JOSEPH SMITH TESTIFIES OF PRIESTHOOD RESTORA-
TION. In this statement, made by Oliver, reference is
made to a prophecy by Joseph of old, son of Jacob, in
which he declared that the priesthood should be restored
in the last days through the administration of an angel
"in the bush." In the *Book of Mormon* we are given a
glimpse at the prophecy by Joseph concerning the restoration, but the prophecy has only been given in part
unto us, and is yet to be revealed.[55] Without doubt, it
was made known to the Prophet in connection with many
other things which have not yet been given to the world.

[55]2 Ne. 3:4-25; *Inspired Version*, Gen.
50:24-38.

The Prophet has, however, added some light concerning this prophecy, and has revealed to us the manner of the ordination to the Melchizedek Priesthood of himself and Oliver Cowdery.

On the 18th day of December, 1833, when the Prophet blessed his father and ordained him to the Patriarchal Priesthood, he also blessed a number of others, among whom was Oliver Cowdery. After pronouncing Oliver's blessing, the Prophet said:

"These blessings shall come upon him [Oliver] according to the blessings of the prophecy of Joseph in ancient days, which he said should come upon the seer of the last days and the scribe that should sit with him, and that should be ordained with him, *by the hands of the angel in the bush,* unto the *lesser* priesthood, and *after* receive the holy priesthood *under the hands* of those who had been held in reserve for a long season, *even those who received it under the hands of the Messiah,* while he should dwell in the flesh upon the earth, and should receive the blessings with him, even the seer of the God of Abraham, Isaac, and Jacob, saith he, even Joseph of old."

This blessing was also recorded in the handwriting of Oliver Cowdery, and was copied by him in the record on the 2nd day of October, 1835, in the city of Kirtland, Ohio, and having been written by an eye-witness of the fulfilment, is certainly strong proof of the ordination. Whether this is the "other place" mentioned by Oliver, where the account of the ordination to the *Melchizedek* Priesthood is recorded is a question. If not, the account of the ordination is either lost or misplaced among the many papers in possession of the Church.

John the Baptist was not ordained to the priesthood by the hand of Messiah, as he received his ordination when eight days of age, under the hands of an angel.[66] Peter, James, and John were called by the Savior and

<hr />

⁶⁶*D. & C.* 84:28.

received their authority from him; and the prophecy of Joseph was fulfilled when they conferred upon Joseph Smith and Oliver Cowdery the keys of the High Priesthood which they had received from Messiah while in the flesh.[57]

---

[57]*Era*, vol. 7, pp. 938-943.

CHAPTER 6

PRIESTHOOD ORGANIZATION

THE PRIESTHOOD AND ITS APPENDAGES

"ALL PRIESTHOOD IS MELCHIZEDEK." How many priesthoods are there? The answer is there is *one priesthood*, but the Lord divided it into *two divisions* known as the *Melchizedek* and the *Aaronic Priesthood*. We sometimes speak of the *Levitical Priesthood* which is a part of the *Aaronic Priesthood*.[1] The Aaronic Priesthood embraces the *offices* that have to do with the temporal matters of the Church, the crying of repentance and baptism for the remission of sins.[2]

When the Lord says there are two priesthoods, he is speaking of divisions of the priesthood. The Prophet Joseph Smith has explained this as recorded in the conference minutes, October 5, 1840: "Its institution was prior to 'the foundations of this earth, or the morning stars sang together, or the sons of God shouted for joy,' and is the highest and holiest priesthood, and is after the order of the Son of God, and *all other priesthoods are only parts, ramifications, powers, and blessings belonging to the same, and are held, controlled and directed by it.*"[3]

The Prophet also said, "*All priesthood is Melchizedek, but there are different portions or degrees of it. That portion which brought Moses to speak with God face to face was taken away, but that which brought the ministry of angels remained.*"[4]

MELCHIZEDEK PRIESTHOOD INCLUDES AARONIC. When a person holds the Melchizedek Priesthood as an

---

[1] D. & C. 107:1-6.
[2] D. & C. 20:46-59; 84:26-30; 107:20.
[3] Joseph Fielding Smith, *Teachings of the Prophet Joseph Smith*, p. 167.
[4] Smith, *op. cit.*, pp. 180-181.

elder, seventy or high priest, he holds the Aaronic Priesthood. When a person is ordained to an office in the
Aaronic Priesthood, and then receives an office in the
Melchizedek Priesthood, none of the former authority
is taken away. The Melchizedek has authority to officiate
in the Aaronic.

PATRIARCHAL ORDER PART OF MELCHIZEDEK
PRIESTHOOD. The priesthood which prevailed from
Adam to Moses was the *Patriarchal Order*, yet it was
only a *part* of the Melchizedek Priesthood. *All of the
ancient patriarchs were high priests, but the direction of
the Church in those days was by patriarchs.*⁵ After the
time of Moses, when the Melchizedek Priesthood was
withdrawn from Israel, this *order* as it is called, of
Patriarchal Priesthood, did not continue. There came,
then, the Aaronic Priesthood, with the prophets holding
the Melchizedek Priesthood as high priests. The bestowal of this higher authority, however, had to come by
special designation; it was not generally given to the
male members of the tribes.

After our Savior established his Church, he placed
in it all the officers as we have them today, with presiding
high priests at the head, and apostles, patriarchs, high
priests (the patriarch being a high priest), seventies, and
elders. All priesthood is divine authority, but it is divided
into the two grand heads, Melchizedek and Aaronic, although we speak of the order of the evangelist, or
patriarch, and the order of the Levites. We could also
speak of the order of high priests, or the order of seventies, or of elders, meaning the *calling* of those who hold
these offices.⁶

POWER AND OFFICES OF MELCHIZEDEK PRIEST-
HOOD. The Melchizedek Priesthood "holds the right of
presidency, and has power and authority over all the
offices in the church in all ages of the world, to admin-

⁵*D. & C.* 107:39-57.   ⁶Pers. Corresp.

ister in spiritual things." The First Presidency of the Church are also known as "the Presidency of the High Priesthood," and they "have a right to officiate in all the offices," and they "hold the keys of all the spiritual blessings of the church."

The offices in the Melchizedek Priesthood are as follows: elder, seventy, and high priest. The First Presidency are "three Presiding High Priests." Apostles are also high priests, with the special calling and ordination in addition of apostles, or special witnesses for Christ. They, next to the First Presidency, hold all the keys of authority in the Church and are called to build it up in all the earth. Evangelists, or patriarchs, are high priests with the special ordination as patriarchs, by right of which they bless the people of the Church. The seventy, under the direction of the Twelve Apostles, are the missionaries of the Church. There are seven presidents in each quorum of seventy, and over all the quorums a presiding presidency of seven who are known as the First Council of Seventy. Elders and high priests are appointed to officiate in the ministry in spiritual things in the stakes of Zion, and from among the high priests come the presiding officers of the Church and in the stakes and wards of the Church.[7]

ALL OFFICES ARE APPENDAGES TO PRIESTHOOD. When an elder is ordained, he receives the Melchizedek Priesthood and then the office of elder, seventy, or high priest, as the case may be, and the *office* which he receives designates the *nature* of his duties. Not only is the office of bishop and elder an *appendage* to the priesthood but so is every other office, for they all grow out of the priesthood. *The apostle, high priest, seventy, and every other office is an appendage to the priesthood.*[8]

The Lord has, himself, declared that *all authorities or offices in the Church are appendages to the priest-*

----

[7]*Church News*, Sept. 9, 1933, p. 4;   [8]*Pers. Corresp.* D. & C. 107:6-38, 89-98.

hood.[9] That is to say, *they are circumscribed by priesthood and grow out of it.*

Paul has informed us that both the gifts and the offices of the Church, in their fulness, are essential to the welfare of the Church. "For the body is not one member, but many"; and the foot cannot say, therefore, because it is not the hand, it is not of the body; nor the ear to the eye, nor the head to the feet. "But now hath God set the members every one of them in the body, as it hath pleased him." "And whether one member suffer, all the members suffer with it; or one member be honoured, all the members rejoice with it."[10]

PRIESTHOOD CALLINGS AND ORDINATIONS

PREREQUISITES TO PRIESTHOOD ORDINATIONS. Before any man is ordained to any office in the priesthood, those who call him should carefully consider the following:

1. *Worthiness* of the individual to hold the priesthood.[11]

2. His *willingness to serve* in the calling whereunto he is to be called, and his *previous faithfulness* to the Church and to responsibility.[12]

3. He must be *sustained* by the vote of the people concerned.[13]

USE OF WORD "ORDAIN" IN EARLY DAYS. When the Prophet received the Presidency of the High Priesthood, the history says that he was *ordained.*[14] Today we would say *set apart.* They used the term *ordain* in the early days of the Church for everything,[15] even when sisters were *set apart* to preside in the Relief Society.

President Brigham Young and the other members of the Council of the Twelve had the *fulness* of the keys

---

[9]*D. & C.* 84:29-30; 107:5, 14.
[10]*Church News*, Sept. 9, 1933, p. 4; 1 Cor. 12:1-31.
[11]*D. & C.* 95:5-6, 12-13; 121:34-36; 130:20-21; 132:7.
[12]*D. & C.* 107:99-100.
[13]*Era,* vol. 41, p. 653; *D. & C.* 20:65.
[14]*D. & C.* 107:22.
[15]*D. & C.* 20:67.

and priesthood conferred upon them by the Prophet *before* his death, so that any one of them could act, each in turn, should he come to the Presidency, and all he would then need would be the setting apart. All of the members of the Council of the Twelve today have had conferred upon them all the keys and authority necessary to be exercised by anyone who might reach the Presidency, and then he would be set apart.

CLASS TEACHERS SHOULD NOT BE SET APART. Today we use the term *setting apart* when men are appointed to preside in stakes and wards and in auxiliary organizations. There is no reason to set apart teachers in classes or chairmen of groups. If we continue to do this, after awhile some may think these positions have become permanent offices in the priesthood.

USE OF RIGHT HAND IN ORDINANCES. The custom, evidently by divine direction, from the very earliest time, has been to associate the right hand with the taking of oaths, and in witnessing or acknowledging obligations. The right hand has been used, in preference to the left hand, in officiating in sacred ordinances where only one hand is used.

The earliest reference we have to the superiority of the right hand over the left, in blessing, is found in the blessing of Jacob to his two grandsons, Ephraim and Manasseh, when he placed his hand "wittingly" upon the heads of the boys.[16]

Earlier, when Abraham sent his servant to Abraham's own kindred to find a wife for Isaac, he had the servant place his hand under his (Abraham's) thigh, and swear to him that he would accomplish his mission.[17] Evidently, this was the servant's right hand.

The Lord said through Isaiah: "Fear thou not; for I am with thee: be not dismayed; for I am thy God: I will strengthen thee; yea, I will help thee; yea, I will

---

[16]Gen. 48:13-14.   [17]Gen. 24:1-9.

uphold thee with the *right hand* of my righteousness."[18]

In the Psalms we read: "The Lord said unto my Lord, Sit thou at my *right hand,* until I make thine enemies thy footstool."[19]

It is the custom to extend the right hand in token of fellowship.[20] The right hand is called the *dexter,* and the left, the *sinister;* dexter means *right* and sinister means *left.* Dexter, or right, means *favorable* or *propitious.* Sinister is associated with evil, rather than good. Sinister means *perverse.*

We take the sacrament with the right hand. We sustain the authorities with the right hand. We make acknowledgment with the right hand raised.

An Evangelist Is a Patriarch. According to the dictionary and in the generally accepted view of the word, an *evangelist* is "a preacher who goes from place to place holding services especially with a view of church revivals." He is a "preacher of the gospel." The term *evangel* means gospel, or good news. But dictionaries also contain such definitions as this: "A Mormon officer of the Melchizedek or Higher Priesthood, whose special function is to bless."

The Prophet's explanation in relation to the evangelist is: *"An evangelist is a patriarch,* even the oldest man of the blood of Joseph or of the seed of Abraham. Wherever the Church of Christ is established in the earth, there should be a patriarch for the benefit of the posterity of the saints, as it was with Jacob in giving his patriarchal blessings unto his sons."[21]

Who Are Pastors? The dictionary definition of a *pastor* is a correct one, even from our understanding of this term; it is, "a Christian minister who has a church or congregation under his official charge." *The term pastor does not refer to an order in the priesthood,* like

[18]Isa. 41:10.
[19]Ps. 110:1; Matt. 22:44; 25:33-46; Acts 7:55; Rom. 8:34; 1 Pet. 3:22.
[20]Gal. 2:9.
[21]Pers. Corresp.; Smith, *op. cit.,* p. 151.

deacon, priest, elder, seventy, and so on, but is a general
term applied to an officer who presides over a ward,
branch in a mission or a stake, and it could even be applied to a president of a stake. There are several references to pastors in the Old Testament, particularly in the
Book of Jeremiah. I quote one or two of these showing
that this is a general term applied to the priests and
teachers in Israel and not to an order of the priesthood:

"And I will give you pastors according to mine
heart, which shall feed you with knowledge and
understanding."[22]

"For the pastors are become brutish, and have not
sought the Lord: therefore they shall not prosper, and
all their flocks shall be scattered."[23]

"As for me, I have not hastened from being a pastor
to follow thee: neither have I desired the woeful day;
thou knowest: that which came out of my lips was right
before thee."[24]

From these passages you will see that it is clear that
the Lord has reference to the priests and rulers over the
children of Israel and not to an order, or office, in the
priesthood. The Prophet Joseph Smith in the Sixth
Article of Faith was following Paul's expression and had
reference to those who had jurisdiction over the flocks,
or branches, of the Church.[25] We can say truthfully that
a bishop is a pastor; so is an elder who has charge of a
branch of the Church, or a president of a stake who has
direction of a number of wards and branches.[26]

We used to have pastors, so named, in Great Britain;
they were men appointed to preside over two or more
conferences, now called districts.[27]

PAUL'S TEACHING THAT DEACONS SHOULD BE
MARRIED. It was the judgment of Paul that a deacon
in that day should be a married man.[28] That does not

22Jer. 3:15.
23Jer. 10:21.
24Jer. 17:16.
25Eph. 4:11; Jer. 23:1-2.

26Era, vol. 56, p. 826.
27 Pers. Corresp.
281 Tim. 3:8-13.

apply to our day. Conditions were different in the days
of Paul. In that day a minister was not considered qual-
ified to take part in the ministry until he was 30 years
of age. Under those conditions deacons, teachers, and
priests were mature men. This is not the requirement
today.

There are in all kinds of churches today ministers
who are under that age, and there is no requirement in
the Church in this dispensation that a person must be a
matured man before he can take part in the ministry or
hold the priesthood. Nor was it the rule in very ancient
times, for we learn that Noah was only 10 years of age
when he was given the priesthood under the hands of
Methuselah.[29] John the Baptist was ordained when only
eight days old by an angel, "to overthrow the kingdom of
the Jews, and to make straight the way of the Lord before
the face of his people,"[30] but John did not enter this ministry until shortly before the coming of Christ to be baptized and enter his ministry. John was a few months
older than our Savior.[31]

SOME YOUNG BOYS ORDAINED ELDERS. Young men
were ordained and sent out to preach the gospel in the
days of the Prophet Joseph Smith. Several young men
who had not reached their majority, and who were
unmarried, went forth to do missionary work with the
power of the Melchizedek Priesthood upon them. The
Prophet's youngest brother, Don Carlos Smith, was ordained an elder when he was 14 and went out doing
missionary work. He converted, through the help of the
Lord, Solomon Avery who was a Baptist minister. When
he was 19, he was made president of the high priests
quorum, which position he held until his death in 1841.

My own Father, President Joseph F. Smith, was
called and ordained an elder and sent by President
Brigham Young, when he was only 15 years of age, to

---

[29]*D. & C.* 107:52.   [31]*Era*, vol. 57, p. 17.
[30]*D. & C.* 84:28.

fill a mission among the natives of the Hawaiian Islands; and if a missionary was in any manner inclined to be tempted and lose his virtue, surely he had every opportunity among the natives of those islands in that early day. Other young men were also ordained and sent out, under the direction of President Brigham Young. President Anthon H. Lund was ordained an elder when 15 years of age and became a local missionary, in the days of President Brigham Young. Now there would be no logic in refusing to ordain a young, unmarried boy a deacon, if that same boy could be ordained an elder and sent out into the world, away from parents and every good influence and protection, except the guidance of the Lord, to preach the gospel to a benighted people.

Paul's day was far different from our day. Many of the customs which prevailed then cannot be adopted or insisted upon today, but the fundamental *principles* of the gospel have not changed.[32]

ANCIENT AND MODERN LEVITICAL DUTIES

DUTIES OF DEACONS AND TEACHERS. In the Aaronic Priesthood, besides bishops, who hold the keys of presidency, we have the offices of deacon, teacher, and priest. Men holding these offices are appointed to *assist the bishops* in their wards. The duty of the deacon is to assist the teacher and priest, and to be at the service of the bishop when required.[33]

What is the duty of the teacher? As we read here in section 20 of the *Doctrine and Covenants,* which was given the day the Church was organized, it is the duty of the teacher to visit the homes of the people, to teach them, to see that there is no iniquity in the Church; that there is no fault-finding one with another, no backbiting, no false speaking one against another, and, more than that, to see that the members of the Church perform their

[32]Pers. Corresp.   [33]*Church News,* Sept. 9, 1933, p. 4; D. & C. 20:57-60; 84:111.

duty. That great responsibility rests upon the teacher. He is to see that the members pray, that they fast upon the fast day, that they are paying their tithing, in the season thereof, that they are attending their fast meetings in the wards, week by week; and all these things are required of the teacher as he visits in the homes of the people. And if the teacher does not see to these things, then the sin lieth at his door.[34]

DUTIES OF PRIESTS OF AARONIC ORDER. What are the duties of the priest? The duty of the priest is to preach, teach, expound, exhort, baptize, and administer the sacrament. He is to visit the house of each member and exhort all to pray, vocally and in secret, and attend to all family duties. That is the duty of the priest.

Now the good bishops in the wards should see that their priests go into the homes of the people and do this very thing, teaching the members in the spirit of prayer. When they find an individual member of the Church who fails in any one of these particulars, it is the right of these teachers or priests to make the report to the bishop, the common judge. However, they are to labor diligently, and with long suffering, in faith and humility, with these members who do not see the necessity of keeping the commandments of the Lord, and after they have done all in their power, and can do nothing further to bring the non-praying members to repentance, the common judge may cite them before him, and he has the right to take action against them for their fellowship. Of course, our duty is to save souls. We must not be hasty in casting any out. So, I say, after the teachers or the priests have done all that can be done, then the drastic measures may be meted out.[35]

LEVITICAL AND AARONIC DUTIES ANCIENTLY. The tabernacle, sometimes called the temple, was a very ornate though portable building, which the children of

---

[34]D. & C. 20:53-60; 84:111; Ezek. 33:2-9.   [35]Conf. Rep., Oct. 1919, p. 114; D. & C. 20:46-60; 42:78-93; 68:33.

Israel carried with them in the wilderness. It was to this temple that Hannah went to pray and where Samuel ministered.[36] It was the duty of the Levites to take care of this building and keep it in order. They took it apart, carried it and all that pertained to it from place to place as they journeyed in the wilderness, and then set it up again when a new camp was made.

These responsibilities, in some degree *similar* to the duties of deacons today, were divided among the descendants of the three sons of Levi, son of Jacob. They were Gershon, Kohath, and Merari. The sons of Gershon had charge of "the tabernacle, and the tent, the covering thereof, and the hanging for the door of the tabernacle of the congregation, And the hangings of the court, and the curtain for the door of the court, which is by the tabernacle, and by the altar round about, and the cords of it for all the service thereof."

The sons of Kohath in their assignment cared for "the ark, and the table, and the candlestick, and the altars, and the vessels of the sanctuary wherewith they minister, and the hanging, and all the service thereof." Eleazar, son of Aaron, had charge of this group of Levites, and "the oversight of them that keep the charge of the sanctuary." The sons of Merari had charge of "the boards of the tabernacle, and the bars thereof, and the pillars thereof, and the sockets thereof, and all the vessels thereof, and all that serveth thereto, And the pillars of the court round about, and their sockets, and their pins, and their cords."[37]

In a general way the duties and responsibilities of the tabernacle, and of the preparations for sacrifices, were assigned to the descendants of the three sons of Levi. Wagons and oxen were provided for the Gershonites and the Merarites, but the sons of Kohath, "because the service of the sanctuary belonging unto them was that

---

[36]1 Sam. 1:1-18; 3:1-18; Ex. 35; 36;   [37]Num. 3:5-51.
    37; 38; 39; 40.

they should bear upon their shoulders" their burdens—
they had no wagons.[38] Not only were the Levites appointed to take care of the tabernacle and all that pertained to it, but other similar duties were assigned to
them. They could offer sacrifice, although it was Aaron's
place and that of his sons to hold the *keys* of this ministry.

RESTORATION IN THE MERIDIAN OF TIME. According to this assignment and the instructions given to
Moses, the priests (i.e. sons of Aaron) and Levites
officiated from the day of their appointment to the days
of the coming of Jesus Christ. When our Savior came,
he *restored* to the Church all that had been taken away,
and once again the fulness of the priesthood with all of
its blessings was given to men. As Peter said, there
existed again a "chosen generation, a royal priesthood,
an holy nation, a peculiar people," but this condition did
not continue long before apostasy once more destroyed
it all.[39]

ADMINISTRATION OF PRIESTHOOD QUORUMS

PURPOSE OF PRIESTHOOD QUORUMS. Every person
holding an office in the priesthood should be enrolled and
receive membership in the proper quorum where his membership is recorded. One of the main purposes of a
quorum of priesthood is to help every individual member
of that quorum in all things pertaining to the quorum—
in his spirituality, in his temporal salvation, in all his
needs.[40]

Organization is an essential requirement in the government of the Church. The entire universe is organized
on a divine plan. Without organization there would be
confusion, chaos, and that would lead to disorganization
and destruction.

[38]Num. 7:3-9.
[39]*Church News*, Aug. 11, 1945, p. 6;
   1 Pet. 2:9.

[40]*Era*, vol. 41, p. 680.

The quorums of the priesthood are organized for a definite purpose. I have jotted down several of these:

1. To keep the members holding the priesthood active and alert in the performance of every duty which the priesthood requires at their hands;

2. To teach the members how to assume responsibility and magnify their callings;

3. To train them in methods by which they may effectually teach others and officiate in their behalf;

4. To encourage them in their responsibilities pertaining to the salvation of the dead as well as for the living.

A quorum, properly appointed, must seek out the needs of every individual member and attempt to supply these needs that may be discovered, *both temporally and spiritually*. No quorum of the priesthood is assuming the full obligation placed upon it by the Lord which does not sufficiently extend temporal need. Each member should dedicate himself and use his talent to advance the cause of Zion. He must be loyal and faithful to the Church, to the quorum, to the priesthood in general, to his family and to every divine principle of eternal truth.[41]

RESPONSIBILITY FOR QUORUM ADMINISTRATION. The responsibility for the success of priesthood quorums in the stake is placed, first, upon the presidency of the stake and, second, upon the presidency of the priesthood quorum. The General Authorities hold the stake presidency, with the aid of the high council, responsible for the condition of the quorums of elders, seventies, and the quorum of high priests. It is the duty of the stake presidency to see that these quorums are properly officered with men who understand the nature of their callings and the responsibilities of the priesthood. . . .

Moreover, the presidency of the stake, aided by their high council and the stake priesthood committee, are

41Conf. Rep., Oct., 1945, p. 95;
    D. & C. 107:21-40, 58-100.

under the responsibility of seeing that quorums are fully organized, not only with presiding officers, but with live, active committees which are faithfully functioning. Where a quorum of priesthood has failed to function, and has been indifferent to the responsibilities assigned to it, the presidency of the stake will be held responsible *first*, and then officers of the quorum *next*. If officers refuse to work, or are incapable, then they should be released, and faithful and willing men called to act in their stead.

BEST MEN TO BE PRIESTHOOD PRESIDENTS. Too frequently in the past, the best material has been taken to officer the auxiliary organizations, and then what was left was considered good enough to officer priesthood quorums. It is hoped sincerely that this day has perished and that no vestige of it now remains. The presidency of the stake should see that the very best available material is called to positions of presidency in priesthood quorums. Auxiliary organizations are the *helps* to the priesthood in the Church.[42]

RESPONSIBILITY OF QUORUM PRESIDENTS. The responsibility of the quorum president is, as stated in this revelation, to sit in counsel, to advise and instruct and teach those who are under his direction.[43] *The Lord has placed the responsibility for the training and the conduct of the members of the quorum upon the shoulders of the president of the quorum.* He has given him two counselors to assist him in that work. This direction and care of the quorum may not be transferred to the shoulders of some other. Men who are the most capable for these positions of presidency should be sought.

Too frequently it is thought that the supervision of a quorum, especially of elders, is not of great importance, but *the Lord thinks otherwise.* There should be, however, a division of responsibility among the presidency. The

---

[42]*Era*, vol. 41, p. 653.   [43]*D. & C.* 107:21, 60-66, 85-100.

presidency should see that the quorum is fully organized and that every man is performing his duty. If there are delinquent or wayward members, these should be labored with until brought to repentance and full fellowship.[44]

DILIGENT PRIESTHOOD SERVICE REQUIRED

STEWARDSHIP OF PRIESTHOOD BEARERS. It is our duty to save the world. That is our mission, insofar as they will listen unto us and receive our testimony. All those who reject the testimony of the elders of Israel will be held responsible and will have to give an accounting for their stewardship, just as we will give an accounting of our stewardship as elders and teachers of the people.[45]

RESPONSIBILITY OF PRIESTHOOD BEARERS. Never before in the history of the Church has the responsibility which has been given to the priesthood been more necessary of fulfilment than today. Never before have we been under greater obligation to serve the Lord, and keep his commandments, and magnify the callings which have been assigned to us.

The world today is torn asunder. Evil is rampant upon the face of the earth. The members of the Church need to be humble and prayerful and diligent. We who have been called to these positions in the priesthood have that responsibility upon our shoulders to teach and direct the members of the Church in righteousness.[46]

EMBARKING IN SERVICE OF GOD. If we do not serve him with all our heart, might, mind, and strength, if we are not loyal to this calling which we have received, we are not going to be blameless when we stand before that judgment seat. It is a very serious thing to hold the priesthood. I wish when our young men were called and ordained, that is. recommended to be ordained to the office of elder in the Church, they could be impressed

---

before they were ordained with the importance of the calling which they are about to receive.[47]

SAVE PRIESTHOOD MEMBERS FROM SPIRITUAL DEATH. Many wayward souls may be lost, who, with a little help from these committees, could be saved from the spiritual death which awaits them. Spiritual death is the most terrible of all deaths, yet we see our fellow quorum members dying for want of a little sympathetic and brotherly attention. Many of these wayward men, if not all, could be saved by this careful attention. Truly "the worth of souls is great in the sight of God."[48] *To save the souls of those who have strayed from the fold is just as worthy and commendable, and causes just as much rejoicing in heaven, as to save souls in far away parts of the earth.*

SOURCE OF PRIESTHOOD RESPONSIBILITY. Brethren of the priesthood, these are your responsibilities. The Council of the Twelve did not place them upon you; the Presidency of the Church did not place them upon you— it is true that they, or their representatives, called you and ordained you to this ministry—but the responsibility to perform this labor came to you from the Son of God! You are his servants. You will be held accountable to him for your stewardship, and unless you magnify your callings and prove yourselves worthy and faithful in all things, you will not stand blameless before him at the last day.[49]

HOLDERS OF ALL PRIESTHOOD OFFICES TO BE FAITHFUL. It is a very strange thing that the idea should prevail in the Church that the higher a man advances in authority in the priesthood, the greater is his responsibility to be faithful in keeping the commandments of the Lord, and the less authority which he has, the less is his responsibility to be faithful before the Lord. In other words, if a man is called to act as a bishop, a high coun-

[47]Conf. Rep., Oct., 1945, p. 98;   [48]D. & C. 18:10-16.
      D. & C. 4:1-7.   [49]Era, vol. 41, p. 680.

cilor or president of a stake, he is expected to walk circumspectly and obediently in the discharge of the office which he holds.

One of the presiding authorities, the apostle, for instance, is expected to be a consistent and faithful Latter-day Saint. He must eschew every evil practice and keep every commandment. Should he fail, or even should the bishop or the high councilor fail to walk consistently with the commandments of the Lord, the whole Church would rise up and declare that he should speedily be brought into the line of his duty or be relieved of his responsibility.

But if it happens to be an ordinary elder, seventy, or even a high priest, who has not been given special responsibility, the majority of the people of the Church seem to feel that his conduct is not a matter of very serious consequence. It seems that the body of the Church has been trained—but erroneously—to think that an elder in the Church, who has not been called to some position of prominence or authority, may be guilty of almost any violation of the commandments and regulations of the Church, and he should not be called into very serious question.

OBEDIENCE REQUIRED OF ELDERS AS WELL AS APOSTLES. What the Lord has revealed in relation to the priesthood teaches us that the elder, even if he is not given some special responsibility, is under just as great a responsibility to be true to "every word that proceedeth forth from the mouth of God,"[50] as is the man who is called to preside over a stake, or even over the Church. *The apostle is under no greater commandment to be true to his covenant and membership in the Church than is the ordinary elder, or seventy, or any other individual holding the priesthood*. It is true the apostle has a greater responsibility, or calling, in the priesthood, but no greater responsibility to be true to gospel principles and com-

---

[50]*D. & C.* 84:44.

mandments. Especially is this so, if the elder has received
the ordinances of the house of the Lord. . . .

The punishment for the violation of this covenant
of the priesthood will come as readily and as surely upon
the ordained elder as it will upon the apostle in the
Church, who may turn away into forbidden paths and
to the neglect of duty.[51]

USE OF SACRED NAMES

REVERENCE FOR NAME OF SUPREME BEING. In the
revelation on priesthood given March 28, 1835, the Lord
declared that there are "two priesthoods, namely, the
Melchizedek and Aaronic, including the Levitical Priesthood." The first, or greater, is called the *Melchizedek
Priesthood* after the name of the righteous king of Salem
because he was such a great high priest. This is done,
the Lord declares, "out of respect or reverence to the
name of Supreme Being, to *avoid the too frequent
repetition of his name.*"[52]

From the very beginning of time, the sacred name
of the Supreme Being has been held in the greatest reverence and respect by the servants of the Lord. We are
informed that the true pronunciation of one of his names
by the Hebrews was lost, because they scrupulously
avoided mentioning it, substituting in its stead "one or
other of the words with whose proper vowel-points it
may happen to be written."[53]

One of the commandments of the decalogue is:
"Thou shalt not take the name of the Lord thy God in

---

[51]*Era*, vol. 41, p. 653; *D. & C.* 84:33-
42   [52]*D. & C.* 107:1-4.

[53]In Hebrew and certain other Eastern languages, a "vowel point" was a mark
placed above or below a consonant, representing the vowel sound which
precedes or follows the consonant sound. The "incommunicable name" of
Deity has been preserved only in the form of four consonants. Traditionally
this name of the Supreme Being was not pronounced except with the vowel
points of *Adonai* or *Elohim*, so that the true pronunciation was lost. The
four consonants are variously written IHVH, JHVH, JHWH, YHVH,
YHWH. Numerous attempts have been made to represent the supposed
original form, as Jahaveh, Jahvah, Jahve, Javeh, Yahve, Yahveh, Yahwe,
Yahweh, etc.

vain; for the Lord will not hold him guiltless that taketh his name in vain."[54] This commandment he repeated frequently through his servants the prophets, and it is further written in the commandments given to Moses, "He that blasphemeth the name of the Lord, he shall surely be put to death."[55]

VULGARITY BEGETS BLASPHEMY. There is nothing that should be held in more sacred reverence and respect than the name of the Supreme Being and the name of his beloved Son, our Redeemer. Satan puts it into the hearts of men to blaspheme the name of the Lord, and the more vulgar and obscene a man becomes the greater is his tendency to violate this sacred commandment. It seems a strange thing that characters of this kind are never satisfied to swear in the name of mortal men, but always in the name of Deity, which rebellion seems to be in keeping with their wickedness.

USE OF NAMES OF DEITY WHEN PREACHING. Even in the preaching of the gospel, the elders of Israel should exercise great care not to repeat these sacred names too frequently and needlessly when other terms of designation will suffice. There are occasions when the use of these sacred names or titles may properly be used, and the Lord himself, has given us this privilege, for instance, in the blessings of the sacrament; but it is well for those who address the congregations of the people to use these holy names sparingly when other expressions will suffice. The term *Lord* whether applied to the Father or the Son is permissible, and in speaking of the Son we may properly refer to him as our Savior or Redeemer and not always by the familiar use of his name.

REVERENCE FOR SACRED PRIESTHOOD TITLES. Reverence should also be given to other sacred titles or names. Frequently we hear the brethren of the General Authorities addressed on the street and in private con-

---

[54]Ex. 20:7; Deut. 5:11; Mosiah 13:15.   [55]Lev. 24:16.

versations as well as in public by their titles or the offices which they hold in the priesthood. This should be avoided except at the time and place when such usage would be proper. For example, it is not the best form to refer to a member of the Quorum of the Twelve as *Apostle* ...., either in speaking of him or to him. The Lord has given us the general designation of *Elder* which may be applied to any man holding the Melchizedek Priesthood, and no matter what office a man may hold, it is an honor for him to be so designated and addressed.

It has become customary through long established usage to refer to the first President of the Church as *The Prophet Joseph Smith*, or *Joseph Smith, the Prophet*. This is permissible because of the great honor which was bestowed upon him and the great work which he accomplished under the hand of the Lord and the fact that he long since departed this mortal life. If he were here, he would be happy to be called, as he was by members of the Church in his day, *Brother Joseph*. This was not said in the spirit of familiarity but in the spirit of love and respect.

PROPER TITLES FOR CHURCH OFFICERS.   In addressing a member of the First Presidency, it is perfectly proper to say, President Grant, President Clark, or President McKay, and the same designation should be applied to the President of the Council of the Twelve Apostles. These brethren will take no offense or consider it an act of disrespect if they should be called *Brother*, for it is also an honor to belong to the brotherhood of the Church and be in fellowship with the faithful members. The proper title by which the members of the Council of the Twelve Apostles and the First Council of Seventy may be called is that of *Elder*. This title may also be applied to the members of the Presiding Bishopric, although the title *Bishop* has been used from the beginning and may be without offense, whether applied to the Presiding Bishopric or to other bishops in the Church.

In introducing one of the members of the Council of the Twelve Apostles or of the First Council of Seventy, the brother conducting the exercises in the meeting may say, Elder ...., or Brother ...., of the Council of the Twelve Apostles, or of the First Council of the Seventy.

PROPRIETY IN INTRODUCING SPEAKERS. The presiding officer in a meeting when introducing a speaker, especially one of the General Authorities of the Church, should not indulge in flattering remarks or make a long eulogy. What may be said should be brief; if there is occasion to make a remark better to identify the speaker, it should be given as a matter of explanation or identification without any word that may cause embarrassment to the person so introduced. It has happened at times that the brother conducting the exercises when giving an introduction has taken a good part of the time allotted to the speaker. This is a fault frequently indulged in by *inexperienced* presiding officers. *Brief* introductions will be appreciated by the brethren, and very brief comments, if any, are necessary at the close of their remarks.[56]

PRIESTHOOD AND COMMON CONSENT

OPERATION OF LAW OF COMMON CONSENT. No man can preside in this Church in any capacity without the consent of the people. The Lord has placed upon us the responsibility of sustaining by vote those who are called to various positions of responsibility. No man, should the people decide to the contrary, could preside over any body of Latter-day Saints in this Church, and yet it is not the right of the people to nominate, to choose, for that is the right of the priesthood.

The priesthood selects, under the inspiration of our

[56]*Era,* vol. 44, p. 204.

Father in heaven, and then it is the duty of the Latter-day
Saints, as they are assembled in conference, or other
capacity, by the uplifted hand, to sustain or to reject; and
I take it that no man has the right to raise his hand in
opposition, or with contrary vote, *unless he has a reason
for doing so that would be valid if presented before those
who stand at the head.* In other words, I have no right
to raise my hand in opposition to a man who is appointed
to any position in this Church, simply because I may not
like him, or because of some personal disagreement or
feeling I may have, but *only on the grounds that he is
guilty of wrong doing, of transgression of the laws of the
Church which would disqualify him for the position
which he is called to hold.*[57]

---

[57]Conf. Rep., June, 1919, p. 92;
D. & C. 20:60-67; 26:2.

CHAPTER 7

KEYS AND COVENANT OF PRIESTHOOD

RESTORATION OF PRIESTHOOD KEYS

KEYS INCLUDED IN RESTORATION OF ALL THINGS. We are living in the dispensation of the fulness of times. In this dispensation, we have been informed by the prophets of old, *all things* are to be restored, "both which are in heaven, and which are on earth," all things are to be gathered in one in Jesus Christ.[1] The Savior himself declared, when he came down from the mount with Peter, James, and John, that the time would come when Elias should be sent to restore all things.[2] Peter told the Jews that all the prophets since the world began had spoken of this restoration.[3] We are living in that day.

The keys of priesthood had to be restored. It was not sufficient that John the Baptist came with the keys of the Aaronic Priesthood, and Peter, James, and John with the keys of the Melchizedek Priesthood, by virtue of which the Church was organized, but there had to be an opening of the heavens and a restoration of keys held by *all the prophets who have headed dispensations* from the days of Adam down to the days of Peter, James, and John. These prophets came in their turn, and each bestowed the authority which he held. . . .

COMPLETE RESTORATION OF ALL KEYS. All the keys of all dispensations had to be brought in order to fulfil the words of the prophets and the purposes of the Lord in bringing to pass a *complete restoration of all things*. Therefore the father of the human family, the

[1]Eph. 1:9-10.
[2]Matt. 17:10-13; *Inspired Version,*
Matt. 17:9-14.

[3]Acts 3:19-21.

first man on the earth, Adam, had to come, and he came
with his power. Moses came, and others. *All who had
keys came and bestowed their authorities.* Our revelations do not tell us just when. We have not the dates
when some of these authorities were made manifest, but
the Prophet Joseph Smith in writing to the saints in
Nauvoo in regard to the salvation of the dead declared,
as we have it recorded in section 128 of the *Doctrine and
Covenants,* that all these prophets came with their keys
in the dispensation in which we live.[4]

Brethren and sisters, this is a glorious dispensation.
All other dispensations flow into it. All authorities, all
powers, are centered in this dispensation in which we live.
*We are privileged to partake of these blessings through
our faithfulness.*[5]

MOSES, ELIAS, AND ELIJAH RESTORED KEYS.
Among the keys of authority and power which were bestowed, there are none of more far reaching or greater
significance than the keys of authority bestowed by
Elijah. It was in the Kirtland Temple, April 3, 1836,
that the Lord sent to the Prophet Joseph Smith and Oliver
Cowdery some of the ancient prophets with their keys.
How many came we do not know. We have been given
the record of the coming of *Moses,* with the keys of the
gathering of Israel and the restoration of the ten tribes;
the coming of *Elias,* who lived in the days of Abraham,
with the restoration of the covenants and authorities given
to Abraham and in his day; and the coming of *Elijah*
who was spoken of by Malachi as having the authority
to restore the power of turning the hearts of the fathers
to the children, and the hearts of the children to their
fathers. This was to come before the great and dreadful
day of the Lord and to save the earth from being smitten
with a curse.[6]

---

[4]*D. & C.* 110:11-16; 112:30-33; 128:18-
21.
[5]*Gen. & Hist. Mag.,* vol. 27, pp. 98-99,
101.

[6]*Gen. & Hist. Mag.,* vol. 27, pp. 49-
50; *D. & C.* 2:1-3; 110:11-16; Mal.
4:5-6.

ELIAS RESTORED GOSPEL POWER OF ABRAHAM'S
DAY. Elias came, after Moses had conferred his keys,
and brought the gospel of the dispensation in which
Abraham lived. *Everything that pertains to that dispensation, the blessings that were conferred upon Abraham,
the promises that were given to his posterity, all had to
be restored,* and Elias, who held the keys of that
dispensation, came.[7]

This Elias was a prophet who lived in the days of
Abraham and who held the keys of that dispensation. He
came and bestowed the gifts and the blessings that were
pronounced upon Abraham's head, both for himself and
his posterity after him. This Elias restored all that pertained to that dispensation, for in the dispensation of the
fulness of times in which we live, all dispensations had to
be revealed, all keys had to be restored; and hence the
prophets of old, having the keys of dispensation, had to
come declaring their honors, their authority, the power
of their priesthood.[8]

ELIJAH HELD KEYS OF KINGDOM. The Lord gave
unto Elijah the *keys of presidency* in his time—the *keys
of the kingdom,* the *keys of the sealing power;* and it is
that sealing power which gave him the right and authority to officiate. And the Lord said unto him, "That which
you bind on earth shall be bound in heaven." That is
how great his power was, and in that day Elijah stood
up and officiated for the people in the sealing power.[9]

Since the latter-day bestowal of these keys, the work
of salvation for the dead has been proclaimed, has taken
hold of the hearts of the children of men, both in the
Church and out of it. There are thousands who are
working in the gathering of the records of the dead, and
why they do it they do not know.

I asked one man in the city of Salem, Massachusetts,

[7]*Gen. & Hist. Mag.*, vol. 27, p. 100;
    D. & C. 110:12.
[8]Conf. Rep., Apr., 1936, p. 74.

[9]*Gen. & Hist. Mag.*, vol. 13, p. 57;
    D. & C. 27:9; 1 Kings 17; 18; 19;
    2 Kings 1; 2:1-15.

in the year 1902, why he was gathering the records of
the dead. He was undertaking a marvelous work. He
said to me, "I do not know, but I got started and I cannot
quit." I *know why*.[10]

JOSEPH SMITH HOLDS KEYS IN TIME AND ETERNITY.
The Prophet holds the keys of this dispensation through
all time and eternity. Moses holds the keys of his dispensation, and 3,000 years after his departure, he came
and bestowed those keys upon the Prophet Joseph Smith
for this dispensation. Elijah came over 2,500 years after
his departure and bestowed the keys of his authority, and
so likewise all the prophets who held dispensations; but
this did not rob them of any authority whatever, and they
still hold the keys that were given to them and which
they conferred upon Joseph Smith and his associates.

The Prophet does not stand at the head of former
dispensations, but of the dispensation of the fulness of
times. President Brigham Young and succeeding presidents of the Church held the keys and authorities while
living, but the keys held by the Prophet, as holding the
keys of the dispensation for time and eternity, were never
transferred and are still held by him.[11]

KEYS OF SEALING POWER

WHY ELIJAH RESTORED SEALING KEYS. Joseph
Smith, the Prophet, said: "Elijah was the last prophet
that held the keys of the priesthood, and who will, before
the last dispensation, restore the authority and deliver
the keys of the priesthood, in order that all the ordinances
may be attended to in righteousness. It is true that the
Savior had authority and power to bestow this blessing;
but the sons of Levi were too prejudiced. 'And I will
send Elijah the Prophet before the great and terrible day
of the Lord,' etc. *Why send Elijah? Because he holds*

---

[10]Conf. Rep., Apr., 1936, p. 74.   [11]Pers. Corresp.; *D. & C.* 90:3; 112:30-
33.

*the keys of the authority to administer in all the ordi-
nances of the priesthood: and without the authority is
given, the ordinances could not be administered in
righteousness.*"[12] . . .

The higher ordinances, the greater blessings which
are essential to exaltation in the kingdom of God, and
which can only be obtained in certain places, no man has
a right to perform except as he receives the authority to
do it from the one who holds the keys. It makes no difference how great an office you have, what position in
the Church you hold, you cannot officiate unless the keys,
the sealing power, is there back of it. That is the thing
that counts, and that is why Elijah came; that is why
Moses came, for he also held keys of the priesthood;
that is why they (Moses and Elijah) conferred upon the
heads of Peter, James, and John, in that dispensation,
these privileges or these powers, these keys, that they
might go forth and perform this labor; and that is why
they (Moses and Elijah) came to the Prophet Joseph
Smith.[13]

NATURE OF SEALING POWER. Elijah restored to
this Church and, if they would receive it, to the world,
the keys of the sealing power; and that sealing power puts
the stamp of approval upon *every ordinance* that is done
in this Church and *more particularly those that are performed in the temples of the Lord*. Through that restoration, each of you, my brethren, has the privilege of going
into this house or one of the other temples (I believe
most of you have done so) to have your wife sealed to
you for time and for all eternity, and your children sealed
to you also, or better, have them born under that covenant.

What a glorious privilege it is to know that the
family organization will remain intact. It is not destroyed. It does not come to an end when we have com-

---

[12]Joseph Fielding Smith, *Teachings of
the Prophet Joseph Smith,* p. 172.

[13]*Elijah the Prophet and His Mission,*
pp. 18-20; Smith, *op. cit.,* p. 158;
Matt. 17:1-13.

plied with the divine law, by virtue of the keys which
are held by the President of the Church.[14]

SEALING POWER EMBRACES LIVING AND DEAD.
Elijah, the last of the prophets who held the keys of the
sealing power in ancient Israel, came and bestowed that
power, the power of sealing. Some members of the
Church have been confused in thinking that Elijah came
with the keys of baptism for the dead or of salvation
for the dead. Elijah's keys were *greater* than that. They
were the keys of *sealing,* and *those keys of sealing pertain to the living and embrace the dead who are willing
to repent.*

I think sometimes we look at this work for the salvation of the dead rather narrowly. It is a wrong conception to think of the people for whom we are doing
work in the temple of the Lord as being dead. We should
think of them as *living;* and the living proxy but repre-
sents them in receiving the blessings which they should
have received, and would have received *in this life,* had
they been living in a gospel dispensation. Therefore,
every dead person for whom work is done in the temple
is considered to be living at the time the ordinance is
given; and those keys and blessings, which are conferred
upon the dead by proxy, are given to the living who represent the dead in ordinance work which pertains to the
gospel of Jesus Christ in this mortal life.

So Elijah came, having the keys of sealing, and the
power has been given unto us by which we may reach
out after the dead. This sealing power embraces those
who are *dead,* who are willing to *repent* and to receive
the gospel, who died without that knowledge, just the
same as it reaches out for those who *repent* who are
living. That is the work of Elijah.[15]

[14]Conf. Rep., Apr., 1948, p. 135.   [15]Gen. & Hist. Mag., vol. 27, pp. 100-
101.

FULNESS OF THE PRIESTHOOD

How Christ Gained Fulness of Priesthood. Joseph Smith said: *"If a man get a fulness of the priesthood of God, he has to get it in the same way that Jesus Christ obtained it, and that was by keeping all the commandments and obeying all the ordinances of the house of the Lord."*[16]

I hope we understand that. If we want to receive the fulness of the priesthood of God, then we must receive the fulness of the ordinances of the house of the Lord and keep his commandments.[17] This idea that we can put off our salvation because of some weaknesses of the flesh until the end, and then our children will go and do this work for us in the temple of the Lord when we are dead, will get us nowhere. Salvation for the dead is for those who died without a knowledge of the gospel so far as celestial glory is concerned. And those who have rejected the truth and who have fought the truth, who would not have it, are not destined to receive celestial glory. Now, the Lord says this—it is not my saying, I am glad to say, although I fully believe it.[18]

Fulness of Priesthood Not Dependent on Office Held. Let me put this in a little different way. I do not care what *office* you hold in this Church—you may be an apostle, you may be a patriarch, a high priest, or anything else—you cannot receive the *fulness of the priesthood* unless you go into the temple of the Lord and receive these ordinances of which the Prophet speaks. *No man can get the fulness of the priesthood outside of the temple of the Lord.* There was a time when that could be done, for the Lord could give these things on the mountain tops—no doubt that is where Moses got it, that is no doubt where Elijah got it—and the Lord said that in the days of poverty, when there was no house prepared

---

[16]Smith, *op. cit.*, p. 308.
[17]D. & C. 124:28-42.
[18]Smith, *op. cit.*, p. 107.

in which to receive these things, that they can be received on the mountain tops.

But now we have temples, and you cannot get these blessings on the mountain tops; you will have to go into the house of the Lord, and you cannot get the fulness of the priesthood unless you go there. Do not think because somebody has a higher office in this Church than you have that you are barred from blessings, because you can go into the temple of the Lord and get *all* the blessings there are that have been revealed, if you are faithful; you can have them sealed upon you as an *elder* in this Church, and then you have *all* that any man can get. There have to be offices in the Church, and we are not all called to the same calling, but you can get the fulness of the priesthood in the temple of the Lord by obeying this which I have read to you. I want to make this emphatic.[19]

FULNESS OF PRIESTHOOD REQUIRED FOR EXALTATION. There is no exaltation in the kingdom of God without the fulness of priesthood. How could a man be an *heir* in that kingdom without priesthood? While the sisters do not hold the priesthood, they share in the fulness of its blessings in the celestial kingdom with their husbands. These blessings are obtained through obedience to the ordinances and covenants of the house of the Lord. . . .

To obtain the fulness of the priesthood does not mean that a man must become President of the Church. Every man who is faithful and will receive these ordinances and blessings obtains a fulness of the priesthood, and the Lord has said that "he makes them equal in power, and in might, and in dominion."[20] Only one man at a time on the earth holds the *keys* of the priesthood; only one man at a time has the power to receive revelations for the Church; but the Lord has made it possible for

---

[19]*Elijah the Prophet and His Mission,*   [20]*D. & C.* 76:95; 88:107.
pp. 28-29.

every man in this Church, through his obedience, to receive the fulness of the priesthood through the ordinances of the temple of the Lord. This cannot be received anywhere else.[21]

FULNESS OF PRIESTHOOD FOR LIVING AND DEAD. Only in the temple of the Lord can the fulness of the priesthood be received. Now that temples are on the earth, there is no other place where the endowment and the sealing powers for all eternity can be given. No man can receive the *keys of exaltation* in any other place.

Joseph Smith has said that, "the saints have not too much time to save and redeem their dead, and gather together their living relatives, that they may be saved also, before the earth will be smitten, and the consumption decreed falls upon the world."[22] When that day comes, those who have *professed* to believe in the latter-day work, and who have *rejected* the doctrine of temple building and the ceremonial endowments therein, will find themselves shut out of the kingdom of God. This subject occupied the mind of the Prophet Joseph Smith for several years before his death, for the Lord revealed to him all things pertaining to the work in the temples, and he revealed them unto others that the work might go on.

In the temples the saints are performing the ordinances which will insure, through faithfulness, the fulness of the blessings of the kingdom of God. During the past century the Church has been true to this calling, and the prospect for the future is good. This work will go on through the millennium, until redemption shall come to all who are worthy to receive it. In the words of the Prophet: "Let the dead speak forth anthems of eternal praise to the King Immanuel, who hath ordained, before the world was, that which would enable us to redeem them out of their prison; for the prisoners shall go free."[23]

---

[21]*Gen. & Hist. Mag.*, vol. 21, pp. 99-100.

[22]Smith, *op. cit.*, p. 330.

[23]*Gen. & Hist. Mag.*, vol. 21, p. 57; D. & C. 128:22.

FULNESS OF PRIESTHOOD IS IN SEALING POWER OF
ELIJAH. But now we have the fulness of the *power* of
the priesthood. The Lord has restored the keys and
authorities of all the dispensations and has made it possible, *by the power of Elijah,* to make every act performed
by authority of force when men are dead or out of the
world. Let us remember that all contracts, bonds, oaths,
or performances, which are not entered into by the
authority of this sealing power, are of no efficacy or virtue
after men are dead. The house of the Lord is a house of
order and everything in it is obedient to divine law.[24]

When a man assumes authority which he does not
have and becomes a law unto himself, according to the
word of the Lord, he is not justified and must remain
filthy still.[25] Let each member of the Church reflect carefully upon these things and see to it that he or she is
in perfect harmony with that which the Lord has revealed,
and that all ordinances are received *under the hands of
those who are officially called and endowed with power
from on high.*[26]

PRIESTHOOD KEYS CENTER IN ONE MAN

KEYS AND PRIESTHOOD COMPARED. President Joseph F. Smith has said: "The priesthood in general is the
authority *given to man to act for God.* Every man ordained to any degree of the priesthood has this authority
delegated to him. But it is necessary that every act performed under this authority shall be done at the proper
time and place, in the proper way, and after the proper
order. *The power of directing these labors constitutes
the keys of the priesthood.* In their fulness, the keys are
held by only one person at a time, the prophet and President of the Church. He may delegate any portion of this
power to another, in which case that person holds the
keys of that particular labor."[27]

---

[24]*D. & C.* 132:6-14.
[25]*D. & C.* 88:35.
[26]*Gen. & Hist. Mag.,* vol. 27, p. 53.

[27]Joseph F. Smith, *Gospel Doctrine,*
4th ed., p. 168.

The president of a quorum holds the keys, or the right to direct, in that quorum of priesthood. The bishop holds the keys of authority in his ward. The president of a stake holds the keys of authority in his stake. The apostles hold the keys of authority to preach the gospel in all the world and to have it preached by authority.[28] The President of the Church holds the keys over all the Church. In him is concentrated the power of the priesthood. He holds all the keys of every nature, pertaining to the dispensation of the fulness of times. All the keys of former dispensations which have been revealed are vested in him.

We are taught that the new and everlasting covenant of the gospel embraces the fulness of the gospel— every covenant, contract, bond, obligation, vow, authority—and that the keys of this authority are held by the President of the Church, who is president of the High Priesthood, "and there is never but one on the earth at a time on whom this power and the keys of this priesthood are conferred."[29]

KEYS CENTER IN CHURCH PRESIDENT. I wish we could get it firmly fixed in our minds that only one man upon the face of the earth at a time holds, in their fulness, the powers, the keys, the authorities, of this glorious priesthood. The man who holds these keys by virtue of his right, that right which God himself has vested in him, has the right to *delegate* authority and to *withdraw* authority as he sees fit and receives inspiration so to do.

No man, I do not care who he is or how much priesthood he holds, has any right to officiate in any ordinance of this gospel for any soul contrary to the sanction and the approval of the man who holds the keys of authority in this Church. Now the Lord has told us that.

The priesthood is concentrated, centered if you please, in one man, and it radiates from him, so far as the

---

[28]*D. & C.* 112:21-22.　　　　[29]*Church News,* Sept. 16, 1933, p. 4; *D. & C.* 132:7.

Church is concerned upon the face of the earth, just as it radiates from Jesus Christ to him. He has the right to speak, to give counsel, to say what we shall do and what we shall not do by virtue of the priesthood, and he who goes contrary to that counsel is under condemnation in the sight of God.[30]

CANNOT USE PRIESTHOOD WITHOUT KEYS. I have no right, there is no man upon the face of this earth who has the right to go forth and administer in *any* of the ordinances of this gospel unless the President of the Church, who holds the keys, sanctions it. He has given us authority; he has put the sealing power in our priesthood, because he holds those keys; and if the President of the Church should say to us, "You shall not baptize in this state or in that state, or in this nation," any man that would go forth to baptize contrary to that command would be violating a command of God and going contrary to authority and power; *and that which he did would not be sealed.* Oh, I wish we could understand that. We would not have some going around, as they have been doing in the past, claiming that they have authority to do certain things when they have no authority. They do not understand this thing.

The man who holds the keys can bestow and he can withdraw; he can give the power, and he may take it again; and if he takes it, that *ends* our right to officiate. That has been done; it may be done again. . . .

Remember there is only one on the face of the earth who holds the sealing power of the priesthood, and he can delegate that power unto others that they may act, and they may seal on earth and it is valid, it is binding, *so long as he sanctions it;* if he withdraws it, no man can exercise that power.[31]

ORDINANCES PERFORMED WITHOUT AUTHORITY ARE INVALID. I have no right, notwithstanding I belong

[30]*Gen. & Hist. Mag.,* vol. 27, pp. 101-102.

[31]*Elijah the Prophet and His Mission,* pp. 24, 31.

to the Council of the Twelve, to baptize one of my own children without first going to the bishop in the ward where I live and getting his consent, because he holds the keys for that ward to which I belong as a member. I have never baptized any of my children except—and I have baptized nearly all of them as far as I could do and on their birthdays, too, when they were eight years old—except I have gone to the bishop and gained his sanction to perform that ordinance and to confirm them members of the Church.

I have no right to go into a stake of Zion and ordain a man an elder without the appointment coming to me from the presidency of the stake, after the man to be ordained has been voted upon by those who have the right to vote to sustain him in that stake. *If a man goes into a stake to perform an ordinance and he is not sent, if he is not called, he is violating authority, he is doing that which he has no right to do, and it is not valid.*

All this authority radiates from the President of the Church. The President of this Church could say, if the Lord gave him that inspiration, that we shall not preach the gospel any more in the New England states, or in the United States, or in Europe, and there would not be an elder in this Church that would have any authority, notwithstanding his priesthood, to go into any place where he had been forbidden to go and preach the gospel, if the President of the Church *withdrew* the authority. . . .

CELESTIAL MARRIAGES VALID ONLY WHEN AUTHORIZED. No man in this Church has a right to perform a marriage for time and eternity unless he is designated or set apart by the President of the Church. No president of a stake, no bishop, no man has that authority unless he gets it from the President of the Church, just as it reads in this revelation.

I have no authority to perform a marriage for anybody in this Church, or out of it, outside of the temples of the Lord, because I have been told by the President of the Church that I am not to perform marriages outside of the temples; but I have all the authority in the world to perform those marriages for time and for eternity in the temples of the Lord, because I have received that authority from the President of the Church.

The bishops and the presidents of stakes have authority to perform marriages *for time only* outside of the temples, but they have no authority to go into the temples to perform those ordinances for time and eternity unless they have been especially designated to do it. And so with other men who labor in the house of the Lord, they have to be chosen and set apart for that labor.[32]

POWER OF PRESIDENT TO WITHDRAW SEALING POWER. The power and the authority held by Elijah, then, lies in the sealing ordinances, and more particularly those pertaining to the holy temple. Only one man at a time holds the keys of this sealing power on the earth. According to the revelation, "all covenants, contracts, bonds, obligations, oaths, vows, performances, connections, associations, or expectations" that pertain to the exaltation must be entered into and made with the *sanction* and *approval* of the *sealing authority* of the *one* who holds the keys of priesthood in the Church.[33] This one is *always* the President of the Church who is President of the High Priesthood. He may, and does, delegate the sealing authority to others so that they may officiate in the temples in all the ordinances which pertain to the exaltation in the celestial kingdom; but no man can take this honor unto himself.

The President may at any time he is so disposed *revoke* the privilege and bring an *end* to the authority of any individual who may be called and set apart to perform these sacred ordinances. Any man who *presumes* to have authority to perform these sealing ordinances which belong to the house of the Lord, when it has not been given

---

[32]*Church News,* May 6, 1939, pp. 5, 7.   [33]*D. & C.* 132:7.

him by the one who holds the keys of authority, is an *impostor* and a *fraud*. It is a most astonishing thing that in view of what the Lord has revealed, there are those who rise up from time to time claiming that they have authority and no one can take it from them. There is order in the Church.

KEYS CAUSE SEALING OF ORDINANCES IN HEAVEN. While the majority of the male members hold the priesthood and are called to officiate in a general way in the ordinances of the gospel, yet we, one and all, should realize that *it is the power vested in the President of the Church by virtue of the keys he holds, which come from Elijah in particular and from the other prophets of old in general, which makes valid the authority which we possess.* Without that central authority with its commanding keys and the privilege extended to the men holding the priesthood by this one person who presides, the acts of those who are ordained to the priesthood could not be administered in righteousness.

Peter, James, and John restored the Melchizedek Priesthood, out of which all the offices come; but the ordinances of the gospel which are performed by virtue of that High Priesthood receive their *final sanction* and *approval* by virtue of the keys of authority. In other words *they are bound in heaven as well as on earth by virtue of the sealing power.*[34]

OATH AND COVENANT OF PRIESTHOOD

EXALTATION PROMISED IN PRIESTHOOD COVENANT. In section 84 of the *Doctrine and Covenants*, the Lord has this to say: "For whoso is faithful unto the obtaining these two priesthoods of which I have spoken, and the magnifying their calling, are sanctified by the Spirit unto the renewing of their bodies. They become the sons of Moses and of Aaron and the seed of Abraham, and the

[34]*Gen. & Hist. Mag.*, vol. 27, pp. 51-52.

church and kingdom, and the elect of God. And also all they who receive this priesthood receive me, saith the Lord."

And if we receive the Lord, then, surely the Lord receives us, and we are in fellowship with him, "For he that receiveth my servants receiveth me; And he that receiveth me receiveth my Father."

Now, here is the great blessing, which I think many of us have overlooked, and especially these young men when they are called and sustained to be ordained to the office of elder: "And he that receiveth my Father"—and of course we receive the Father through our faithfulness and our obedience—"*receiveth my Father's kingdom; therefore all that my Father hath shall be given unto him.*"[35]

Can you think of a greater blessing the Lord could offer to any man holding the priesthood? But this is based upon faithfulness and the magnifying of the calling.

In other revelations, you know, the Lord says: "And [they] who overcome by faith, and are sealed by the Holy Spirit of promise, . . . They are they into whose hands the Father has given all things— . . . they are gods, even the sons of God."[36]

"And this is according to the oath and covenant which belongeth to the priesthood. Therefore, all those who receive the priesthood, receive this oath and covenant of my Father, which he cannot break, neither can it be moved."

Here is a definite, positive statement that every man who receives the priesthood receives it with an oath and covenant that he will magnify his calling, that he will be faithful and true, and *his reward will be to become a son of God and a joint-heir with Jesus Christ in having the fulness of the Father's kingdom.* No greater blessing could be offered.

And then the Lord has said: "Therefore, *all those*

[35]D. & C. 84:33-38.   [36]D. & C. 76:53-58.

who receive the priesthood, receive this oath and covenant of my Father, which he cannot break, neither can it be moved."

PENALTY FOR BREAKING COVENANT OF PRIESTHOOD. Now, these promises were not made to high priests alone, but to *all* who receive the priesthood. And then the Lord is promising us *everything that he has* if we will be faithful. Is it not fair that the punishment for violation of that covenant, and the trampling of that priesthood under our feet, should bring a punishment, on one hand, as severe as the reward will be glorious on the other? And so the Lord says: "But whoso breaketh this covenant after he hath received it, and altogether turneth therefrom, shall not have forgiveness of sins in this world nor in the world to come."[37]

Oh, if we could only impress that upon the mind of every man when he is called to receive the priesthood! Now, only those who magnify their callings will be chosen.[38]

Thus when a man is ordained to the Melchizedek Priesthood, he receives it with an oath and covenant that he will magnify his calling and be faithful before the Lord. That does not follow in the case of the Aaronic Priesthood, so the Prophet tells us.[39] They who are faithful in receiving these two priesthoods become the sons of Moses and of Aaron, and the elect of God in regard to the Melchizedek Priesthood.

Now when a man makes a covenant that he will receive the priesthood and magnify it, and then he violates that covenant, "and altogether turneth therefrom" —there is a chance to repent if he does not altogether turn therefrom—then there is no "forgiveness of sins in this world nor in the world to come." That does *not* mean that man is going to become a son of perdition, but the meaning is that *he will never again have the oppor-*

---

[37]*D. & C.* 84:39-41.
[38]Conf. Rep., Oct., 1945, pp. 98-99.
[39]Smith, *op. cit.,* pp. 322-323; Heb. 7:17-28.

*tunity of exercising the priesthood and reaching exalta-
tion.* That is where his forgiveness ends. He will not
again have the priesthood conferred upon him, because
he has trampled it under his feet; but as far as other
things are concerned, he may be forgiven.[40]

PRIESTHOOD: KEY TO KNOWLEDGE OF GOD

No KNOWLEDGE OF GOD WITHOUT PRIESTHOOD.
The Lord—speaking of the priesthood, and the power
of the priesthood, and the ordinances of the Church
which we receive through the priesthood—had this to
say: *"And this greater priesthood administereth the gospel and holdeth the key of the mysteries of the kingdom,
even the key of the knowledge of God."*

So *if there is no priesthood, there is no knowledge
of God.* And that is why the world is in darkness today,
because they have no priesthood. They have lost the
knowledge of God. And so they have been teaching all
manner of tradition, all manner of false doctrine, all manner of man-made philosophy in relation to God and the
principles of truth pertaining to the salvation of men.
These principles can only be received, if you please,
through the power of the priesthood, for it is by that
power that the keys of the knowledge of God are
obtained.

Let me read that again: "And this greater priesthood
administereth the gospel and holdeth the key of the mysteries of the kingdom, even the key of the knowledge of
God. Therefore, in the ordinances thereof, the power
of godliness is manifest. And without the ordinances
thereof, and the authority of the priesthood, the power
of godliness is not manifest unto men in the flesh; For
without this, no man can see the face of God, even the
Father, and live."[41]

When we read things of this nature, it ought to make
every man among us who holds the priesthood rejoice

---

[40]*Church News,* Mar. 30, 1935, p. 6.   [41]*D. & C.* 84:19-22.

to think that we have that great authority by which *we may know* God. Not only the men holding the priesthood know that great truth, but because of that priesthood and the *ordinances thereof*, every member of the Church, men and women alike, may know God.[42]

---

[42]*Church News*, Mar. 30, 1940, p. 4.

CHAPTER 8

THE HOLY APOSTLESHIP

NATURE OF APOSTOLIC CALLING

WHAT IS AN APOSTLE? An *apostle,* the dictionary states, is "one of the twelve chosen by Christ to proclaim his gospel; also a Christian missionary who first evangelizes a certain nation; any zealous advocate of a doctrine or cause." We frequently hear a man spoken of as the apostle of some great undertaking because he was the *pioneer* in his particular field.

The true calling of the apostles of Jesus Christ is to hold the fulness of the priesthood and to proclaim the gospel in all the world. They hold the *keys,* to open the door by the proclamation of the gospel of Jesus Christ, and first unto the Gentiles and then unto the Jews.[1] In this dispensation there is a reversal of this commandment given to the Twelve in former days; then they were commanded to go first to the Jews and then to the Gentiles.[2] The Lord said that in these last days the first should be last and the last should be first.[3] Since the restoration of the gospel it has been carried to the Gentile nations, and soon it will be taken to the Jews. Fulfilment of prophecy indicates that the *days,* or "times of the Gentiles," are about fulfilled, and the days of Judah are now at hand.[4]

TWO KINDS OF APOSTLES DISTINGUISHED. The term *apostle* is recognized in the Church in the sense in which it is defined in the dictionary. *Men have been called apostles who have been sent forth with the gospel*

---

[1]D. & C. 107:23-24, 33-35; 112:21; 124:128.
[2]Matt. 10:1-6; 15:21-28; Mark 7:24-30; Acts 10:1-48.
[3]D. & C. 90:9; 1 Ne. 13:42; Matt. 19:30; 20:1-16; Mark 10:28-31; Luke 13:23-30.
[4]Luke 21:24; Rom. 11:25-27; D. & C. 45:24-30.

message even when they have not been ordained to that particular office. The seventies of the Church are at times referred to as the *seventy apostles,* because they are the missionaries of the Church and are sent out with the message of salvation and as witnesses for Christ into all the world, although *they do not hold the office of apostle in the restricted sense.*

In like manner the Lord spoke of the brethren who were ordained *high priests:* "Therefore, go ye into all the world; and unto whatsoever place ye cannot go ye shall send, that the testimony may go from you into all the world unto every creature. And as I said unto mine apostles, even so I say unto you, for *you are mine apostles, even God's high priests;* ye are they whom my Father hath given me; ye are my friends."[5]

This revelation was given two years and four months *before* the first men were *ordained* to the *special calling as apostles* in the Church, but as they were commissioned to go forth proclaiming the gospel as witnesses for Christ, he designated them as his *apostles.*

In a discourse by President Wilford Woodruff in 1856, he said, speaking to the brethren holding the priesthood: "Let the *twelve apostles,* and the *seventy apostles,* and *high priest apostles* and *all other apostles* rise up and keep pace with the work of the Lord God, for we have no time to sleep. What is a man's life good for, or his words or work good for when he stands in the way of men's salvation, exaltation, and glory? They are of no use at all."[6]

To think that President Woodruff believed and intended to convey the thought that there were apostles who were of the Twelve, and some of the seventies, and some of the high priests, is absurd. He merely desired to call attention to the fact that men holding these offices in the priesthood who were called to carry the gospel into

the world as *witnesses of its restoration* should be alert
and alive to their great responsibility.

SPECIAL STATUS OF "ORDAINED" APOSTLES. The
fact is well established that Christ chose twelve men and
conferred upon them the apostleship, and these twelve
men constituted the only Council of Apostles in the
Church in that day, and *there is but one Council of
Apostles in the Church today.* These twelve men are
endowed with the power and responsibility to serve as
the *special witnesses for Christ.* They are entitled to
have the inspiration and necessary guidance of the Holy
Ghost to fit and qualify them for this important mission.

*All men may, by virtue of the priesthood and the
gift of the Holy Ghost, become witnesses for Christ.* In
fact that is just what *every elder* in the Church should be,
but *there is a special calling which is given to the Twelve
special witnesses that separates them from other elders
of the Church in the nature of their calling as witnesses.*
These twelve men hold the *fulness of authority, keys,*
and *priesthood,* to open up the way for the preaching
of the gospel to every nation, kindred, and tongue.
Others who go forth go under their direction and are
subject unto them. This work of proselyting is in their
hands, and under the counsel of the First Presidency
they are called upon to conduct *all the affairs of the
Church* and the preaching of the gospel to every
creature.[7]

JOSEPH SMITH BECAME AN APOSTLE IN 1820. In
the spring of 1820, after the vision was given to Joseph
Smith of the Father and the Son, he stood as the only
witness among men who could testify with knowledge
that God lives and Jesus Christ is verily his Son. In this
knowledge *he became a special witness for Christ, and
thus an apostle before the priesthood had been restored.*
With the coming of John the Baptist, and Peter, James,

---
[7]*D. & C.* 107:21-39; 112:14-34.

and John, the priesthood was restored; then Oliver Cowdery, as well as Joseph Smith, became *a special witness for Christ, and hence an apostle.*

These men were not ordained to the special calling, or office, as apostles. When John the Baptist came, we know what happened for his exact words are given. He conferred upon Joseph Smith and Oliver Cowdery the Aaronic Priesthood.[8] In similar manner *Peter, James, and John conferred upon them the Melchizedek Priesthood, and not an office.* Oliver Cowdery has said that this was so. Having received the priesthood, *they had power to ordain each other, after the organization of the Church, to offices in this priesthood, for the Lord had said that all offices are appendages of the priesthood* and grow out of it.[9] . . .

JOSEPH AND OLIVER ORDAINED ELDERS, NOT APOSTLES. In the *Doctrine and Covenants*, section 27:12-13, the Lord says that he sent Peter, James, and John to ordain Joseph Smith and Oliver Cowdery and that by virtue of that ordination they became apostles and special witnesses.[10] This is true, but as previously stated *these men were not ordained to the specific office in the priesthood, but received the priesthood itself out of which the offices come.* Joseph Smith and Oliver Cowdery were therefore, *by virtue of the conferring of priesthood,* apostles or special witnesses, for Jesus Christ, and *the only men among men who could testify from knowledge and personal contact as did the Twelve in the meridian of time.*[11]

On the day of the organization of the Church, Joseph Smith ordained Oliver Cowdery to the office of *elder,* and Oliver Cowdery ordained Joseph Smith to that same office, in keeping with the instructions they had received from the heavenly messengers who had first

---

[8]*D. & C.* 13.
[9]*D. & C.* 84:29-30; 107:5; Joseph F. Smith, *Gospel Doctrine,* 4th ed., pp. 169, 184.

[10]*D. & C.* 20:1-4; 27:12-13.
[11]*Era,* vol. 38, pp. 208-209.

come to them. . . . When the Church was organized, Joseph Smith and Oliver Cowdery received the *first offices coming out of the priesthood* and bestowed for the necessary government of the Church. These offices were conferred by unanimous vote of the little band of worshipers who organized the Church.

No Ordained Offices Outside Church. The priesthood, under certain conditions, may be held independent of the Church. Such was the case from the 15th of May, 1829, to the 6th of April, 1830. This had to be the case for the Church could not be organized without the authority for the organization *preceding* it. *The offices, which grow out of the priesthood, for they are appendages to it, belong also to the Church and therefore are not conferred independent of the Church.*

There can be no Church of Jesus Christ without priesthood. Wherever the Church is there must be divine authority for its government. This same divine authority must also be exercised, in all its ramifications, within the Church and in the work of proselyting, for the Church has the mission to carry the gospel to every nation, kindred, tongue, and people, as well as caring for those who have come into its fold. It is by virtue of the priesthood sent from heaven that ordinances of salvation are performed in behalf of men. There could be no ordinance of baptism and remission of sins without it; there could be no bestowal of the gift of the Holy Ghost; no one could properly preach the gospel, for *any preaching without the authority back of it would be impotent and lifeless.*

Growth of Offices in the Church. After the organization of the Church, proselyting commenced and the Church grew in numbers, in spite of bitter opposition and persecution, for all sects and parties were arrayed against it. At the beginning two elders could take care of the little flock, but the Lord revealed piecemeal, line upon line, until the fulness of organization came. There was in the beginning need for officers of the Aaronic priesthood, and *deacons, teachers,* and *priests* were soon ordained. As development came other *elders* were needed to preside over the early branches which were organized.

Later there came the need for *bishops* to take charge of the temporal affairs. The bishop is the presiding officer of the Aaronic Priesthood, whose duty is essentially, but not exclusively, to look after the temporal affairs of the Church. *High priests* were also ordained, and later *patriarchs,* or *evangelists, seventies,* the *First Presidency*—the presiding quorum of the Church—and the *Council of Twelve Apostles.* In this manner, in the course of a very brief time, the same organization which existed in the primitive Church was fully established. Branches grew into stakes of Zion. Missions were opened and the word began to be preached with success in various parts of the world.[12]

THREE WITNESSES CHOOSE FIRST COUNCIL OF TWELVE. After the opening of the dispensation of the fulness of times the Lord made it known that the organization of the primitive Church of Jesus Christ was to be restored. As early as June, 1829, before the Church was organized, a revelation came calling the witnesses of the *Book of Mormon* to choose the Twelve who should constitute the Council of Apostles.[13] . . .

It was nearly six years after this revelation that the apostles were chosen. After the return of Zion's camp from Missouri to Kirtland, the Prophet Joseph Smith called all the brethren who went forth on that journey together. From these men who had been willing to risk their lives in the service of the Lord, the Three Witnesses, who were set apart to choose out the Twelve, made the selection of the Apostles. This was on the 14th day of

[12]*Church News,* Sept. 9, 1933, p. 4.   [13]*D. & C.* 18:26-40.

February, 1835, and the men were chosen in the following order:

1. Lyman E. Johnson, 2. Brigham Young, 3. Heber C. Kimball, 4. Orson Hyde, 5. David W. Patten, 6. Luke S. Johnson, 7. William E. McLellin, 8. John F. Boynton, 9. Orson Pratt, 10. William Smith, 11. Thomas B. Marsh, 12. Parley P. Pratt.

ORDINATION OF FIRST LATTER-DAY APOSTLES. Lyman E. Johnson, Brigham Young, and Heber C. Kimball were then called forward, ordained, and instructed in that order, after which the meeting adjourned. The following day, February 15th, the ordinations continued. Orson Hyde, David W. Patten and Luke S. Johnson were called forward and ordained. William E. McLellin, John F. Boynton and William Smith were also each ordained after which the congregation adjourned. Some of the brethren were absent on this occasion. February 21, 1835, Parley P. Pratt was ordained. Elders Thomas B. Marsh and Orson Pratt, being away on missions, it was not until near the end of April when they were ordained. Elder Marsh returned to Kirtland, April 25th, and Elder Orson Pratt on the following day.

After the Twelve had all been selected and ordained they were organized according to age in the council. Thomas B. Marsh the oldest became the senior, and the first man ordained, Lyman E. Johnson, the junior.[14]

FILLING VACANCIES IN COUNCIL OF TWELVE. There is no set rule in regard to the choosing of apostles. For instance: The first Twelve chosen in this dispensation were selected by the Three Witnesses. Others, both in the day of the Prophet and since his day, have been chosen by direct revelation through the President of the Church. Others have been chosen as was Matthias in the days of the ancient apostles. At other times, the members of the Presidency and the Twelve present names

---

[14]*Era*, vol. 38, p. 212.

which are considered by the First Presidency and one
chosen by "lot" much as Matthias was.[15]

APOSTOLIC POWER IN FORMER DAYS

ANCIENT PROPHETS AND THE APOSTOLIC POWER.
The question has arisen at times, *Do the apostles hold
greater authority and keys than were given to ancient
prophets?* The answer to this question is that they do not.
Many of the prophets of old had conferred upon them
the *fulness of the power of the priesthood.* Adam was
chosen, under Jesus Christ, to hold the keys of salvation
on this earth. . . .

Then we know that Enoch, Melchizedek, Abraham,
Moses, and Elijah held the fulness of the priesthood and
officiated in its ordinances. Elijah was the last of the
prophets in ancient Israel who held the fulness of the
priesthood, that is to say, the last of the prophets clothed
with the fulness of the sealing power. The prophets who
came after him did not hold this fulness. The fact that
Elijah was the last connotes that there were prophets
before him who also held the keys of the priesthood, and
this we have learned from the revelations given to Joseph
Smith the Prophet.[16]

HISTORY OF ANCIENT APOSTLES. The history of
the apostles chosen in the days of Christ is vaguely
known. Tradition, which is faulty, has told us some
things about them and how each met his death. We know
that Judas Iscariot lost his standing because of his treacherous betrayal of the Master, and Matthias was called
to take his place.[17] We know that James, the son of Zeb-
edee, was killed with the sword not long after the resurrection of our Lord. John was given the privilege of
remaining on the earth with a translated body until Christ
shall come again.[18] Peter was crucified, and at his own

---

[15]Pers. Corresp.; Acts 1:15-26.
[16]Joseph Fielding Smith, *Teachings of
the Prophet Joseph Smith,* pp. 157-
159, 166-173.

[17]Acts 1:15-26.
[18]John 21:20-23; Rev. 10:8-11; *D. & C.*
7:1-8; 77:14.

request, tradition states, upside down because of his humiliation in denying the Lord.[19] Paul met his death in Rome.[20]

We know that it was the custom in the beginning to *fill vacancies* in this presiding council, *for the quorum of the Twelve was to remain in the Church during its entire existence.*[21] We know that in course of time there came a "falling away," and the Church was taken from the earth, and the priesthood went back to God for a season.[22]

PETER, JAMES, AND JOHN SERVED AS FIRST PRESIDENCY. In the days of Christ's ministry he called the first apostles who were ever ordained to that office so far as we have any knowledge. He conferred upon them all the power and authority of the priesthood. He also appointed three of these Twelve to take the keys of presidency. *Peter, James, and John, acted as the First Presidency of the Church in their day.*[23]

There is no evidence in any scripture or prophecy declaring that these three men acted independently, or apart from the Council of the Twelve Apostles. All the information we have indicates that they served in this capacity while serving at the same time as three of the Council of the Twelve.

In this last dispensation we have received the added information, and perhaps the added order of priesthood, and we have in the Church of Jesus Christ today the quorum of the First Presidency, separate from the Council of the Apostles. It is under the direction of the First Presidency that the apostles act in all matters in the priesthood and in the Church. In the dispensation of the fulness of times, when the keys and authorities of the dispensations from the beginning of time have been revealed and restored, it is noteworthy that the order of priesthood in all its ramifications, powers, and offices,

[19]John 21:15-19.
[20]Acts 21:10-40; 22; 23; 24; 25; 26; 27; 28.
[21]Eph. 4:11-16.
[22]Rev. 12:1-17.
[23]Matt. 16:13-19; 17:1-13; *D. & C.* 81:1-2; Smith, *op. cit.*, 158.

should be given to the Church in the whole and complete manner in which we find it today.[24]

ADDITIONS TO COUNCIL OF TWELVE ANCIENTLY. We have no record that states that in the days of the apostles of old that any one was ever ordained to be an apostle and not to be a member of the Council of the Twelve. The Savior chose Twelve Apostles, and *this quorum was to continue,* according to the revelations,[25] but at no place has the Lord said that others more than the Twelve and a Presidency of three should be called.

Paul was an *ordained apostle,* and without question he took the place of one of the other brethren in that Council.[26]

APOSTOLIC TESTIMONY OF CHRIST. It is questionable if all of the apostles in the former dispensation were "personal" witnesses of the resurrection of Jesus Christ, if by that is meant that he appeared to them after his resurrection. This is certainly true of the original eleven.[27] Paul saw in vision,[28] but we have evidence that the Council of the Apostles was maintained for some time after the death of some of the original Twelve.[29] Whether these ever had a visitation from the Savior the records do not state.

Every member of the Council of the Twelve Apostles should have, and I feel sure have had, the *knowledge of the resurrection of Jesus Christ.* This does not have to come by *direct visitation* of the Savior, but it does come from the testimony of the Holy Ghost. Let me call your attention to the statement of the Savior in Matthew 12:31-32. *The testimony of the Holy Ghost is the strongest testimony that can be given. It is better than a personal visit.* It is for this reason that the Savior

24*Era*, vol. 38, pp. 209, 212.
25Acts 1:15-26; Eph. 4:11-16.
261 Tim. 2:7.
27Luke 24:36-53; Acts 1:1-14; 1 Cor. 15:5-7.
28Acts 9:1-9; 22:6-16.
29Acts 1:15-26; Eph. 4:11-16; Rom. 16:7; 1 Cor. 12:28-29; Gal. 1:19.

said that all manner of sin and blasphemy against the Holy Ghost could *not* be forgiven.[30]

VESTING OF THE KEYS OF THE KINGDOM

JOSEPH SMITH CONFERRED ALL KEYS ON ALL THE TWELVE. A short time before his martyrdom, the Prophet bestowed upon the Twelve Apostles—who constitute the second quorum in the Church—all the keys and all the ordinances and priesthood necessary for them to hold in order to carry on this great and glorious work of universal salvation.

That the Twelve did receive these keys and powers we learn from the following quotations from the *Times and Seasons*. Orson Hyde, one of that quorum, said:

"Before I went east on the 4th of April [1844] last, we were in council with Brother Joseph almost every day for weeks; said Brother Joseph in one of those councils, 'There is something going to happen; I don't know what it is, but the Lord bids me to hasten and give you your endowment before the Temple is finished.' He conducted us through every ordinance of the holy priesthood, and when he had gone through with all the ordinance he rejoiced very much, and said, 'Now if they kill me, *you have got all the keys, and all the ordinances, and you can confer them upon others, and the hosts of Satan will not be able to tear down the kingdom as fast you will be able to build it up'*; and now, said he, 'On your shoulders will the responsibility of leading this people rest.' "[31]

This testimony is corroborated by the testimony of Elder Wilford Woodruff who says: "They [the Twelve] received their endowments, and actually *received the keys of the kingdom of God*, and oracles of God, keys of revelation, and the pattern of heavenly things; and thus addressing the Twelve [Joseph] exclaimed, 'Upon your

---

[30]Pers. Corresp.   [31]*Times and Seasons*, vol. 5, p. 651.

shoulders the kingdom rests, and you must round up your shoulders and bear it, for I have had to do it until now.' "[32]

Sister Bathsheba W. Smith, wife of George A. Smith, one of the Twelve to whom these keys were given, was present in the council meetings above referred to, and in an affidavit, dated November 19, 1903, she says:

"In the year 1844, a short time before the death of the Prophet Joseph Smith, it was my privilege to attend a regular prayer circle meeting in the upper room over the Prophet's store. There were present at this meeting most of the Twelve Apostles, their wives and a number of other prominent brethren and their wives. On that occasion the Prophet arose and spoke at great length, and during his remarks I heard him say that he had conferred on the heads of the Twelve Apostles all the keys and powers pertaining to the priesthood, and that upon the heads of the Twelve Apostles the burden of the kingdom rested, and that they would have to carry it."[33]

CHOOSING A CHURCH PRESIDENT. The Prophet, in anticipation of his death, conferred upon the Twelve all the keys and authorities which he held. He did not bestow the keys on any one member, but upon them *all*, so that *each held the keys* and authorities. All members of the Council of the Twelve since that day have also been given all of these keys and powers. But these powers cannot be exercised by any one of them *until*, if the occasion arises, he is called to be the *presiding officer* of the Church. The Twelve, therefore, in the setting apart of the President do not give him any additional priesthood, but *confirm* upon him that which he has *already* received; they *set him apart* to the office, which it is their right to do.

On the death of the President, the Council of the Twelve becomes the presiding quorum in the Church *until* by their action they organize again the First Presidency.

---

[32]*Times and Seasons*, vol. 5, p. 698.   [33]*The "Reorganized" Church vs. Salvation for the Dead*, pp. 7-9.

This is a consistent order. If only one man held this binding and loosing power, then the Lord would be under the necessity of restoring it each time a new President of the Church was called.

There is no mystery about the choosing of the successor to the President of the Church. The Lord settled this a long time ago, and the *senior apostle automatically becomes the presiding officer of the Church*, and he is so sustained by the Council of the Twelve which becomes the presiding body of the Church when there is no First Presidency. The president is *not elected*, but he has to be *sustained* both by his brethren of the Council and by the members of the Church.

PROPRIETY OF IMMEDIATE REORGANIZATION OF PRESIDENCY. In regard to the length of time which elapsed from the death of the Prophet Joseph Smith and the organization of the First Presidency in the days of President Brigham Young, I would like to say that every move was new. Never before had such a condition arisen, and the brethren were slow to act. President John Taylor followed the same course and also President Wilford Woodruff, but some time before the death of President Woodruff he gave instruction that there should be no delay in the reorganization of the Presidency, and this was the will of the Lord. Since that time the First Presidency has been completed as soon as convenient, which is the proper order of the Church.

STATUS OF THE TWELVE AS REVELATORS FOR CHURCH. The Twelve Apostles have been sustained as prophets, seers, and revelators ever since the time of the dedication of the Kirtland Temple. *There is only one man at a time who holds the keys of revelation for the Church.*[34] The Twelve Apostles may receive revelation to guide them *in their labors* and to assist them in setting in order the priesthood and organizations of the

---

[34]*D. & C.* 43:3-7.

Church. When they are sent out into a stake by authority, they have all the power to receive revelation, to make changes, and to conduct the affairs according to the will of the Lord. But they do not receive revelations for the guidance of the whole Church, only wherein one of them may succeed to the Presidency. In other words the right to receive revelation and guidance for the whole Church is vested in each one of the Twelve which he could exercise should he succeed to the Presidency. But this power is *dormant* while the President of the Church is living.

APOSTLES ARE ALWAYS HIGH PRIESTS. *All of the apostles are high priests and are so ordained.* They belong to a quorum of high priests separate and distinct from the high priests quorum in a stake. The First Presidency is a *presidency of high priests,* as stated in the revelation[35] and since every apostle has the priesthood and keys to enable him to serve as President of the Church, he necessarily must be a high priest.

COUNSELORS IN PRESIDENCY NEED NOT BE APOSTLES. Counselors in the First Presidency may or may not be ordained apostles. We have had some who were not, including: John R. Winder, Charles W. Nibley, William Law, Frederick G. Williams, and Sidney Rigdon.[36]

APOSTLES AMONG NEPHITES AND LOST TRIBES

CALLING AND MISSION OF NEPHITE TWELVE. The Twelve men chosen by our Savior among the Nephites are called *disciples* in the *Book of Mormon.* Nephi wrote of his vision given nearly 600 years before the birth of the Lord as follows:

"And the angel spake unto me, saying: Behold the *twelve disciples* of the Lamb, who are chosen to minister unto thy seed. And he said unto me: Thou rememberest the *twelve apostles* of the Lamb? Behold they are they

---

[35]*D. & C.* 107:8, 22, 64-66.   [36]Pers. Corresp.

who shall judge the twelve tribes of Israel; wherefore, the *twelve ministers* of thy seed shall be judged of them; for ye are of the house of Israel. And these *twelve ministers* whom thou beholdest shall judge thy seed. And, behold, they are righteous forever; for because of their faith in the Lamb of God their garments are made white in his blood."[37]

In fulfilment of this prophecy, when the Savior came to the Nephites, he chose twelve men and gave them authority to minister in his name among the Nephites on this American continent in *all the ordinances essential to their salvation*. These twelve went forth healing the sick, performing many miracles, and administering the ordinances as they had been commanded to do. The fulness of the gospel, with the power and the authority of the Melchizedek Priesthood, was given to the Nephites the same as it was to the Church on the Eastern Hemisphere. Moreover, the Lord informed the Nephites that the law that had been given to Moses, including the offering of sacrifices by the shedding of blood, had been done away in him.[38]

While in every instance the Nephite Twelve are spoken of as *disciples,* the fact remains that *they had been endowed with divine authority to be special witnesses for Christ among their own people.* Therefore, they were *virtually apostles to the Nephite race,* although their jurisdiction was, as revealed to Nephi, eventually to be subject to the authority and jurisdiction of Peter and the Twelve chosen in Palestine.

According to the definition prevailing in the world, an apostle is a witness for Christ, or one who evangelizes a certain nation or people, "a zealous advocate of a doctrine or cause." Therefore, in this sense the Nephite Twelve became apostles, as special witnesses, just as did

---

[37]1 Ne. 12:8-10.

[38]3 Ne. 11:18-41; 12:1-2; 13:25-34; 15:4-9; 18:1-37; 19:1-36; 28:1-40.

Joseph Smith and Oliver Cowdery in the dispensation of the fulness of times.

MINISTERS AMONG LOST TRIBES. When the Savior taught the Nephites, he informed them that he had "other sheep" which were not of the Nephites, neither of the land of Jerusalem, and these also were to hear his voice and be ministered to by him. It is reasonable for us to conclude that among these others, who were hidden from the rest of the world, he likewise chose *disciples*—perhaps *twelve*—to perform like functions and minister unto their people with the same fulness of divine authority.[39]

[39]*Era*, vol. 57, p. 702; 3 Ne. 16:1-4; 17:4.

CHAPTER 9

PATRIARCHS, BLESSINGS, AND ADMINISTRATIONS

LAW OF PATRIARCHAL LINEAGE

TWO HEREDITARY OFFICES IN CHURCH. The office of *Patriarch to the Church* is one of two *hereditary offices* in the Church, the other being that of *Presiding Bishop.*[1] In the case of the Presiding Bishop, however, the Lord has not revealed the line of descent, and since one holding the office of high priest may serve, this order has been followed from the beginning in this dispensation. . . . In case of the Patriarchal office, the Lord has designated the line of descent. By revelation and commandment Joseph Smith, Sr., was called and ordained to this office.[2]

From the days of Adam the office of patriarch has descended from father to son. Adam is the great Patriarch of the human family and will preside over his posterity forever.[3]

PATRIARCHAL ORDER: FROM ADAM TO MOSES. The order of this priesthood which was established in the beginning was patriarchal. The authority descended from father to son, and those who held it were high priests. This order of descent from Adam to Noah is given in the *Doctrine and Covenants.*[4] Noah, who stands next to Adam in authority, brought this priesthood through the flood, and it continued from generation to generation.[5] Abraham, the 10th from Noah, received special blessings from the Lord, and the priesthood continued through him and his seed with the promise that

---

[1]*D. & C.* 68:14-24; 107:15-17, 39-41.
[2]*Era,* vol. 45, p. 695.
[3]*Era,* vol. 38, p. 216; *D. & C.* 107:55.

[4]*D. & C.* 107:41-52.
[5]Joseph Fielding Smith, *Teachings of the Prophet Joseph Smith,* p. 157.

all who received the gospel should be counted as Abraham's seed and partake of his blessings.[6]

The patriarchal authority has come down from Abraham through Isaac, Jacob, Joseph, and Ephraim. Why Manasseh, the older son of Joseph, was not chosen we do not know. If we had the full record, this matter would no doubt be made clear.[7] All through the centuries from the beginning to the days of Moses, the patriarchal priesthood prevailed. Those who held this authority were high priests.

PATRIARCHAL ORDER TAKEN FROM ANCIENT ISRAEL. When the children of Israel—the descendants of Jacob, grandson of Abraham—were in the wilderness, after their deliverance from Egypt, the Lord offered them, on conditions that they would serve him, the fulness of this priesthood with all its blessings, and they would have become a nation of priests under this patriarchal order.

However, the children of Israel rebelled; they showed themselves *unworthy* of this great honor, and *the Lord in his anger denied them this fulness of priesthood with all the rites that would prepare them for the exaltation in his presence.* When Moses went up into the mount and remained 40 days, the Lord gave him two tables of stone on which were carved his holy commandments, with the promise to Israel of blessings, through their faithfulness, that would permit them "to enter into his rest."

When Moses returned and found the people worshiping the golden calf, the God of the Egyptians, in his anger he threw down the tables and broke them. Then, later, at the command of the Lord, he went back into the mountain and received *other tables,* also written by the finger of God; but *these did not contain the same commandments in all particulars that were on the first. The*

[6]*Church News,* Aug. 11, 1945, p. 1;   [7]*Era,* vol. 38, p. 216; Gen. 48:1-22.
Abra. 1:1-4; 2:6-11; *D. & C.* 84:6-16.

Lord had eliminated that which pertained to the higher blessings.[8]

BIRTHRIGHT IN ANCIENT ISRAEL. In this dispensation it was made known to Joseph Smith that the right to hold the keys of this patriarchal office belonged to his father, Joseph Smith, Sr. This authority was conferred upon Joseph Smith, father of the Prophet, by right of his being *"the oldest man of the blood of Joseph, or of the seed of Abraham."*

It is well understood by Latter-day Saints that the birthright (which usually is conferred upon the oldest son in the family) passed by Reuben, the firstborn son of Jacob, because of his transgression, and it was placed upon the head of Joseph by divine revelation.[9] Joseph was the eldest son of Rachel and by long odds the most worthy son of Jacob. Because of his worthiness and his integrity, and, perhaps, the fact that he was the firstborn son of Rachel, he was chosen to occupy this exalted position among the sons of Israel.

However, for reasons which we do not understand for the history of those events is very brief, this authority came down through the lineage of Joseph's second son, Ephraim. It was Ephraim who was called to occupy the position held by his father, and he is spoken of in the scriptures as the firstborn in Israel.[10] Since that day the record of descent of the patriarchal power is very meager.

LATTER-DAY PATRIARCHAL LINEAGE

JOSEPH SMITH, SR., FIRST LATTER-DAY PATRIARCH. It is sufficient for us to know that in this day the Lord by revelation declared it was the right of Joseph Smith, father of the Prophet, to stand in this important office as *the Patriarch holding the keys of this ministry.* He was, as we have said, the first man called to occupy this

---

[8]*Church News*, Aug. 11, 1945, pp. 1, 6; *D. & C.* 84:18-27; *Inspired Version*, Ex. 34:1-2.

[9]Gen. 35:21-22; 49:3-4, 22-26; 1 Chron. 5:1-2.

[10]Gen. 48:1-22; Deut. 33:13-17; Jer. 31:9; *D. & C.* 133:34.

position in this dispensation.[11] He was ordained by his illustrious and honored son, Joseph, to this position, December 18, 1833, and held this office with honor and with the inspiration of the Lord resting upon him, until his death, September 14, 1840, at the age of 69 years. His life was shortened by persecution and mobocracy.[12]

PROPHET'S BLESSING UPON HIS FATHER. In the blessing pronounced upon his father's head, given December 18, 1833, the Prophet said:

"Three years previous to the death of Adam, he called Seth, Enos, Cainan, Mahalaleel, Jared, Enoch, and Methuselah, who were all high priests, with the residue of his posterity who were righteous, into the valley of Adam-ondi-Ahman, and there bestowed upon them his last blessing. And the Lord appeared unto them, and they rose up and blessed Adam, and called him Michael, the prince, the archangel. And the Lord administered comfort unto Adam, and said unto him: I have set thee to be at the head; a multitude of nations shall come of thee, and thou art a prince over them forever.[13]

"So shall it be with my father. He shall be called a prince over his posterity, holding the keys of the Patriarchal Priesthood over the kingdom of God on earth, even the Church of the Latter-day Saints, and he shall sit in the general assembly of patriarchs, even in council with the Ancient of Days, when he shall sit and all the patriarchs with him, and shall enjoy his right and authority under the direction of the Ancient of Days. . . .

"Again, blessed is my father, for the hand of the Lord shall be over him, and he shall be full of the Holy Ghost. . . . Behold, the blessings of Joseph by the hand

---

[11]It has been erroneously stated in the *Doctrine and Covenants Commentary*, old edition, p. 869, that John Young, father of Brigham Young, was the first man ordained to the office of patriarch, and that this was after the return of Zion's Camp in 1834. Joseph Smith, Sen., was ordained December 18, 1833, nearly one year before the ordination of John Young. J.F.S.

[12]*Gen. & Hist. Mag.*, vol. 23, p. 50-53.   [13]*D. & C.* 107:53-55.

of his progenitor shall come upon the head of my father and his seed after him, to the uttermost."[14]

HEREDITARY NATURE OF PATRIARCHAL OFFICE. It has always been understood, and so the revelations declare, that this office is hereditary. In a revelation to Hyrum Smith a few days after the organization of the Church, the Lord foreshadowed the coming of this priesthood as it would descend upon the head of Hyrum Smith, and implied that it would be an office which would pertain to his family, in the following words:

"Behold, I speak unto you, Hyrum, a few words; for thou also art under no condemnation, and thy heart is opened, and thy tongue loosed; and thy calling is to exhortation, and to strengthen the church continually. Wherefore *thy duty is unto the church forever, and this because of thy family.*"[15]

The statement that the duty of Hyrum Smith was to the Church forever, *because of his family,* evidently conveys the thought that he would succeed to the office of Patriarch and that *it should continue in his posterity to the end of time,* for, surely, it would have to continue in this way to last forever in the Church upon the earth among mortal men. Then again, the blessing pronounced upon the head of Hyrum Smith's father, was that this calling was to come upon his head *"and his seed after him, to the uttermost."* And so, down through the history of the Church, this doctrine has been recognized.[16]

HYRUM SMITH GIVEN KEYS OF PATRIARCHAL PRIESTHOOD. Joseph Smith, Sr., was succeeded in this office by his faithful son, Hyrum, who was ordained to this position, January 24, 1841. In the call which came by revelation to Hyrum Smith the Lord said:

"And again, verily I say unto you, let my servant William [Law] be appointed, ordained, and anointed, as a counselor unto my servant Joseph, in the room of

---

[14]Smith, *op. cit.,* pp. 38-39.   [16]*Era,* vol. 45, pp. 695, 737.
[15]*D. & C.* 23:3.

my servant Hyrum, that my servant Hyrum may take the office of Priesthood and Patriarch, which was appointed unto him by his father, *by blessing* and also *by right;* That from henceforth *he shall hold the keys of the patriarchal blessings upon the heads of all my people,* That whosoever he blesses shall be blessed, and whosoever he curses shall be cursed; that whatsoever he shall bind on earth shall be bound in heaven; and whatsoever he shall loose on earth shall be loosed in heaven."[17]

This blessing pertains to the office and calling of the man who holds the *keys of the Patriarchal Priesthood.*

HYRUM ALSO GIVEN KEYS OF KINGDOM. The Lord conferred upon Hyrum Smith, however, another important and special honor, in making him as well as Joseph Smith a holder of the *keys of authority* in this dispensation of the fulness of times. These are the words of that appointment: "And from this time forth I appoint unto him that he may be a prophet, and a seer, and a revelator unto my church, as well as my servant Joseph."[18]

This was a *special* blessing given to Hyrum Smith, and in accepting it he took the place of Oliver Cowdery, upon whom these keys had previously been bestowed. It should be remembered that *whenever the Lord revealed priesthood and the keys of priesthood from the heavens, Oliver Cowdery stood with Joseph Smith in the presence of the heavenly messengers, and was a recipient, as well as Joseph Smith, of all this authority.* They held it *conjointly,* Joseph Smith as the *first* and Oliver Cowdery as the *second* elder of the Church.

HYRUM SMITH: WITNESS OF RESTORATION. Thus the law pertaining to witnesses was fully established, for there were *two witnesses standing with authority, keys, and presidency, at the head of this the greatest of all dispensations.*[19] When through transgression Oliver Cowdery lost this wonderful and exalted blessing,

---

[17]*D. & C.* 124:91-93.
[18]*D. & C.* 124:94.
[19]Joseph Fielding Smith, *Doctrines of Salvation.* vol. 1, chap. 13.

Hyrum Smith was chosen by revelation of the Lord to take his place—the Lord calling him in these words:

"That he [Hyrum Smith] may act in concert also with my servant Joseph; and that he shall receive counsel from my servant Joseph, who shall show unto him the keys whereby he may ask and receive, and be crowned with *the same blessing, and glory, and honor, and priesthood, and gifts of the priesthood, that once were put upon him that was my servant Oliver Cowdery;* That my servant Hyrum may *bear record of the things which I shall show unto him,* that his name may be had in honorable remembrance from generation to generation, forever and ever."[20]

And thus, according to promise, the Lord opened the vision of Hyrum Smith and showed to him those things which were necessary to qualify him for this exalted position, and upon him were conferred by Joseph Smith all the keys and authorities by which he, Hyrum Smith, was able to act in concert with his younger brother as a prophet, seer, and revelator, and president of the Church, "as well as my servant Joseph."[21]

The Prophet Joseph blessed Hyrum as follows: "Blessed of the Lord is my brother Hyrum, for the integrity of his heart. . . . He shall stand in the tracks of his father and be numbered among those who hold *the right of Patriarchal Priesthood, even the Evangelical Priesthood, and power shall be upon him.*"[22]

WILLIAM SMITH NEVER SUSTAINED IN PATRIARCHAL OFFICE. At the time of the martyrdom of Hyrum Smith, his oldest son, John, was but a boy 11 years of age and therefore too young to act in this calling. President Brigham Young said it would have been the right of *Samuel,* brother of Hyrum, to have received this office, but Samuel died in the year 1844, shortly after the martyrdom.

[20]D. & C. 124:95-96.
[21]Gen. & Hist. Mag., vol. 23, pp. 50-53.
[22]Smith, *Teachings of the Prophet Joseph Smith,* p. 40.

William Smith was thus left the only surviving brother of Hyrum Smith, and President Young and the apostles said it was William's right, and they therefore *ordained* him to this office in the summer of 1845, but at the October conference of 1845, the saints *rejected* him. William Smith, therefore, was never legally *installed* in this office.[23]

REBELLION AND EXCOMMUNICATION OF WILLIAM SMITH. There has been some question raised as to the number of men who have held this office of Patriarch to the Church, and some errors have been made in listing them. At the general conference held in October, 1844, President Brigham Young said it was William's right to be ordained to the office of *Patriarch to the Church*. However, because of the unstable attitude of William, no action was taken at this or at the next conference held in April, 1845, although at each of these conferences William was sustained in his calling as an apostle.

At a meeting of the Council of the Apostles held in Nauvoo, May 24, 1845, after a long consultation with William, in which he apparently humbled himself and promised faithfully to support the apostles, William Smith was ordained to this office of Patriarch to the Church. It was only a few days later, however, or on May 29th, that the brethren were under the necessity of severely rebuking William Smith for his rebellious spirit, and from that time forth until the time of the October conference he continued to manifest a dissatisfied spirit and a disposition to disregard the counsels of the priesthood.

The result was that at the October conference, 1845, he was rejected, both as a member of the Council of the Apostles and as Patriarch, by "unanimous vote." William Smith, therefore, was *never sustained* in this office by a vote of the people. President Joseph F. Smith maintained most strenuously that, because of this, *William*

[23]*Era.* vol. 38, p. 216.

Smith should not be classed among the Patriarchs holding this exalted position, and for that reason, in speaking of the Presiding Patriarchs, William Smith has not been included.[24]

The offices of Patriarch and Assistant-President were held by Hyrum Smith until the martyrdom. The office of Patriarch was then offered to William Smith, the only surviving brother of the Prophet, and President Brigham Young declared it was his *by right.* William Smith confirmed the saying of the Lord, "many are called, but few are chosen,"[25] for he failed to magnify this calling, turned against his brethren, and was excommunicated. He was never sustained by the vote of the people, and therefore never did legally act; *he was called, but was not chosen.*[26]

ASAEL SMITH NOT PATRIARCH TO CHURCH. It has also been said that *Asael Smith,* brother of the first Patriarch, had been ordained to this position, but this is not the case. He was ordained a patriarch, but was never called to the position of Presiding Patriarch, having died in the interval between the rejection of William Smith and the ordination of John Smith, Asael's younger brother.

DESCENT OF PATRIARCHAL OFFICE. *John Smith, uncle of the Prophet Joseph,* and younger brother of the first Patriarch, was ordained to this position, January 1, 1849; he died in Salt Lake City, May 23, 1854.

After his death the office reverted to the family of Hyrum Smith, his eldest son, *John,* being ordained February 18, 1855.[27] He was an inexperienced boy 22 years of age at the time of his ordination, and after he was ordained President Brigham Young sent him on a mission that he might gain experience. He died in Salt Lake City,

[24]*Gen. & Hist. Mag.,* vol. 23, pp. 50-53.
[25]*D. & C.* 95:5-6, 12; 121:34-46.
[26]*Era,* vol. 45, pp. 737-738.
[27]*Gen. & Hist. Mag.,* vol. 23, pp. 50-53.

November 6, 1911, after holding the office for over 56 years.

The fifth Patriarch was *Hyrum Gibbs Smith,* grandson of John Smith, and the great-grandson of Hyrum Smith. He was ordained under the hands of President Joseph F. Smith, May 9, 1912. He died February 4, 1932, in Salt Lake City.[28] During the 19 years of his ministry he gave 21,590 blessings which were recorded, or 931 more than his grandfather gave.[29]

PATRIARCHAL OFFICE AND BLESSINGS

PATRIARCH TO CHURCH STANDS AS A FATHER TO ISRAEL. Hyrum Gibbs Smith was a very lovable character, even tempered, fatherly in his advice and instruction, well informed in relation to the principles of the gospel, and admirably adapted to his high and holy calling. He was devoted to his work in the Church. His heart was filled with tender mercy for his fellow beings, and the spirit of blessing, which it was his right to possess, was one of the strongest manifestations of his noble character.

He was called to occupy one of the greatest positions of honor and trust ever conferred upon man. This calling came to him by *divine right* according to the decree of our Eternal Father, and he stood as a *father to Israel,* holding the keys of Patriarchal Priesthood and blessing, with the right to declare by revelation the lineage of each member of the Church, and to seal upon the head of each a blessing with the power, through faithfulness, to come forth in the morning of the resurrection to enter into glory in the presence of the Lord.

PATRIARCHS TO CHURCH SERVE BY LINEAGE AND WORTHINESS. This does not mean that *every man* who is ordained to the office of Patriarch receives an office which should descend to his son after him, but that the

[28]*Era,* vol. 45, pp. 737-738.   [29]*Gen. & Hist. Mag.,* vol. 23, p. 53.

calling of the man who holds the *keys of this ministry and priesthood,* other things being in harmony, shall descend upon his posterity after him, by legal and divine right. It always should be kept in mind, that *worthiness is one of the essential prerequisites upon which right to this office is based.* Only through obedience to gospel truth, and by worthiness in every particular, is a man who is of the rightful lineage entitled to succeed to this exalted office.

A patriarch is a high priest. The first *government* given to man on this earth was patriarchal, and that order continued throughout all generations, we have reason to believe, until the days of Moses, when the Lord took from Israel the higher blessings of the gospel, as well as the general exercise of the Melchizedek Priesthood, and left the people subject to the law of Moses and under the direction of priests of the Aaronic order.[30]

NATURE AND PURPOSE OF PATRIARCHAL BLESSINGS. The Patriarch to the Church holds the *keys of blessing* for the members of the Church. He has the authority to seal blessings upon the heads of the members in all parts of the Church, that they may, if they prove faithful, enjoy whatever is pronounced upon their heads and come forth in the resurrection to obtain eternal life. *To gain such blessings, however, all the ordinances and covenants belonging to the gospel and to exaltation must by them be received.*

A blessing given by a patriarch is intended to point out the path which the recipient should travel. It should be given by the *spirit of revelation* and should be a great *comfort* and *incentive* to the recipient to continue on in faithfulness to the end. The patriarch also holds the key by which the *lineage* of those whom he blesses may be made known. It is a very important and most holy and sacred calling.[31]

---

[30]*Gen. & Hist. Mag.,* vol. 23, pp. 49-
50; *D. & C.* 107:39-42; Smith, *op. cit.,* p. 151.   [31]*Era,* vol. 45, p. 738.

PREPARATION FOR GIVING PATRIARCHAL BLESS-
INGS. Extreme care should be taken in the giving of
patriarchal blessings. They should be given only in the
spirit of prayer and humility. Patriarchs should sit down
with the candidates for blessings and question them in
relation to their lives, what they have done in the Church
and otherwise. They should feel of their spirits, discover if they have been active or inactive in the Church,
learn all about them that they can; then, relying on the
Spirit of the Lord, patriarchs should give them
conservative blessings.

CONDITIONAL NATURE OF PATRIARCH'S SEALING
POWER. It is reported that some patriarchs are blessing
members of the Church as follows: "I bless you and seal
you up to come forth to your exaltation in the world to
come." This is wrong. The patriarch has a right to seal
a member up to come forth in the morning of the first
resurrection, *based upon his or her faithfulness,* and that
is all.

POWER OF PATRIARCHS TO DECLARE LINEAGE. A
patriarch giving a blessing has the right of inspiration to
declare the literal descent of the person receiving the
blessing; he does not have authority to *assign* that individual to any tribe. Through the waters of *baptism* and
the *priesthood,* Church members become heirs of Abraham with all the rights belonging to the children of
Abraham through their faithfulness.[32]

If a patriarch gives a blessing and the lineage is not
designated, is it considered a patriarchal blessing? Yes.
However, a patriarch has the right of discernment to
designate the lineage.

If in a blessing the lineage is not given, the person
may go to the patriarch and ask for that information,
and if the patriarch is so inspired, he may declare it and

---

[32]Abra. 2:9-11; Smith, *op. cit.,* pp.
  149-150.

have it added to the blessing. If the patriarch is deceased, another patriarch could add that part to the blessing.

SACRED NATURE OF PATRIARCHAL BLESSINGS
Groups or classes in auxiliaries, seminaries, and the like, should not be sent to patriarchs. Members should go individually. *Patriarchal blessings are individual blessings, sacred to those who receive them. It is not intended that patriarchal blessings should become public property.*

There is no definite age limit for blessings, but we advise that blessings should not be given to any who are not old enough to understand what a blessing is for. They should at least be old enough to be deacons and sisters of like age. A person should be in the Church at least a year before seeking a blessing.

NEGROES AND PATRIARCHAL BLESSINGS. A man with the blood of Cain, if he should truly repent may be baptized and come into the Church and have a patriarchal blessing. Some Negroes who are members of the Church have received patriarchal blessings.

FATHERS CAN GIVE PATRIARCHAL BLESSINGS. *A faithful father who holds the Melchizedek Priesthood may bless his own children, and that would be a patriarchal (father's) blessing.* Such a blessing could be recorded in the family records, but it would not be preserved in the archives of the Church. *Every father who is true to this priesthood is a patriarch over his own house.* In addition, children may receive a blessing by an *ordained patriarch.* A father blessing his own child could, if he received the inspiration to do so, declare the lineage of the child.[38]

ADMINISTERING TO SICK

ORDINANCE OF ADMINISTRATION IN FORMER DISPENSATIONS. Administering to the sick has been an ordi-

[38]Pers. Corresp

nance of the gospel *practiced from the beginning* when the authority of the priesthood has been found on the earth.

The usual procedure is stated by James: "Is any among you afflicted? let him pray. Is any merry? let him sing psalms. Is any sick among you? let him call for the elders of the church; and let them pray over him, anointing him with oil in the name of the Lord: And the prayer of faith shall save the sick, and the Lord shall raise him up; and if he have committed sins, they shall be forgiven him."[34]

We read in the New Testament how Jesus laid his hands upon individuals and healed them.[35] At times, because of the abundant faith of the afflicted, the Savior healed them by just a word, but his command to his disciples was that they should lay their hands upon the sick. This ordinance was not one that was introduced for the first time in the dispensation of the meridian of time, for in the Old Testament are numerous cases of healing. Two very interesting cases are the raising of the widow's son by Elijah[36] and the similar restoration of the dead son of the Shunammite woman.[37]

This great gift was manifest after the resurrection of Jesus during the sojourn of his apostles on the earth. Following their passing the spiritual gifts ceased and the anointing with oil and the blessing of the sick came to an end—not because these gifts were no longer needed, but because faith had departed from the souls of men and the priesthood had been taken from the earth. Henceforth the cry has been heard that these gifts were only intended for the days of the apostles and are no longer needed. Nevertheless, there have been many times when sincere, devout people, *who have endeavored to observe the commandments of the Lord to the best of their knowledge,* have been blessed and healed through the prayer of faith. The prayers of honest souls who

[34]Jas. 5:13-15.
[35]Mark 6:5, 13; 16:18; Luke 13:12-13.
[36]1 Kings 17:19-24.
[37]2 Kings 4:18-37.

sincerely seek blessings from the Lord are often answered, and the Lord accepts their faith.

ORDINANCE OF ADMINISTRATION RESTORED. In this dispensation the Lord has spoken and given commandment in relation to the administration of the sick in the following words: "And whosoever among you are sick, and have not faith to be healed, but believe, shall be nourished with all tenderness, with herbs and mild food, and that not by the hand of an enemy. And the elders of the church, two or more, shall be called, and shall pray for and lay their hands upon them in my name; and if they die they shall die unto me, and if they live they shall live unto me."[38]

The detail in anointing and blessing the sick is as follows. Two or more elders should be called for the purpose. One elder should pour the oil from the bottle containing *pure olive oil*, which has been consecrated, upon the *crown of the head* of the sick person. (One drop taken from a medicine dropper is improper, nor should the oil be poured from a spoon.) The brother anointing should not seal the anointing but leave that to the second elder who offers the *prayer of administration*. The sick person should be called by name in the anointing, and it should be done in the name of Jesus Christ and by authority of the Melchizedek Priesthood according to the revelation, and to the end that the sick person may be healed.

After the ordinance of anointing is finished, the elders present, two or more, including the one who anointed, will lay their hands upon the head of the sick and offer a prayer in faith in the name of Jesus Christ and by virtue of the priesthood which they hold seal the anointing. If moved upon by the Spirit of the Lord, the brother who is voice may rebuke the illness and bless with life and health. Prayers and blessings for the sick need not be of great length, that which is essential should

---

[38]D. & C. 42:43-44.

be uttered and then the prayer closed in the name of Jesus Christ. After the administration is finished, it is wisdom for the elders who officiate not to prolong their visit but cheerfully withdraw.

INSTRUCTIONS ON ANOINTING AND SEALING. The following is taken from the *MIA Manual* of 1902-3, pages 58-59:

"The ordinance of administering to the sick usually consists of two parts: The *anointing*, and the *prayer of faith*. The first usually is performed by one of the elders. The *sealing of the anointing* is performed by all the elders gathered around the person and laying hands on him or her, one of them offering the prayer. The words to be used are not prescribed. In this anointing it is necessary to use the name of Messiah and to invoke the power of the priesthood, witnessing that the anointing is performed for the purpose of healing. In sealing the anointing the same name and authority should be used, and the statement made that the anointing for the healing of the sick is sealed, the disease rebuked, and the blessing of health promised. Any *additions, conditions,* or *promises* that are dictated by the inspiration of the Lord, should of course be set forth in the prayer. *Those officiating should exercise the strongest possible faith for the patient's recovery, and place themselves thoroughly under the influence of the Spirit of the Lord* because in such cases much depends on the faith of the elders and the spirit that accompanies them. *Faith to heal the sick is one of the most desirable gifts of the gospel and should be sought by all the elders; and they should be in readiness at any time to exercise this power in behalf of the unfortunate.*"

"And these things ye shall not do, except it be required of you by them who desire it, that the scriptures might be fulfilled; for ye shall do according to that which is written."[39]

---

[39]*D. & C.* 24:14.

PROPER ADMINISTRATION PROCEDURES. If a man were alone with a sick person, should he anoint with oil and give the blessing and seal it by himself? If an elder is alone and no help is available, and he is called on to administer to the sick, he has full authority both to anoint and seal the anointing.

Is it proper to anoint the afflicted parts of the body? No. The anointing should be on the crown of the head. (It could be a matter of impropriety to anoint afflicted parts of the body.)

Is it permissible to administer the oil internally? No. Taking the oil internally is not part of the administration. If persons who are ill wish to take oil internally, they are not forbidden, but many sicknesses will not be improved by oil in the stomach.

Is it proper for an elder to take with him a brother holding the Aaronic Priesthood to assist in administering to the sick? This question has been answered by the First Presidency and Council of the Twelve as follows:

"It was the sense of the Council . . . that the practice [of administering] be confined to the elders; but in the case of absolute necessity, that is where an elder finds himself in the situation that he cannot avail himself of the company of another elder, he may, if opportunity affords, avail himself of the company of a member of the Aaronic Priesthood, or even a lay member, but for the purpose only of being supported by the faith of such member or members, *the elder alone to officiate in the ordinance of administration;* or, the elder may administer alone without such assistance of a lay member or one holding the Aaronic Priesthood."[40]

LAYING ON OF HANDS BY WOMEN IN ADMINISTRATIONS. If a man and his wife were alone with a sick person, could he anoint with the oil and then seal the anointing with his wife assisting using the priesthood she

[40]*Journal History,* Feb. 18, 1903.

holds jointly with her husband? President Joseph F. Smith answered this question as follows:

"Does a wife hold the priesthood with her husband, and may she lay hands on the sick with him, with authority? *A wife does not hold the priesthood with her husband, but she enjoys the benefits thereof with him;* and if she is requested to lay hands on the sick with him, or with any other officer holding the Melchizedek Priesthood, she may do so with perfect propriety. *It is no uncommon thing for a man and wife unitedly to administer to their children.*"[41]

When this is done the wife is adding her faith to the administration of her husband. The wife would lay on hands just as would a member of the Aaronic Priesthood, or a faithful brother without the priesthood, she in this manner giving support by faith to the ordinance performed by her husband. The Prophet Joseph Smith said, "Respecting females administering for the healing of the sick, . . . there could be no evil in it, if God gave his sanction by healing; that there could be no more sin in any *female laying hands on and praying for the sick,* than in wetting the face with water; it is no sin for anybody to administer that has faith, or if the sick have faith to be healed by their administration."[42] *Such an administration would not be by virtue of the priesthood, but a manifestation of faith.*

ADMINISTRATIONS AND FORGIVENESS OF SINS. James says when a man administers to a sick person he has power to remit his sins; how does the elder get power to remit sins?

It is not the elder who remits or forgives the sick man's sins, but the Lord. *If by the power of faith and through the administration by the elders the man is healed, it is evidence that his sins have been forgiven.* It is hardly reasonable to think that the Lord will forgive

---

[41]*Era*, vol. 10, p. 308.   [42]Smith, *op. cit.,* pp. 224-225.

the sins of a man who is healed if he has not repented. *Naturally he would repent of his sins if he seeks for the blessing by the elders.*[43]

WOMEN AND THE PRIESTHOOD. There is nothing in the teachings of the gospel which declares that men are superior to women. The Lord has given unto men the power of priesthood and sent them forth to labor in his service. A woman's calling is in a *different* direction. *The most noble, exalting calling of all is that which has been given to women as the mothers of men. Women do not hold the priesthood, but if they are faithful and true, they will become priestesses and queens in the kingdom of God, and that implies that they will be given authority.* The women do not hold the priesthood with their husbands, but they do reap the *benefits* coming from that priesthood.

WOMEN NOT TO ANOINT OR SEAL BLESSINGS. The Brethren do not consider it necessary or wise for the women of the Relief Society to wash and anoint women who are sick. The Lord has given us directions in matters of this kind; we are to call in the elders, and they are to anoint with oil on the head and bless by the laying on of hands.

The Church teaches that a woman may lay on hands upon the head of a sick child and ask the Lord to bless it, *in the case when those holding the priesthood cannot be present. A man might under such conditions invite his wife to lay on hands with him in blessing their sick child.* This would be merely to exercise her faith and not because of any inherent right to lay on hands. *A woman would have no authority to anoint or seal a blessing,* and where elders can be called in, that would be the proper way to have an administration performed.

REPEATED ANOINTINGS NOT NECESSARY. If a sick person has been anointed and the following day seeks

[43]*Era,* vol. 58, pp. 558-559, 607.

another blessing, it is not necessary to anoint with oil the second time. President Joseph F. Smith has left us this counsel: "In the matter of administering to the sick, according to the order and practice established in the Church, *care should be taken to avoid unwarranted repetitions.* When an administration is made, and when the blessing pronounced upon the afflicted one has been received, the ordinance should not be repeated, rather let the time be given to prayer and thanksgiving for the manifestation of divine power already granted and realized. No limit should be or can be set to the offering of prayer and the rendering of praise to the Giver of Good, for we are specially told to pray without ceasing, and no special authority of the priesthood or standing in the Church is essential to the offering of prayer; but *the actual administration by anointing with oil and by the imposition of hands by those who hold the proper office in the priesthood is an authoritative ordinance, too sacred in its nature to be performed lightly, or to be repeated loosely when the blessing has been gained."*[44]

SICK NOT DEDICATED TO LORD. The elders are to bless and comfort the sick and acknowledge the hand of the Lord in all things; but they are not to dedicate a person to the Lord. In regard to the dedicating of the very sick, or the suffering, to the Lord when they are administered to (thus presumably giving them up to death), and as to the advisability of this custom, we have this definite information from the First Presidency:

"The custom which is growing in the Church to dedicate those who appear to be beyond recovery, to the Lord, has no place among the ordinances of the Church. The Lord has instructed us, where people are sick, to call in the elders, two or more, who should pray for and lay their hands upon them in the name of the Lord; and 'if they die,' says the Lord, 'they shall die unto me, and

[44]Joseph F. Smith, *Gospel Doctrine,*
    4th ed., pp. 256-257.

if they live they shall live unto me.'[45] *No possible advantage can result from dedicating faithful members of
the Church to the Lord prior to their death.* Their membership in the Church, their devotion to the faith which
they have espoused, are sufficient guarantee, so far as
their future welfare is concerned.

"*The administration of the ordinances of the gospel
to the sick is for the purpose of healing them, that they
may continue lives of usefulness until the Lord shall call
them hence.* This is as far as we should go. If we adhere
strictly to that which the Lord has revealed in regard to
this matter, no mistake will be made."[46]

USE OF CONSECRATED OIL

OLIVE OIL: AN EMBLEM OF PURITY AND PEACE.
Why is olive oil, instead of some other kind, used in
administering to the sick? When was this practice first
instituted? By what authority was it instituted?

Oil used in the anointing of the sick and for other
holy purposes, including the anointing in the house of
the Lord, must be *pure oil, free from all unsavory conditions and impure elements.* For this reason it is very
evident that oil produced from animal bodies could not
be used. The purest oils come from the higher forms of
plant life, and among these the olive tree stands pre-
eminently first.

*The olive tree from the earliest times has been the
emblem of peace and purity.* It has, perhaps, been considered more nearly sacred than any other tree or form
of vegetation by the inspired writers of all ages through
whom we have received the word of the Lord. In parables
in the scriptures the House of Israel, or the people who
have made covenant with the Lord, have been compared
to the olive tree.[47]

We, even in this modern day when things are turned

[45]*D. & C.* 42:44.   [47]Jacob 5; *D. & C.* 101:43-54; Jer.
[46]Pers. Corresp.; *Era*, vol. 25, p. 1122.   11:16; Rev. 11:4.

upside down, speak of the olive branch as being the emblem of peace, and it is usually portrayed as being carried in the bill of the dove of peace. When the Prophet Joseph Smith sent to the saints in Missouri a copy of section 88 of the *Doctrine and Covenants*, one of the greatest revelations ever given to man, he said: "I send you the olive leaf which we have plucked from the Tree of Paradise."[48]

ANCIENT USE OF OLIVE OIL FOR HOLY PURPOSES.
Just when olive oil was first used in anointing we do not know, for the record is silent as to the original use of oil for this purpose; but we do have the word of the Lord given to Israel through Moses some 1500 years before the birth of our Lord, wherein the use of olive oil is commanded for *holy purposes*, as the following will show:

"And thou shalt command the children of Israel, that they bring thee *pure oil olive* beaten for the light, to cause the lamp to burn always."[49]

"And of cassia five hundred shekels, after the shekel of the sanctuary, and of oil olive an hin: And thou shalt make it *an oil of holy ointment*, an ointment compound after the art of the apothecary: it shall be *an holy anointing oil*."[50]

"And he made *the holy anointing oil*, and the pure incense of sweet spices, according to the work of the apothecary."[51]

Zechariah, also, wrote: "Then answered I, and said unto him, What are these two *olive trees* upon the right side of the candlestick and upon the left side thereof? And I answered again, and said unto him, What be these two *olive branches* which through the two golden pipes empty the golden oil out of themselves? And he answered me and said, Knowest thou not what these be? And I

48*Church History*, vol. 1, p. 316.   50Ex. 30:24-25.
49Ex. 27:20.   51Ex. 37:29.

said, No, my lord. Then said he, These are the two anointed ones, that stand by the Lord of the whole earth."[52]

From these quotations from the scriptures we discover that the pure oil of the olive was commanded to be used in the lamps in the Temple, or Tabernacle, in the wilderness when Israel was waiting to enter the promised land, and also to be used for holy anointing. This practice was continued in Solomon's Temple.

REBELLIOUS ISRAEL DENIED USE OF ANOINTING OIL. It is well known that *the oil of gladness,* or of *anointing,* which is spoken of in the Psalms and other scriptures, and with which the kings and prophets were anointed, was the pure oil of the olive which grew abundantly in Palestine.[53]

One of the curses which Moses predicted would come upon Israel, if the children of Israel turned from the commandments of the Lord, was that they would have olive trees throughout all their coasts, but they should not anoint themselves with the oil, for their olive trees would cast their fruit.[54]

Micah, at a later day, when Israel had turned from the Lord, again warned the people of Israel and said: "Thou shalt sow, but thou shalt not reap; *thou shalt tread the olives, but thou shalt not anoint thee with oil;* and sweet wine, but shalt not drink wine."[55] This was to come upon them as a punishment for their transgressions.

ANOINTING WITH OIL IN MERIDIAN OF TIME. The use of olive oil for the anointing of the sick was in vogue in the Church of Jesus Christ of former days. James says: "Is any sick among you? let him call for the elders of the church; and let them pray over him, *anointing him with oil* in the name of the Lord: And the prayer of faith

---

[52]Zech. 4:11-14.   [54]Deut. 28:40.
[53]Ps. 23:5; 45:7; 89:20; 92:10; Heb.   [55]Micah 6:15.
    1:9.

shall save the sick, and the Lord shall raise him up; and if he have committed sins, they shall be forgiven him."[56]

PRIESTHOOD BLESSINGS WITHOUT USE OF OIL. This same practice was instituted in the Church of Jesus Christ of Latter-day Saints in the beginning and has continued until now, and *will continue as an ordinance as long as present conditions endure.*

There have been cases, sad to relate, where elders of the Church, through lack of understanding, have refused to administer to the sick under conditions where oil could not be had. It is the privilege and duty of the elders to bless the sick by the laying on of hands. If they have pure olive oil which has been consecrated for this purpose, one of them should use it in anointing the sick, and then they should by the laying on of hands seal the anointing. *If no oil is to be had, then they should administer by the laying on of hands in the power of the priesthood and in the prayer of faith,* that the blessing sought may come through the power of the Spirit of the Lord. This is in accordance with the divine plan inaugurated in the beginning.[57]

---

[56]Jas. 5:14-15.   [57]*Church News,* Sept. 1, 1934.

CHAPTER 10

BOOKS THE LORD APPROVES

CLERGY AND CRITICS FIGHT BIBLE

CRITICS OF BIBLE INSPIRED BY SATAN. *The Holy Bible has had a greater influence on the world for good than any other book ever published.* It has been printed in more editions and translated into more languages and read by more people than any other book. *No other publication has been more severely and critically* examined. The reason for the *Bible's* great influence for good is because it is *inspired* and contains the word of the Lord delivered to his prophets, who wrote and spoke as they were moved upon by the Holy Ghost, since the world began.[1]

It has drawn the fire of adverse criticism for the self-same reason. *Had it not been an inspired record less attention would have been paid to it by the opposing critics,* who have drawn their inspiration from the *author of evil,* who in the very beginning swore in his wrath that he would endeavor to destroy the work of God.[2]

APOSTATE CLERGY RESIST PRINTING OF BIBLE. As late as the 14th century, when the world was dominated by *a despotic power that feared not God nor served him,* there were few outside of the clergy who were educated enough to read and write. *Priests* became the lawyers, diplomats, ambassadors, instructors, and prime ministers of the nations. All learned men talked and wrote in Latin, the language of Rome. It is recorded that for centuries a man convicted of crime in England, by showing that he could read and write, could claim the benefits of a trial in the ecclesiastical courts, which by long abuse came to

---

[1] 2 Pet. 1:20-21.　　　　　　　[2] *Church News,* Jan. 2, 1937, p. 1.

mean exemption from the punishment of the criminal law of the land.

With the invention of the printing press learning revived, and during the days of the reformation many among the common people learned to read and write. By that time the books of the *Bible* had been compiled and several translations had been made in the languages of the people of Europe. *Wycliffe's Bible* appeared in 1330 and was followed by other translations at a later date both in English and other tongues.

At first there was an attempt on the part of the powerful but *corrupt clergy* to destroy these copies which were prepared without authority being granted by the great Catholic Church. Before the time of printing a copy of the *Bible* cost the sum of 500 crowns. Through the aid of printing the price was reduced to five crowns, which made it possible for the people not only to have the privilege of hearing the scriptures read in their native tongue, but also to acquire the understanding by which they could read them for themselves.

MEN BURNED AT STAKE FOR OWNING SCRIPTURES. The English chronicler, Henry Kneighton, many years before had expressed the prevailing notion about the reading of the scriptures, when he denounced the general reading of the *Bible*, lamenting "lest the jewel of the church hitherto the exclusive property of the clergy and divines, should be made common to the laity." Archbishop Arundel, in England, had issued an enactment that "*no part of the scriptures in English should be read, either in public or in private, or be thereafter translated, under pain of the greater excommunication.*" The New Testament translation of Erasmus was forbidden at Cambridge, and the Vicar of Croyden said from his pulpit: "*We must root out printing, or printing will root us out.*"[3]

---

[3]See: J. Paterson Smyth, *How We Got Our Bible*, a brief, excellent work on the early translations of the *Bible* and the historical settings in which they came forth.

In the reign of Henry VIII, the reading of the *Bible*
by the common people, or those who were not of the
privileged class, had been *prohibited by act of parliament,*
and *men were burned at the stake in England as well as
in the Netherlands and elsewhere for having even
fragments of the scriptures in their possession.*

DEATH PENALTY FOR OFFENSE OF READING BIBLE.
For those who were considered derelict in church duties,
or heretical in doctrine, edicts were declared, forbidding
them to gather in private assemblies for devotion, in various parts of Europe. "All *reading of the scriptures,* all
discussion within one's own doors concerning faith, the
sacraments, the papal authority, or other religious matter,
was forbidden under penalty of death," writes Motley,
in *The Rise of the Dutch Republic.* "The edicts were no
dead letter. The fires were kept constantly supplied with
human fuel by *monks* who knew the art of burning re-
formers better than that of arguing with them. The
scaffold was the most conclusive of syllogisms, and used
upon all occasions."[4]

Continuing this woeful account of conditions in the
rebellious Netherlands and other countries under Spanish rule, the same author says: "Charles [V] introduced
and organized a papal inquisition side by side with those
terrible 'placards' of his invention, which constituted a
masked inquisition even more cruel than that of Spain.
The execution of the system was never permitted to lan-
guish. The number of Netherlanders who were *burned,
strangled, beheaded,* or *buried alive,* in obedience to his
edicts, and for the *offense of reading the scriptures,* or
looking askance at a graven image, or of ridiculing the
actual presence of the body and blood of Christ in a
wafer, has been placed as high as one hundred thousand
by distinguished authorities, and has never been put at
a lower mark than fifty thousand."[5]

---

[4]J. L. Motley, *The Rise of the Dutch*   [5]Motley, *op. cit.,* p. 99.
    Republic, Burt's ed., vol. 1, p. 68.

Think of a condition such as this prevailing among those who *professed* to be the ministers of the word of God and the teachers of the revelations of the prophets! The Lord declared that the people should know his will by the study of the scriptures, and his disciples taught that they were given by inspiration of God and were profitable for doctrine in righteousness, and were written expressly for our learning![6]

In spite of the strict and horrible ruling in the ages that were dark, the people continued to print, to read, to study, to learn much in regard to the scriptures, until the prediction of the Vicar of Croyden was fulfilled.[7]

BIBLE APPROVED BY LATTER-DAY REVELATION. Today there is more criticism and doubt thrown on the *Bible*, and especially on the writings of Moses, than at any previous time. *Higher criticism* has endeavored to destroy the authenticity of the five books of Moses and place the writing of them at a much later date. This revelation to Joseph Smith establishes the authenticity of the words of Moses,[8] and to every true Latter-day Saint the question of the validity and authorship of the Book of Genesis, and other books of the scriptures, is a settled question. The Lord has settled it by new revelation in the dispensation of the fulness of times.[9]

SAINTS HAVE ANCIENT AND MODERN SCRIPTURAL WITNESSES. During the past century and longer there has been a tendency to dissect the scriptures. But we are taught that they are not of private interpretation and cannot be understood except by the light of the Holy Spirit.[10] The book of *Doctrine and Covenants*, one of the precious works, has come from the Lord to us. It is the word of God to us who live now. Therefore, we have three witnesses.

---

[6]John 5:39; 2 Tim. 3:16-17.
[7]*Young Woman's Journal*, vol. 28, pp. 592-594.
[8]Moses 1:40-42.

[9]*Church News*, Aug. 1, 1931, p. 2; Eighth Article of Faith.
[10]2 Pet. 1:20-21.

They may assail the *Bible,* as they do, and endeavor to prove that the writings attributed to different men were not written by them. We leave that to them. They can do as they please with their learning; we will cling to the *Bible* because we know that whatever errors there are, they are the errors of uninspired men who have done the translating. But they must not and cannot tread upon other ground that we have.

They have assailed the *Book of Mormon* from an outside standpoint and claim that it was translated, or as they say, written by someone else than Joseph Smith. But we have disproved that, and the *Book of Mormon* comes to us pure, having been translated by divine power, and it contains *incontrovertible internal evidence* to those who read it and know anything about the power and Spirit of God—it comes to them with internal evidence of its divinity and they *know* it is true. Therefore, we have this, besides which we have the *Doctrine and Covenants,* and these *three witnesses* enable us to occupy a different position from any other religious denomination upon the face of the earth.[11]

INTERPRETING THE BIBLE

ALLEGORICAL AND SYMBOLICAL TEACHINGS IN BIBLE. Even the most devout and sincere believers in the *Bible* realize that it is, like most any other book, filled with *metaphor, simile, allegory,* and *parable,* which no intelligent person could be compelled to accept in a literal sense. . . .

When the Lord said to Noah, "Every moving thing that liveth shall be meat for you; even as the green herb have I given you all things,"[12] does any person believe that this permission included the use of unclean animals and every poisonous herb which carries within its leaves or roots the power of agonizing death? Should we not have the liberty to *interpret* this, as we do similar things

---

[11]*Church News,* June 12, 1949, p. 24.   [12]Gen. 9:3.

in other writings, in the light of wisdom and with a sprinkling of reason, guided by what else may be written in the sacred word bearing upon the subject?

When Jacob blessed his sons and said, "Judah is a lion's whelp, . . . Issacher is a strong ass, . . . Joseph is a fruitful bough" by a well,[13] must we be forced to believe that these sons literally became a lion's whelp, a strong ass between two burdens, a serpent, a hind let loose, and a bough of a tree by a well, because a court, in the famous trials in Tennessee involving the teaching of evolution, has ruled that the *Bible* must be interpreted literally?

David said: "My soul is among lions: and I lie even among them that are set on fire, even the sons of men, whose teeth are spears and arrows, and their tongue a sharp sword."[14] Very queer looking enemies were these according to such a ruling. The Preacher said: "A wise man's heart is at his right hand; but a fool's heart at his left."[15] Must we, therefore, take these sayings literally?

SYMBOLISM AND FIGURES ENHANCE BIBLE. If we are forced by constitutional declaration or court decree, or for any other cause, to interpret the *Bible* literally in all that is recorded, then Jesus is a lamb,[16] the Pharisees are whited sepulchers that devour widow's houses,[17] the saints are sheep and lambs,[18] and the unrighteous at the day of judgment are to be turned into goats,[19] while the people of the present day are turned into wheat and tares.[20]

The Lord has not taken from those who believe in his word the power of reason. He expects every man who takes his "yoke" upon him to have common sense enough to accept a figure of speech in its proper setting, and to understand that the holy scriptures are replete with allegorical stories, faith-building parables, and artistic speech. Much of the beauty of the *Bible*, even in the

---

[13]Gen. 49:9-22.
[14]Ps. 57:4.
[15]Eccles. 10:2.
[16]John 1:29.

[17]Matt. 23:13-33.
[18]John 21:15-17.
[19]Matt. 25:31-34.
[20]Matt. 13:24-30, 36-43.

translations which have come to us, is found in the wonderful figures of this kind, which have never been surpassed. For example, read the 19th, the 23rd, and the 24th Psalms; Judah's desperate plea for the liberty of his brother Benjamin;[21] the poetic flights of Isaiah, and the Sermon on the Mount.[22]

Where is there a writing intended to be taken in all its parts literally? Such a writing would be insipid and hence lack natural appeal. To expect a believer in the *Bible* to strike an attitude of this kind and believe all that is written to be a literal rendition is a stupid thought. No person with the natural use of his faculties looks upon the *Bible* in such a light.[23]

MANY TRUTHS LOST FROM BIBLE. In no place in the Hebrew scriptures, as the translations have come to us, is there a well defined definition of such terms as *soul, second death, eternal punishment,* terms over which the religious world contends because of lack of understanding. Why are men without this understanding? Is it not because they proclaim that the heavens are sealed? That there is no more revelation? That the canon of scripture is full, and the Lord has no more doctrine to reveal through prophets for the knowledge and benefit of mankind? Truly do they cry, "A *Bible!* A *Bible!* We have got a *Bible,* and there cannot be any more *Bible."*[24] They have closed the heavens against themselves and say they are in the strait and narrow path while helplessly groping in the dark.

Without doubt these terms were thoroughly understood by the prophets and holy men of old who wrote and spoke "as they were moved by the Holy Ghost."[25] It is very probable that the correct interpretation of these expressions, as used by the ancient prophets, was *lost* in the copying and translating of the scriptures. None can successfully deny that changes were made by translators

[21]Gen. 44:18-34.
[22]Matt. 5; 6; 7.
[23]*Church News,* Oct. 31, 1936, p. 1.
[24]2 Ne. 29:3.
[25]2 Pet. 1:20-21.

and scribes, according to their human understanding. We are informed in the *Book of Mormon* that the Hebrew scriptures went "forth from the Jews in purity unto the Gentiles, according to the truth which is in God," and after they went forth from the Jews many changes were made, and "many parts which are plain and most precious; and also many covenants of the Lord have they taken away."[26]

If the teachers of religion in the various sects are content, under these conditions, to stand united and agreed that the canon of scripture is full, saying "We have got a *Bible*, and we need no more *Bible*," they are bound to garner conflicting notions not in keeping with the saving power of the gospel of our Lord.[27]

VERSIONS OF THE BIBLE. We are all aware that there are errors in the *Bible* due to faulty translations and ignorance on the part of translators; but *the hand of the Lord has been over this volume of scripture* nevertheless, and *it is remarkable that it has come down to us in the excellent condition in which we find it.* Guided by the *Book of Mormon, Doctrine and Covenants,* and the Spirit of the Lord, it is not difficult for one to discern the errors in the *Bible.*

The Church uses the *King James Version* of the *Bible* because it is *the best version translated by the power of man.*

The revision of the *Bible* which was done by Joseph Smith at the command of the Lord was not a complete revision of the *Bible.* There are many parts of the *Bible* in which the Prophet did not change the meaning where it is incorrect. *He revised as far as the Lord permitted him at the time,* and it was his intention to do more, but because of persecution this was not accomplished. However, all that he did is very helpful for the major errors have been corrected.[28]

[26]1 Ne. 13:23-32.
[27]*Era,* vol. 19, p. 196.

[28]Pers. Corresp.; J. Reuben Clark, Jr., *Why the King James Version,* pp. 1-473.

CHOOSING REVELATIONS FOR PUBLICATION

EARLY PREPARATIONS TO PUBLISH THE REVELA-
TIONS. Shortly after the organization of the Church, the
members were desirous of obtaining copies of the revelations given up to that time. In the summer of 1830, the
Prophet, by divine commandment, commenced to copy
and prepare the revelations, no doubt with the thought
in mind of having them published. Some of the elders
were carrying copies in their pockets, as far as the Lord
would permit them, for there were some revelations at
that time they were forbidden to publish to the world.

On November 1st and 2nd, 1831, a conference of
the elders was held at Hiram, Ohio, when it was decided
that the revelations should be compiled and published.
On the first day of the conference the Lord gave approval
to this plan by giving a revelation which he called his
"preface unto the book of my commandments, which I
have given them to publish unto you, O inhabitants of
the earth."[29]

While this was not the first revelation given to
Joseph Smith, it appears as the first revelation in the
Doctrine and Covenants, naturally, as it is the custom
to place the preface of any book today in the beginning
of the volume. Oliver Cowdery and John Whitmer were
appointed to carry the revelations to Independence, Missouri, where they were to be published. The Prophet
made haste in the choosing and preparation of these revelations so that the brethren could start on their journey
to Missouri about the middle of November.

ATTEMPT TO PUBLISH THE BOOK OF COMMAND-
MENTS. W. W. Phelps, one of the early members of
the Church, was by trade a printer. He had gone down
into Missouri. The printing press and type were brought
down the Ohio River from Cincinnati where it was pur-
chased, and across the country to Independence, and the

---

[29]*D. & C.* 1:6.

revelations which had been selected by the Prophet were set in type, that is, most of them. But this was slow work. We must remember that they were living in pioneer times, that Kirtland was about as far from Missouri as we are here in Salt Lake City from Winter Quarters, from which point the pioneers started on their journey to the Rocky Mountains. We do not stop to think of that, and so it took some time. By the summer of 1833 most of these revelations had been printed, but not all.

At that time trouble arose, and a mob destroyed the press, scattered the type, and destroyed most of the copies that had been printed; however, a few were saved. This was known as the *Book of Commandments*. As I have said, very few of the sheets were preserved so that there are very few copies of the book, so far as it was completed, in existence. I only know of five or six copies that are to be found today.

APPROVAL OF DOCTRINE AND COVENANTS FOR PUBLICATION. In the year 1834, a committee was formed, consisting of the Presidency of the Church, and some others, for the purpose of again preparing the revelations and having them published. This selection of revelations went on, and in 1835 it was presented at a conference of the Church held on the 17th day of August and there was approved. When the Prophet made this selection, he made the statement that he prized these revelations beyond the wealth of this whole earth.

I want to read to you just a word or two of the testimony of the Council of the Twelve in relation to these revelations, which were accepted on August 17, 1835: "We, therefore, feel willing to bear testimony to all the world of mankind, to every creature upon the face of all the earth, that the Lord has borne record to our souls, through the Holy Ghost shed forth upon us, that these commandments were given by inspiration of God, and are profitable for all men and are verily true. We give this testimony unto the world, the Lord being our

helper; and it is through the grace of God the Father, and
His Son, Jesus Christ, that we are permitted to have this
privilege of bearing this testimony unto the world, in the
which we rejoice exceedingly, praying the Lord always
that the children of men may be profited thereby."[30]

Each man signed his name, beginning with Thomas
B. Marsh, then President of the Council, and ending with
Lyman E. Johnson, the youngest.

LECTURES AND ARTICLES PUBLISHED WITH REV-
ELATIONS. At this conference it was decided to include
in this publication of the *Doctrine and Covenants* seven
Lectures on Faith. These lectures had been given before
the schools of the elders in Kirtland during the years
1834-1835. In accepting these seven *Lectures on Faith*,
it was made very clear to that conference that they were
not received on a parallel with the revelations, but were
accepted as helps in the study of the doctrines of the
Church, and so they were added to the *Doctrine and
Covenants* with that understanding.

At this conference two other articles were also received, read, approved, and ordered to be printed in the
Doctrine and Covenants, one on *marriage* and the other
on *laws and government*. These two articles appeared in
each edition of the *Doctrine and Covenants* from the first
edition in 1835, until 1876. We should remember that
these *Lectures on Faith* were not revelations and were
not considered so in the beginning. These two articles,
one on *marriage*, and the other on *laws and government*,
were not revelations. I want to impress this upon you,
because this question comes up constantly; especially is
it brought up by members of the "Reorganized" Church,
who accuse us of taking a revelation out of the *Doctrine
and Covenants*. This article on marriage was not a
revelation and I want you never to forget it.

---
[30]*History of the Church*, vol. 2, p. 245;
   Doctrine and Covenants, explana-
   tory introduction, p. v.

OLIVER COWDERY PREPARED ARTICLE ON MAR-
RIAGE. I hold in my hand a copy of the *Doctrine and
Covenants* published in 1869, one of the last before that
article was taken out. Do not forget what I am going
to tell you, that at this conference held on August 17,
1835, Joseph Smith and Frederick G. Williams, one of
the counselors in the Presidency, were not present; they
were in Michigan. That is a matter of recorded history.
We know where they were because we have it in the
documentary history of the Church.[31]

So this article on marriage and this article on laws
and government in general were written by Oliver Cowdery in the absence of the Prophet Joseph Smith, and
the Prophet knew nothing of the action that was taken
ordering them printed with the revelations. These were
not revelations, never were so considered, were ordered
printed in the absence of Joseph Smith, and when Joseph
Smith returned from Michigan and learned what was
done—I am informed by my father, who got this information from Orson Pratt—*the Prophet was very much
troubled*. Orson Pratt and Joseph F. Smith, my father,
were missionary companions; they traveled together, and
my father learned a great many things from Orson Pratt
of these early days. When the Prophet came back from
Michigan, he learned of the order made by the conference
of the Church and let it go through.

Now the Prophet did know something about these
Lectures on Faith, because he helped to prepare them,
and he helped also to revise these lectures before they
were published, but these two other articles, he had
nothing to do with them.

WHY ARTICLE ON MARRIAGE WAS DELETED. In
the days of Nauvoo, the Lord gave Joseph Smith a revelation on marriage; that revelation appears under date
of July 12, 1843. That is not the date that the revelation
was *given*, but the date when the revelation was *recorded*.

---

[31]*History of the Church*, vol. 2, p. 243.

That revelation on marriage was not placed in the *Doctrine and Covenants* until 1876. In the year 1876, the first edition of the *Doctrine and Covenants* published in the west was published by David O. Calder of the *Deseret News*.

Orson Pratt, under the direction of the Presidency of the Church, had added to the body of revelations a great many others as we have them now in the *Doctrine and Covenants*, that were not in these earlier editions, and this section known as section 132, was among those so added. It would not have been consistent to have allowed that article on marriage to stay in when it *contradicted* the revelation given to the Prophet Joseph Smith, so they took it out, and very properly. That is a matter of history that we ought to be familiar with.

FALSE TEACHINGS OF ARTICLE ON MARRIAGE. I want to read from this article on marriage to show you that it is not a revelation and could not be: "According to the custom of all civilized nations, marriage is regulated by laws and ceremonies; therefore, we believe that all marriages in this Church of Christ of Latter-day Saints should be solemnized in a public meeting or feast prepared for that purpose," — (I do not believe that at all. We solemnize marriages in the temple of the Lord, at an altar. We do not have a crowd, and it is not a feast.) — "And that the solemnization should be performed by a presiding high priest, high priest, bishop, elder, or priest, not even prohibiting those persons who are desirous to get married, of being married by other authority."

I do not believe that. I believe every marriage in this Church should be performed by a high priest who is appointed by the one who holds the keys to perform that ceremony for time and eternity, at the altar in the house of the Lord, and it ought not to be performed anywhere else. Of course *they had no temples and no understanding of the ceremonies for time and eternity in the year 1835,* so we will have to excuse Oliver Cowdery for that. However this article is not the doctrine of the Church, and cannot be; you can see that.

"We believe that it is not right to prohibit members of this Church from marrying out of the Church, if it be their determination so to do; but such persons will be considered weak in the faith of our Lord Jesus Christ."

Of course we do not believe that we should prohibit people from marrying outside of the Church; we cannot go to that extent and prohibit them from doing it, but we should counsel against it, and teach against it, and try to persuade them not to do that sort of thing.

"Inasmuch as this Church of Christ has been reproached with the crime of fornication and polygamy, we declare that we believe that one man should have one wife, and one woman but one husband, except in case of death, when either is at liberty to marry again."[32]

FIRST REVELATION OF PLURAL MARRIAGE. Of course there was no doctrine of plural marriage in the Church in 1835, but Orson Pratt said (I get this from my father who was his missionary companion) that the Lord did reveal to Joseph Smith, before 1835, and before 1834, and *as early as 1832,* the doctrine of plural marriage. The Prophet revealed that to some few of the brethren, and Orson Pratt was one of them. He said the Prophet told him that, but *it was revealed as a law or principle that was not at that time to be revealed to the Church, or made public or practiced,* but something that would yet come, that was *future.* I have the confidence that Orson Pratt spoke the truth.

So it would be inconsistent, I say, to keep that article in here, when the revelation known as section 132 came to the Prophet Joseph Smith and was added to the revelations in the *Doctrine and Covenants.*

It is not necessary for me now to go into further

---

[32]*History of the Church,* vol. 2, pp. 246-247.

detail in regard to the history of these revelations more
than to say this, that in 1876 Orson Pratt divided the
Doctrine and Covenants into verses as we have it now.
Before that it was not divided; and then it was sent to
England to be published—both the *Doctrine and Covenants* and the *Book of Mormon,* as we now have them
divided into verses and the *Book of Mormon* into chapters, also with the footnotes. This was in 1879 when the
first editions of the *Doctrine and Covenants* and *Book
of Mormon,* with footnotes, were published in Liverpool,
England. All of the printing of the Church works, after
we were driven from Nauvoo, until 1876, was done in
Great Britain.

REVELATIONS IN THE DOCTRINE AND COVENANTS

IMPORTANCE AND WORTH OF DOCTRINE AND COVE-
NANTS.   The *Doctrine and Covenants,* that is the title
of this book, and how much more significant it is than the
Book of Commandments. A Book of Commandments
means, if we accept the title at its face value, that it contains only commandments. But this title which the Lord
gave when they got out this edition—let me refer to the
title page: "The *Doctrine and Covenants of the Church
of Jesus Christ of Latter-day Saints"*—is very significant
and tells the story of what this book actually is. It contains the *doctrine* of the Church; it contains the *covenants*
the Lord will make with the Church, if we are willing
to receive them.

*In my judgment there is no book on earth yet come
to man as important as the book known as the Doctrine
and Covenants,* with all due respect to the *Book of Mormon,* and the *Bible,* and the *Pearl of Great Price,* which
we say are our *standards in doctrine.* The book of *Doctrine and Covenants* to us stands in a peculiar position
above them all.

I am going to tell you why. When I say that, do
not for a moment think I do not value the *Book of Mor-*

mon, the *Bible*, and the *Pearl of Great Price*, just as much
as any man that lives; I think I do. I do not know of
anybody who has read them more, and I appreciate them;
they are wonderful; they contain doctrine and revelation
and commandments that we should heed; but the *Bible*
is a history containing the doctrine and commandments
given to the people anciently. That applies also to the
Book of Mormon. It is the doctrine and the history and
the commandments of the people who dwelt upon this
continent anciently.

But this *Doctrine and Covenants* contains the word
of God to those who dwell here *now. It is our book.* It
belongs to the Latter-day Saints. More precious than
gold, the Prophet says we should treasure it more than
the riches of the whole earth. I wonder if we do? If we
value it, understand it, and know what it contains, we
will value it more than wealth; it is worth more to us than
the riches of the earth.

How to Study the Doctrine and Covenants.
I heard a brother say he could not read the *Doctrine and
Covenants* because it was so much like a dictionary. It
is not a consecutive story—it changes the subject, and so
on—well of course it does.

Many years ago when I was a president in a quorum
of seventies—and in those days we did not have any
supervision so far as our study was concerned—it was
decided by that quorum of seventies that they would
study the *Doctrine and Covenants*, and I was appointed
to be the class teacher. We took it up section by section.
You are not going to get all there is out of it in any other
way. You may take it up if you want to by topics, or
doctrines, that is good; but you are not going to understand the *Doctrine and Covenants*, you are not going
to get out of it all there is in it unless you take it up *section by section;* and then when you do that, you will have
to study it with its setting as you get it in the history of
the Church.

So when we studied the *Doctrine and Covenants* in those days, we did not take the *Doctrine and Covenants* for our text book, but we took the *Documentary History of the Church*. The first volume had just been published, and it contained the greater part of the revelations in the *Doctrine and Covenants*, with their setting, so that we got the reasons why this revelation was given, and that revelation was given; and with this background, there was greater interest in the things we were studying than there would have been if we had taken the revelations in some other way. . . .

"SEARCH THESE COMMANDMENTS." Here is the word of the Lord in a commandment to every member of this Church: "Search these commandments, for they are true and faithful, and the prophecies and promises which are in them shall all be fulfilled."[33]

Search these commandments, that is the thread that runs through this preface to this *Book of Commandments*. I tell you *there is nothing you ever attempted to study equal to this*, and you will never find anything quite equal to it. You have only scratched at it; that is all you have done.

Of course it is not my place to dictate to you and tell you what to do, but it is my place to warn the people and tell them *the Lord has commanded them to search these things*. I am reading this book all the time; scarcely a day passes that I do not read something and ponder over it and the other standards in doctrine. The Lord has given this book to us; it is our book; it contains the *doctrines* of the Church and the *commandments* and the *covenants*. Many of the covenants could not be written and put in a book; you get these in the temple of the Lord; but I am reading these things because I want to know what the Lord has to say, and what he would have me do. It is a wonderful study.[34]

---

[33]*D. & C.* 1:37.   [34]*Rel. Soc. Mag.*, vol. 21, pp. 22-28.

DOCTRINE AND COVENANTS FOR WORLD. The Lord has given many revelations in our own day. We have this *Doctrine and Covenants* full of them, all pertaining unto the Latter-day Saints and to the world. For, *this is not our book alone.* This *Doctrine and Covenants* is my book and your book; but more than that, it belongs to all the world, to the Catholics, to the Presbyterians, to the Methodists, to the infidel, to the nonbeliever. It is his book if he will accept it, if he will receive it.

The Lord has given it unto the world for their salvation. If you do not believe it, you read the first section in this book, the preface, and you will find that the Lord has sent this book and the things which it contains unto the people afar off, on the islands of the sea, in foreign lands; and his voice is unto all people, that all may hear.[35]

And so I say it belongs to all the world, not only to the Latter-day Saints; and *they will be judged by it,* and you will be judged by it. We will all be judged by it, by the things which this book contains and by the things which the other books contain which are holy scripture, which the Lord has given unto us; and if we fail to comprehend these things, if we will not search, if we will not take hold on the things which the Lord has revealed unto us, then his condemnation shall rest upon us, and we shall be removed from his presence and from his kingdom. And I say that in all soberness, because it is true.[36]

REVELATIONS WITHHELD BECAUSE OF UNBELIEF. Now the Lord is withholding from us a great many truths that he would gladly reveal if we were ready to receive them. Did you know that a portion of the record from which the *Book of Mormon* is taken is sealed? The Prophet was not permitted to break the seals, and we will not receive the sealed record until the time comes when the people will show by their faith their willingness to accept it.[37]

How many have read the *Book of Mormon* through? How many have made themselves familiar with the things revealed to us in the *Doctrine and Covenants* regarding what the Lord has said of our duties as members of the Church and what he has said regarding our salvation and exaltation and how it may be obtained? Until we are prepared to receive the things already given. I fear the Lord will hold from us those other things which one time will be revealed.[38]

If we had on record all that had been written by inspired historians, then we would have the truth concerning the gospel of Jesus Christ in such a way that it would astonish the world. Because of unbelief the Lord withdrew from the people many truths, and so they were left without the knowledge concerning the principles of the gospel and the true Church of Jesus Christ.[39]

MORE REVELATIONS IN FUTURE. Not all of the revelations given to the Prophet Joseph Smith are in the *Doctrine and Covenants.* He made a selection for this book by revelation. The Church has had many other revelations, but we have in the *Doctrine and Covenants* revelations sufficient to bring to pass our exaltation if we will but heed them. When we, the members of the Church, reach the point that we are willing to live by all that the Lord has revealed, *he will give us more that can be placed in the Doctrine and Covenants. The Lord is withholding from us great and mighty truths because of the hardness of our hearts.* Why should we clamor for more when we will not abide in what we already have? We are led by revelation today just as much as they were anciently.[40]

---

[37]3 Ne. 26:6-12; Ether 3:21-28; 4:4-8.   [39]Gen. & Hist. Mag., vol. 16, p. 67.
[38]D. & C. 59:4; 101:32-34.   [40]Pers. Corresp.

HOME LIBRARIES

HAVE STANDARD WORKS IN THE HOME. One of the influences in the home that leads to faith and prayer and proper religious understanding is to have in the home the standard works of the Church, not hidden, but where they can be found, on a table or some place where they are in evidence and can be referred to, where they will be seen; and then the members of the family ought to be invited from time to time to read them. I go into homes sometimes where they do not have these things. I always like to know, when I go into anybody's home and they have books, what kind of books they have. If I have been in some of your homes, you know that. I take a look at the books you have and find out what it is that you are reading. I am glad to say that in the majority of the houses I find books that can be approved. We ought to have the standard works of the Church, and we ought to encourage the reading of them.[41]

STANDARD WORKS JUDGE TEACHINGS OF ALL MEN. It makes no difference what is written or what *anyone* has said, if what has been said is in *conflict* with what the Lord has revealed, we can set it aside. *My words, and the teachings of any other member of the Church, high or low, if they do not square with the revelations, we need not accept them.* Let us have this matter clear. We have accepted the four *standard works* as the measuring yardsticks, or balances, by which we *measure every man's doctrine.*

You cannot accept the books written by the authorities of the Church as standards in doctrine, only in so far as they accord with the revealed word in the standard works.

Every man who writes is responsible, not the Church, for what he writes. If Joseph Fielding Smith writes something which is out of harmony with the rev-

elations, then every member of the Church is duty bound
to reject it. If he writes that which is in perfect harmony
with the revealed word of the Lord, then it should be
accepted.[42]

HOME LIBRARIES SHOULD BE PROVIDED. It is within
our power to guide our youth in their reading and to cul-
tivate in their hearts a desire for *good books*. It is most
unfortunate where a person is not possessed with the
desire for good reading. The reading habit, like charity,
should begin at home. *It is the duty of every parent to
provide in his home a library of suitable books to be at
the service of the family.* The library need not be large,
nor the books of the most expensive binding, but there
should be a well chosen variety of the most select that
can be obtained.

Children should be encouraged in the home to read
and be instructed in the value of good books and how
to discriminate between the good and the bad in literature. It is far better for a home to be thus provided where
the children can be entertained with a good, wholesome
story than to more than waste their time playing cards—a
habit that cannot too severely be condemned—or spend-
ing their time in poolhalls or upon the streets in company
of evil associates. . . .

Not one of us is so poor but that we are able to purchase a few good books for the home. A small library
of the most worthy books in this day of cheap printing
may be had for a trifling sum. There is scarcely a family
in the land that does not spend for amusement, or in
pleasure that could be dispensed with, a sum each year
that would purchase a suitable course of reading.

I have been in the habitations of some of our people
where even the standard works of the Church could not
be found, and these are *absolutely indispensable* to a
Latter-day Saint home. There may be some excuse for
an absence of the "commonest English classics," but

---
[42]Pers. Corresp.

there is no excuse for an absence of the standard works of the Church and the writings of our ablest authors on the principles of the gospel.

POOR LITERATURE TO BE AVOIDED. Many books have been spoiled because of too much *padding.* Most novels are padded with matter that does not pertain to the theme and clouds the thought and destroys the efficacy of the story. Many of our present day story writers also spoil what they write by the frequent interjection of *profanity.* The common use of the name of Deity in nearly every exclamation seems to them to be an essential feature to give the proper emphasis and vigor. Many books written by capable and distinguished authors have been marred in this manner.

If authors were more familiar with the commandment, "Thou shalt not take the name of the Lord thy God in vain; for the Lord will not hold him guiltless that taketh his name in vain,"[43] it would greatly improve their works and help their readers in keeping this commandment. Books of this class merit *censure,* and where this difficulty is very marked should utterly be condemned.

Other books contain *problem stories,* are *sensational,* or deal with *immoral themes.* These should always be condemned. Among a certain class such books are very popular, but they corrupt the morals and appeal to the *baser passions of mankind.* There are other books that are perhaps free from immoral thought, as we understand that term, but are filled with *vulgar slang.*

One prominent writer has said: "Slang is to a people's language what an epidemic disease is to their bodily constitution, just as catching and just as inevitable in its course. Like a disease, too, it is severest where the sanitary conditions are most neglected, where there is least culture and thought to counteract it."

---

[43]Ex. 20:7.

DESTRUCTIVE POWER OF BAD LITERATURE. A book
may not be classed as bad, but we should ask ourselves
if it contains any thought that will benefit us intellectually,
morally, or spiritually, if we read it. I do not mean to say
that a book written solely to amuse is necessarily bad
and to be condemned, for some of our most worthy
authors have given to the world good books of this kind
that can safely be recommended. But *if the aim of a book
is not uplifting or helpful to the reader it should be
avoided.*[44] There are so many books that have been tried
and proved to be good that we need not waste our time
with those we may consider doubtful.

"He who writes for fools," it has been said, "finds
an enormous audience." The best sellers advertised at
times among the popular books are not always the *best*.
Among them we may find the sensational, vicious, and
immoral, which *poison the mind and destroy the soul*.
Many of these books are written by contract made between publisher and author at so much per word for the
purpose of getting gain. To be sure, they are made at-
tractive and filled with catchy sayings that appeal to the
simple minded of that enormous class to which reference
has been made.

These books are like spiders' webs, built to inveigle
silly flies who know no better than to be ensnared within
their meshes. They are sold largely on the strength of
the extensive advertising they receive, and while they
may pass through several editions while the craze is on,
seldom live but a few short years and are soon dead and
forgotten. Not so, however, with the mischief they can
do, for the impressions on the mind for evil may endure.

READ SYSTEMATICALLY. Desultory reading as a
habit is not good. Such reading impairs the power of
thought and is enervating to the mind. *Reading should
be done systematically*. Reading that requires study and
reflection should not be done in haste. It is better to read

---
[44]*D. & C.* 50:23.

a little and understand it than to read a great deal without getting the thought.

We sometimes hear the complaint, "I haven't time." But we all have time to read and study which is our *solemn duty.* Can we not arrange to find at least 15 minutes in each day to devote to systematic reading and reflection? This would be but a trifling amount of time, yet it would be one hour and 45 minutes in a week; seven and one-half hours in a month of 30 days, and 91 hours and a quarter in the year. This is equal to 11 and one-half days of eight hours each during the entire year. I am sure we can all find more time than that to read, yet this amount is all Dr. Eliot felt was necessary for a man to spend to receive the "essentials of a liberal education" from his recommended five foot shelf of books. . . .

Very few among us read too much; most of us read too little. The Lord has said: *"And as all have not faith, seek ye diligently and teach one another words of wisdom; yea, seek ye out of the best books words of wisdom; seek learning, even by study and also by faith."*[45]

VALUE OF READING CLUBS. Reading clubs might be organized with profit. The young men could meet at some selected time and place, and one could read while the others listen. There is virtue in reading aloud; let each boy take a turn. It will teach them to read well, to think more clearly, and properly to pronounce their words. It trains the ear as well as the eye, and then, there is the social intercourse and exchange of ideas, which is a benefit to them. This, of course, must be done under the direction of some responsible person connected with the Mutual work. When a book is read, all who were present at the reading should have credit as having read the book.

There is a verse in the 8th chapter of Nehemiah that has a bearing on this subject. When the Jews returned from the captivity, we read that the people were

---

[45]*D. & C.* 88:118.

called together and Ezra and the priests stood before
them to instruct them. This is the passage: *"So they read
in the book in the law of God distinctly, and gave the
sense, and caused them to understand the reading."*[46]
This verse is a perfect treatise, in a sentence, of the art
of reading aloud. Let our young men remember the passage in their reading. See that the books of the reading
course are placed in your public libraries and reading
rooms. A number of young men forming a reading club
may purchase the entire set among them, and the expense
will not be very great. It would be well for each home
to secure the reading course and that each association
also be provided with a set.[47]

---

[46]Neh. 8:8.   [47]*Era*, vol. 16, pp. 1000-1005.

CHAPTER 11

COMING FORTH OF BOOK OF MORMON

RESTORATION OF BOOK OF MORMON

INSPIRED NATURE OF BOOK OF MORMON. The *Book of Mormon* is the *sacred history* of the ancient inhabitants of the American continent; it contains the predictions of their prophets, the commandments of the Lord to them, and the history and destiny of those ancient peoples. It is the American volume of scripture and is just as sacred and inspired as is the *Bible,* which contains the sacred records of the Hebrew race on the Eastern Hemisphere.

No other book has been so sharply, bitterly, and relentlessly attacked as the *Book of Mormon*. Yet, like gold tried many times in the furnace, it has passed through all attacks unscathed. Every weapon raised against it has perished, and the wisdom of the self-righteous who have attacked it has come to naught.

There is an inspiration and feeling of peaceful joy and satisfaction which accompany the sincere and prayerful reading of this book. Its *doctrines* and *literary merit* are in keeping with the writings of the Jewish prophets. The sincere student who is willing to put Moroni's promise to the test is forced to say, "Surely this is the work of the Lord and not the work of man, for no man could have written it."[1]

STICK OF JOSEPH IN HANDS OF EPHRAIM. Ezekiel saw in vision the great nation of the Nephites, the house of Joseph, when he wrote by prophecy concerning the joining of the records of Joseph with that of Judah.[2] . . .

It is very apparent that the *Bible* is the record, or

---

[1]*Era,* vol. 23, pp. 503-504; Moro. 10:3-5.   [2]Ezek. 37:15-28; 2 Ne. 3:12; 29:13; D. & C. 27:5.

stick of Judah; moreover, that it does *not* contain a history
of the nations which were to come of Ephraim and Manasseh. That stick, or history must be sought for elsewhere. And from whence? It has been declared by some
that the *Bible* as we have it today fulfils this prediction,
that this commandment to Ezekiel was a local commandment to him, and he was to write and join the writings
of the two nations of Judah and Israel and hold them
forth before the people of his day. A careful study of
this prophecy, however, reveals that this joining of the
records was to be in the *latter-day,* not in the time of
Ezekiel. . . .

One significant expression in the prophecy of
Ezekiel is that the *stick of Joseph* and his fellows was to
be in the *hand of Ephraim.* Ephraim was to stand at the
head of the tribes of Israel in the *latter-days,* according
to his birthright. Joseph Smith, unto whom the record
of the Nephites was delivered and who translated it, is
of the tribe of Ephraim. The Lord so revealed it. So are
most of those who have received the gospel in this dispensation. Therefore this stick of Joseph is in the hand
of Ephraim and by him has been joined to the stick of
Judah, fulfilling the prophecy of Ezekiel.[3]

The *Book of Mormon* is the record of Joseph. It
contains the history of the descendants of Joseph on this
land, both of Ephraim and of Manasseh. It was in the
hands of Ephraim when it was given to Joseph Smith,
and it is still in the hands of Ephraim when our missionaries go forth proclaiming its truths to the world, for
they also are of Ephraim.[4]

KNOWLEDGE OF CHRIST RESTORED IN BOOK OF
MORMON. It was necessary in the restoration of *all
things* that the people of this continent, who anciently had
received the favor and blessing of the Almighty, should
be brought to light through their history which contained
the prophesying and commandments they received from

God. Although it should be, as stated by one of their prophets, as a voice speaking from the dead, out of the dust of the ground, they were nevertheless to *speak* and *bear witness for Christ*.[5]

In the title-page-preface the promise is made that this record would be preserved to come forth by the power of God to the convincing of the Lamanite, and also the Jew, and also the Gentile, that Jesus Christ is the Son of God. Throughout the *Book of Mormon* the prediction is made that this record would be preserved for that purpose and, moreover, to bear witness of the inspiration and sacredness of the Hebrew scriptures.[6]

BOOK OF MORMON FOR ALL NATIONS. *The promise was made that the contents of this record would be made known among all nations.* Nephi wrote that the day would come "that the words of the book which were sealed shall be read upon the house tops; and they shall be read by the power of Christ."[7]

Joseph Smith and the witnesses to the *Book of Mormon* were deeply impressed with this fact, for in giving to the world their testimonies they worded their address as follows: "Be it known unto all nations, kindreds, tongues, and people, unto whom this work shall come"; and then follows their positive statements concerning the record. Had it not been for the *spirit of prophecy* they would not have dared to have made their address in such manner, nor would Joseph Smith have dared to have declared that *the book would be distributed in all the world as a witness for Christ*. He had no power in himself, even with the help of the 11 witnesses, to bring to pass such a bold and remarkable prediction. Had the *Book of Mormon* been a fraud and these men deceivers, it is very probable that the book would not have been known beyond a radius of a very few miles from Palmyra.

Moroni, when he appeared to Joseph Smith, in Sep-

---

[5]*Church News*, Aug. 26, 1933, p. 4;   [6]Morm. 5:12-15; 7:8-9.
  2 Ne. 27; Isa. 29.   [7]2 Ne. 27:11.

tember, 1823, told Joseph Smith that his name should
be known for both good and for evil among all peoples.
Today no one will say that this has not been fulfilled. So
also has knowledge of the *Book of Mormon* penetrated
the nations of the earth. Wherever the name of Joseph
Smith is known the *Book of Mormon* is also known.
Those who have sincerely read it accept it as a divinely
inspired record; among those who reject it, it may be
looked upon in ignorance as a cunning fraud. However,
the word of the Lord spoken anciently has been, and is
still being, fulfilled.[8]

BIBLE TELLS OF BOOK OF MORMON

BOOK OF MORMON FULFILS PROMISES OF JACOB. It
is reasonable to believe that if the *Book of Mormon* contains the message of salvation as given to the ancient
peoples of this continent and is a witness for the *Bible*,
there also must be some inspired utterances in the *Bible*
bearing witness to the *Book of Mormon*. If there were
no such references, there would be a serious defect in the
testimony of the record of the Nephites.

There is strong presumptive evidence in the blessings
given by Israel to his son Joseph, and his grandsons
Ephraim and Manasseh, as recorded in Genesis, that they
were to inherit a land *far from Jerusalem* and become a
multitude of nations. Joseph was promised that his inheritance should be to the "utmost bound of the everlasting hills"; that he was "a fruitful bough, even a fruitful
bough by a well; whose branches run over the wall."
Moreover, *he was to receive a greater inheritance than
his progenitors,* who were given the land of Palestine.[9]

The *Book of Mormon* is the record of the descendants of Joseph who were led across the "great waters"
to inherit this western land, which land is designated as
being choice above all other lands. Surely these blessings

[8]*Rel. Soc. Mag.,* vol. 14, pp. 424-425.   [9]Gen. 48:3-22; 49:22-26; *Inspired Version,* Gen. 50:24-38; 2 Ne. 3:1-25.

could not be realized in Palestine. Joseph and his sons did not become a multitude of nations there; the tribes of Ephraim and Manasseh did not receive a more wonderful inheritance in Palestine than any other of the tribes of Israel. There the chief honors were conferred first on Benjamin and then on Judah. Here in America all these promises were fulfilled when the descendants of Joseph possessed the land given as their inheritance. . . .

ISAIAH PROPHESIES OF BOOK OF MORMON. One of the most important predictions regarding the *Book of Mormon* is that found in the 29th chapter of Isaiah. The prophet here speaks of a people who should be like Ariel, the city where David dwelt. They should have heaviness and sorrow and should be brought down to speak out of the ground, and their speech was to be low out of the dust, and their voice was to be as of one that had a familiar spirit. Later in this same prophecy Isaiah refers to the words of "a book that is sealed, which men deliver to one that is learned, saying, Read this, I pray thee: and he saith, I cannot; for it is sealed: And the book is delivered to him that is not learned, saying, Read this, I pray thee: and he saith, I am not learned."[10]

This prophecy was literally fulfilled when Martin Harris took copies of the engravings of the plates of the *Book of Mormon* to Professor Anthon in New York. Mr. Anthon answered Martin in almost the language of Isaiah, when he was informed that the book from which the characters were taken was sealed. Said he: "I cannot read a sealed book."[11] How remarkable it is that Isaiah said that the *words* of the book were delivered to one who was learned and that the *book* was delivered to the one who was not learned. How perfectly this harmonizes with the history of the case respecting Mr. Anthon and Joseph Smith!

At the time this should take place, the Lord was to commence a marvelous work and a wonder because the

---

[10]Isa. 29:11-12; 2 Ne. 27.   [11]Jos. Smith 2:63-65.

people drew near to him with their mouths and with their lips honored him, but their hearts were far removed from him, and their fear towards him was taught by the precepts of men. The marvelous work has commenced, and of all times in the history of the world, *now* is the time when the conditions of the people warrant the fulfilment of this prophecy.

NEPHITES: LORD'S "OTHER SHEEP." One other passage of great import, having reference to the people dwelling in America in early times, is the remark of the Savior in that beautiful discourse in relation to his death: "And other sheep I have, which are not of this fold: them also I must bring, and they shall hear my voice; and there shall be one fold, and one shepherd."[12]

It is thought by some that he had reference to the Gentiles, but he said himself that he was not sent to the Gentiles, but to the lost sheep of the house of Israel.[13] He must have referred to Israelites who were not in Palestine, and the visitation must have been one after his resurrection. There is no reference to such a visit in any of the four gospels, and the remark was made shortly before his death. When the Savior visited the Nephites, he told them plainly that this reference to other sheep was a reference to them; but because of the hardness of the hearts of the disciples in Jerusalem, his Father commanded him to make no further reference to the nation of Nephites while instructing the Jews.[14]

Perhaps this reference to other sheep of the house of Israel and the work of the Lord among them would have been stated more clearly if the people had been willing to understand. For the same reason many references to the *Book of Mormon* and the people of the Lord in other lands than Palestine were so expressed that their true significance was hidden. The Savior taught in parables many things so that those who were unprepared

---

[12]John 10:16.   [14]3 Ne. 15:11-24.
[13]Matt. 10:5-6; 15:24.

should not understand.[15] Even today the people of the world, unaided by the Spirit of the Lord, cannot see the true meaning of these passages of scripture here presented. The reason for the discourses of the Savior in parables is equally applicable in the dispensation of the fulness of times.[16]

TRANSLATION OF BOOK OF MORMON

EARLY TRANSLATING DONE INTERMITTENTLY. The idea seems to prevail quite generally among members of the Church that the Prophet Joseph Smith spent the greater part of his time between September, 1827, when he received the plates, and the fall of 1829, translating the *Book of Mormon*.

Because of lack of dates it is impossible to tell exactly how long it took him to complete the translation, but we know from the historical information at hand that there were many days spent in other work, when no attempt was made to translate after that labor had been undertaken. There were times when the Lord commanded him to cease translating. For instance, the Lord said on one occasion: "I say unto thee Joseph, when thou hast translated a few more pages thou shalt stop for a season, even until I command thee again."[17] The reason given for this is that his enemies were lying in wait to destroy him and the work. Again the Lord said: "Do not run faster or labor more than you have strength and means provided to enable you to translate; but be diligent unto the end."[18]

PROPHET'S PREPARATION TO TRANSLATE. Joseph Smith received the plates and the Urim and Thummim September 22, 1827. Because of persecution, poverty, and the necessity of "laboring with his hands" for a living, nothing was done towards translating the record that year. However, he was busy *studying the characters* and

---

[15]Matt. 13:10-13.   [17]*D. & C.* 5:30.
[16]*Era*, vol. 26, pp. 959-962.   [18]*D. & C.* 10:4.

making himself *familiar* with *them* and the *use of the Urim and Thummim*. He had a great deal more to do than merely to sit down and with the use of the instrument prepared for that purpose translate the characters on the plates.

Nothing worth while comes to us merely for the asking. All knowledge and skill are obtained by consistent and determined study and practice, and so the Prophet found it to be the case in the translating of the *Book of Mormon*. It will be remembered that the Lord said to Oliver Cowdery when he desired to translate: "But, behold, I say unto you, that you must study it out in your mind."[19] Oliver thought it would be easy, but found it difficult and therefore was content to accept the advice from the Lord and continue as scribe to Joseph Smith.

It was between December, 1827, and February, 1828, that the Prophet copied the characters from the plates; and, in the month of February, Martin Harris carried them to New York to Professor Charles Anthon.[20] April 12, 1828, Martin Harris commenced to write, and the Prophet to translate, the abridgment giving the history of Lehi and down to the days of King Benjamin. These pages Martin Harris lost, and because of his disobedience he was not permitted to act again as scribe and the Prophet Joseph lost his gift for a season.

OLIVER COWDERY ACTS AS SCRIBE IN TRANSLATING. Oliver Cowdery came to the Prophet at Harmony, Pennsylvania, April 5, 1829, and two days later commenced to write at Joseph Smith's dictation. It must be remembered that they had to commence once more at the beginning and cover the same ground that had been covered in the lost manuscript, but in more detail, for they were now translating the small plates of Nephi.

The translating with Oliver Cowdery as scribe, continued without interruption until May 15, 1829, when

---

[19]*D. & C.* 9:8.   [20]Jos. Smith 2:63-65.

these two men having a desire to know something more about baptism went into the woods to pray and received the Aaronic Priesthood from John the Baptist.[21] Following this important event, it became necessary for Joseph Smith and Oliver Cowdery to change their place of residence because of opposition, and they therefore moved from Harmony, Pennsylvania, to Fayette, Seneca County, New York, to the home of the Whitmers.

It was early in June, 1829, that Oliver Cowdery, David Whitmer, and Martin Harris, with Joseph Smith retired to the woods and sought the Lord in prayer and were visited by the angel who revealed to them the plates. It was also on this occasion that they heard the voice of the Lord declaring unto them that the record *had been translated* by the gift and power of God.

About this time Joseph Smith also writes: "Meantime, our translation drawing to a close, we went to Palmyra, Wayne County, New York, secured the copyright, and agreed with Mr. Egbert B. Grandin to print five thousand copies for the sum of three thousand dollars."[22]

I think we may conclude that the copyright was not secured until the translation was completed, and these words of the Prophet Joseph indicate that this is the case. The copyright bears the date of June 11, 1829.

Total of Two Months Spent Translating. After completing the translation it took some time to make arrangements with Mr. Grandin and to raise the sum required to print the book, the funds being furnished by Martin Harris through the sale of his personal property. In the meantime Oliver Cowdery, at the request of Joseph Smith, made a complete *copy of the manuscript,* and it was this manuscript copy that was taken to the printer, a sheet at a time, until the *Book of Mormon* was printed. Mr. Grandin commenced the printing in August, 1829,

---

[21]Jos. Smith 2:66-68; *History of the Church,* vol. 1, pp. 35, 39.   [22]*History of the Church,* vol. 1, p. 71.

and the *Book of Mormon* was ready for distribution about the first of March, 1830.

We may conclude from the evidence that the *actual time of translating the record*, as we have it in the *Book of Mormon*, was between April 7, 1829, and the first week of June of that same year, or *not to exceed two full months*.[23]

ORIGINAL MANUSCRIPT OF BOOK OF MORMON. After the plates were translated, the Prophet received a commandment from the Lord that the entire manuscript should be *copied*, that the copy should go to the printer, and the original manuscript should not be permitted to go out of his hands. . . .

The original manuscript was in this manner carefully guarded, and the copy struck off by Oliver Cowdery was used in the printing of the *Book of Mormon*. The original was never in the hands of the printer. . . .

The original manuscript remained in the possession of the Prophet Joseph Smith and was by his own hand placed in the cornerstone of the Nauvoo House, October 2, 1841, in the presence of numerous witnesses. . . .

The Nauvoo House, which was begun in the days of Joseph Smith, was never finished, and in the course of time the walls were torn down by Mr. Lewis C. Bidamon, second husband of Emma Smith, and the contents of this cornerstone, which had so long been exposed to the elements, were found to be nearly ruined. Some of the articles, however, were preserved and have been widely distributed.

SCATTERING OF ORIGINAL MANUSCRIPT. President Joseph F. Smith had in his possession Lyman Wight's memorial, and also pages three to 22 of the original manuscript of the *Book of Mormon*, which are, considering all things, fairly well preserved. These pages from the original manuscript are now in the Church Historian's

[23]*Era*, vol. 30, pp. 946-948.

Office. Elders Andrew Jenson, Edward Stevenson, Joseph W. Summerhays and others also obtained portions of the original manuscript. Some of it, we understand, was also in the possession of Joseph Smith of the "Reorganization," but only a *small fragment*. Thus the *original manuscript, that portion that was not destroyed by the elements, has been scattered*. . . .

After all, what does it matter what became of the original manuscript of the *Book of Mormon*? It is valueless, save as a relic. The statement has gone forth that the Church offered a large sum for the printer's copy. No such offer was ever made. The *Book of Mormon* has been translated into more than a dozen languages, and hundreds of thousands of copies have been published at a price so reasonable that it is within the reach of all— the same truths being in each copy as are in the original manuscript. *If the Prophet had considered the original* manuscript of any value as a work of reference, he would *not have placed it in the foundation of the Nauvoo House*.[24]

PUBLISHING THE BOOK OF MORMON

JOSEPH SMITH: "AUTHOR AND PROPRIETOR" OF BOOK OF MORMON. The first edition of the *Book of Mormon* was printed by Egbert B. Grandin at Palmyra, New York, in 1830. The edition was of 5,000 copies and the cost was $3,000. On the title page of this edition the following appears, "By Joseph Smith, Junior, Author and Proprietor," and on the next page the copyright appears in full. The expression *Author and Proprietor* has caused some adverse criticism by enemies of the Church, but in making this statement Joseph Smith was merely *complying with the law at that time governing copyrights*. This book contains 588 pages and the testimonies of the witnesses are in the back of the book. A few of the copies

---

[24]*Era.* vol. 10, pp. 572-576.

contain an index but most of them were published without this addition.[25]

SAMUEL H. SMITH'S MISSION AND BOOK OF MORMON. In the first year or two of the existence of the Church, the missionaries were without tracts and other printed information on the principles of the gospel and the restoration and therefore depended almost solely on the *Book of Mormon*. Each missionary took several copies of the *Book of Mormon* and tried to dispose of them among the people usually with excellent results.

Among the first missionaries to go out, if not actually the first, was Samuel H. Smith, younger brother of the Prophet Joseph. Samuel carried several copies of the *Book of Mormon*, but met with indifferences among the people. Finally he reached the home of a Methodist preacher named John P. Greene and tried to interest that gentleman in the story of Joseph Smith and the coming forth of the *Book of Mormon*. Mr. Greene informed him that he had neither the time to read nor the means to buy the book as he was about to leave on an important preaching tour. However, said he, if Samuel desired to leave a copy of the book he would try to dispose of it for him. The book was left and Samuel promised to call again in about two weeks to see what success had been obtained, and feeling somewhat discouraged departed.

In the meantime Mr. Greene started to read the *Book of Mormon*, more out of curiosity than from any desire to gain information, for he had no faith in the story that had been told him. The more he read the more he became interested, and when he had finished the book was convinced of its truth. He took the book to the family of John Young, father of Brigham Young, and they read it; it was also read by the Kimball family, and others, with the result that the family of John Young, Heber C. Kimball, John P. Greene (grandfather of Lulu Greene Richards) and others were eventually brought

[25]*Rel. Soc. Mag.*, vol. 14, p. 425.

into the Church. So the mission of Samuel H. Smith performed in June, 1830, and which he felt was a complete failure, added to the Church some of the most prominent members that ever embraced the gospel. This identical copy of the *Book of Mormon* presented to John P. Greene is now in the possession of the writer of this work.[26]

EARLY EDITIONS OF BOOK OF MORMON. The second edition of the *Book of Mormon* was published by Parley P. Pratt and John Goodson, at Kirtland. This issue contains a preface by the publishers in which they state that they have "obtained leave to issue 5,000 copies of the same, from those holding the copyright." The third edition was published by Don Carlos Smith and Ebenezer Robinson in Nauvoo, in 1840, from plates made by Shepherd and Stearns of Cincinnati, Ohio. Another edition was printed from these plates in Nauvoo, in 1842.

In 1841 Brigham Young and the apostles who were then in England published the first European edition. In the first three American editions the testimonies of the witnesses were printed in the back of the book, but in the first European edition the testimonies were transferred to the front of the book as they have appeared in all editions since. This issue was to have been of 5,000 copies, but only 4,050 were delivered; the printing was done by J. Tompkins and Co., of Liverpool. The second European edition was published by Orson Pratt, in Liverpool, in 1849.

Elder Franklin D. Richards published the third European edition, in 1852. In this edition Elder Richards numbered the verses in the chapters of the book. In 1879 Orson Pratt published an electrotyped edition of the *Book of Mormon* dividing the chapters and the verses and adding the footnote references as we have the book today. After these plates were made many editions appeared

---

[26]*Rel. Soc. Mag.*, vol. 17, pp. 425-426.

in Liverpool, which became for many years the publishing
headquarters of the Church.[27]

The first edition in the English language to be published by any mission, in the United States, was the
Kansas City edition, published by James G. Duffin in
1902. Since that time many editions have been published
by the missions and have been sold by the thousands. . . .
In 1869 an edition was published in the Deseret Alphabet,
under the direction of Elder Orson Pratt, by Russel
Brothers, in New York.

The first edition to be published in any foreign
tongue was that published by Elder Erastus Snow, in
Danish, in 1851. It was published in Welsh, French,
German, and Italian in 1852; Hawaiian, in 1855; Swed-
ish, in 1878; Spanish, in 1886; Maori, in 1889; Dutch,
in 1890; Samoan, in 1903, and since 1903, in Tahitian,
and Armenian, and other foreign languages.[28]

THE URIM AND THUMMIM

ABRAHAM, ISRAELITES, AND JAREDITES HAD URIM
AND THUMMIM. The history concerning the *Urim and
Thummim*, or *Interpreters* as they are called in the *Book
of Mormon*,[29] is not very clear. Abraham had the Urim
and Thummim by which he received revelations of the
heavenly bodies, as he has recorded in the Book of
Abraham.[30] What became of these after his death we
do not know. Aaron also had the Urim and Thummim,
and these were, evidently from the reading of the *Bible*,
handed down among the priests of Aaron from generation to generation.[31] The Lord gave to the Brother of
Jared the Urim and Thummim which he brought with him
to this continent. *These were separate and distinct from
the Urim and Thummim had by Abraham and in Israel
in the days of Aaron.*

---

[27]*Rel. Soc. Mag.*, vol. 14, pp. 426-429.   [31]Ex. 28:30; Lev. 8:8; Num. 27:21;
[28]*Era*, vol. 12, pp. 558-559.   Deut. 33:8; 1 Sam. 28:6; Ezra 2:63;
[29]Mosiah 8:13-17.   Neh. 7:65.
[30]Abra. 3:1-4.

The account of this set, in part, is as follows: "And behold, when ye shall come unto me, ye shall write them [revelations] and shall seal them up, that no one can interpret them; for ye shall write them in a language that they cannot be read. And behold, these *two stones* will I give unto thee, and *ye shall seal them up also* with the things which ye shall write. For behold, the language which ye shall write I have confounded; wherefore I will cause in my own due time that *these stones shall magnify to the eyes of men these things which ye shall write.* . . .

"And the Lord said unto him: Write these things and seal them up; and I will show them in mine own due time unto the children of men. And it came to pass that the Lord commanded him that he should *seal up the two stones* which he had received, and show them not, until the Lord should show them unto the children of men."[32]

JAREDITE URIM AND THUMMIM HAD BY NEPHITES. We have no record of Lehi bringing with him to America the Urim and Thummim. The Lord did give to Lehi the *Liahona,* which was a ball which directed him the way he should go, and writing appeared on it from time to time, but this was not the Urim and Thummim.[33]

King Mosiah possessed "two stones which were fastened into the two rims of a bow," called by the Nephites *Interpreters,* with which he translated the Jaredite record,[34] and these were handed down from generation to generation *for the purposes of interpreting languages.* How Mosiah came into possession of these *two stones* or Urim and Thummim the record does not tell us, more than to say that it was a "gift from God."[35] Mosiah had this *gift* or Urim and Thummim *before* the people of Limhi discovered the record of Ether. They may have been received when the "large stone" was brought to Mosiah with engravings upon it, which he interpreted

[32]Ether 3:22-24, 27-28.   [34]Mosiah 28:11-14.
[33]D. & C. 17:1.   [35]Mosiah 21:28.

by the "gift and power of God."[86] They may have been
given to him, or to some other prophet before his day, just
as the Brother of Jared received them—from the Lord.

That the Urim and Thummim, or two stones, given
to the Brother of Jared were those in the possession of
Mosiah appears evident from *Book of Mormon* teachings.
The Brother of Jared was commanded to seal up his
writings of the vision he had when Christ appeared to
him, so that they could not be read by his people. This
vision was recorded in a language which was confounded,
for it was not to go forth until after the resurrection of
Christ. The Urim and Thummim were also sealed up
so that they could not be used for the purpose of interpreting those sacred writings of this vision, until such
time as the Lord should grant to man to interpret them.
When they were to be revealed, they were to be
interpreted by the aid of the *same* Urim and Thummim.[37]

JOSEPH SMITH RECEIVED JAREDITE URIM AND
THUMMIM. The people of Limhi brought to Mosiah a
record, "engraven on plates of ore,"[38] which record
Mosiah translated, by the aid of "two stones which were
fastened into the two rims of a bow," and which gave an
account of the Jaredites.[39] In translating this record
Mosiah kept from going forth to the people that particular part forbidden by the Lord to be revealed until
after he was lifted up upon the cross.[40] These sacred
revelations given to the Brother of Jared were kept from
the Nephite people, as well as many other things, until
after the resurrection of Christ.[41] After the appearing of
the Savior to the Nephites, the vision of the Brother of
Jared was revealed to the Nephites. When Moroni made
his abridgment of the record of Ether, he copied on his
record the vision of the Brother of Jared.[42]

At the command of the Lord, however, Moroni also

[86]Omni 1:20-21.   [40]Ether 4:1.
[37]Ether 3:21-28.   [41]Alma 63:12.
[38]Mosiah 21:27.   [42]Ether 4:2-7.
[39]Mosiah 28:11-19.

sealed up the greater things in this vision and also the *interpreters—which were the same "two stones" had by the Brother of Jared—*so that this vision should not be made known even in our day among the Gentiles, in the day of their wickedness;[43] it could not be revealed "until the day that they shall repent of their iniquity, and become clean before the Lord."[44] So we today do not have the fulness of the account written and sealed up by the Brother of Jared and again sealed by Moroni. This part of the record the Prophet Joseph Smith was forbidden to translate. We have, then, received but the "lesser part."[45]

Joseph Smith received with the *breastplate* and the plates of the *Book of Mormon,* the Urim and Thummim, which were hid up by Moroni to come forth in the last days as a means by which the ancient record might be translated, which Urim and Thummim were given to the Brother of Jared.[46]

SEER STONE NOT USED IN BOOK OF MORMON TRANSLATION. We have been taught since the days of the Prophet that *the Urim and Thummim were returned with the plates to the angel.* We have no record of the Prophet having the Urim and Thummim after the organization of the Church. Statements of translations by the Urim and Thummim after that date are evidently *errors.* The statement has been made that the Urim and Thummim was on the altar in the Manti Temple when that building was dedicated. The Urim and Thummim so spoken of, however, was the seer stone which was in the possession of the Prophet Joseph Smith in early days. This seer stone is now in the possession of the Church.[47]

While the statement has been made by some writers that the Prophet Joseph Smith used a *seer stone* part of

[43]2 Ne. 27:8.
[44]Ether 4:6.
[45]3 Ne. 26:8-11.
[46]*Era,* vol. 57, pp. 382-383; *D. & C.* 17:1.

[47]B. H. Roberts, *A Comprehensive History of the Church,* vol. 6, pp. 230-231.

the time in his translating of the record, and information points to the fact that he did have in his possession such a stone, yet there is no authentic statement in the history of the Church which states that the use of such a stone was made in that translation. The information is all *hearsay*, and personally, I do not believe that this stone was used for this purpose. The reason I give for this conclusion is found in the statement of the Lord to the Brother of Jared as recorded in Ether 3:22-24.

These stones, the Urim and Thummim which were given to the Brother of Jared, were preserved for this *very purpose of translating the record,* both of the Jaredites and the Nephites. Then again the Prophet was impressed by Moroni with the fact that these stones were given for that very purpose.[48] It hardly seems reasonable to suppose that the Prophet would substitute something evidently *inferior* under these circumstances. It may have been so, but it is so easy for a story of this kind to be circulated due to the fact that the Prophet did possess a *seer stone,* which he may have used for some other purposes.[49]

---

[48]Jos. Smith 2:34-35.   [49]Pers. Corresp.

Chapter 12

A VOICE FROM CUMORAH

WITNESSES OF BOOK OF MORMON

WHY PLATES WERE RETURNED TO MORONI. The question has been asked many times of our elders: *Where are the plates?* Does the Church have in its possession the plates from which the *Book of Mormon* was translated by Joseph Smith?

When the answer is given that the plates were received again by the Angel Moroni, who through the centuries since they were hid up unto the Lord has been their special guardian, the reply is generally made: What a wonderful aid it would be to your people in convincing the world of the truth of your story if you could show the plates to prove that Joseph Smith really had them.

Perhaps it is natural for a man who hears for the first time the story of Joseph Smith and the coming forth of the *Book of Mormon* to propound such a question and to think that the plates, if they had been placed in some museum where the public could examine them, would have added much to prove the authenticity of the Prophet's story. With deeper reflection we discover that this would not have been the case, for *it is not the way the Lord proves his truth, now or at any other time*. However, in surprise, and in some cases with an incredulous smile, the propounder of this question turns away feeling that such an answer as he has received is an admission that Joseph Smith never had the plates and practiced a fraud upon the public.

EXISTENCE OF PLATES WOULD NOT PROVE DIVINITY OF BOOK. It is well in considering this matter to remember the words of the Lord to Isaiah: "For my thoughts are not your thoughts, neither are your ways my ways, saith the Lord. For as the heavens are higher than the earth, so are my ways higher than your ways, and my thoughts than your thoughts."[1]

If the Lord had followed the thoughts of men and had commanded Joseph Smith to place the plates in some repository where they could have been inspected by the curious public, it would have led to *endless disputations. Enemies of the Church would not have been convinced and would have contended most bitterly that the plates were spurious.* No one could have read them for the characters engraved on them are unknown to the savants of the present age.

The Lord does not convince men of his truth by placing before their eyes and in their hands *tangible evidence,* as a lawyer may do before the court, marking it *exhibit A* and *exhibit B,* and then expect it to be accepted. The Lord expects the searcher after truth to approach him with a contrite spirit and with sincerity of purpose; if he will do this and keep the commandments of the Lord, he shall receive the *witness through the Holy Spirit* and shall know the truth. This testimony will come with such force and clearness that it cannot be denied. For this reason the Lord said, "Whosoever speaketh a word against the Son of man, it shall be forgiven him: but whosoever speaketh against the Holy Ghost, it shall not be forgiven him, neither in this world, neither in the world to come."[2]

WITNESSES OF BOOK OF MORMON TO BE RAISED UP. Nephi, one of the earliest prophets of the Israelitish colony, predicted nearly 600 years before the Christian era, that when the records containing the history of his people should be revealed from the dust, it would be in a day when the people would "deny the power of God, the Holy One of Israel," and they would say: "Hearken unto us, and hear ye our precept; for behold there is no God

---

[1]Isa. 55:8-9.   [2]*Era,* vol. 30, pp. 948-949; Matt. 12:32.

today, for the Lord and the Redeemer hath done his work, and he hath given his power unto men."[3] Again, many among them would say when presented with a new volume of scripture containing the history of the people of this western world: "A *Bible! A Bible!* We have got a *Bible,* and there cannot be any more *Bible.*"[4]

Because of this attitude towards this new record the Lord promised to raise up "as many witnesses as seemeth him good," to "establish his word; and wo be unto him that rejecteth the word of God." In that day when these things should be accomplished the Lord would proceed to do a marvelous work and a wonder which would prove to be a testimony against those who "seek deep to hide their counsel from the Lord."[5]

Moreover, this new volume of scripture was to be a witness, not only for Christ and to contain the everlasting gospel, but was also to be a witness for the Jewish scriptures, the *Bible;* and these two records—according to the prophesying of Nephi, his father, and also Joseph, son of Israel—were to grow together bearing testimony of the everlasting gospel.[6] As such a witness these records stand today testifying of the truth to the condemnation of all who reject their teachings.[7]

THE THREE WITNESSES. The three men called to serve as special witnesses of the coming forth of the *Book of Mormon* by the power of God are Oliver Cowdery, David Whitmer, and Martin Harris. . . . They were associated with Joseph Smith in the establishing of this marvelous work in this dispensation. Later *all three witnesses became estranged and left the Church.*[8] Oliver

---

[3] 2 Ne. 28:5.
[4] 2 Ne. 29:3.
[5] 2 Ne. 27:14, 26-27.
[6] 2 Ne. 3; 4; 25; 26; 27; 28; 29.
[7] *Era,* vol. 26, pp. 958-959.

[8] It is well known that Oliver Cowdery and David Whitmer left the Church, but it has been generally supposed that Martin Harris was never excommunicated. The *Journal History* of the Church under date of Jan. 1, 1838, however, tells of his excommunication by the High Council in Kirtland in Dec., 1837. He was rebaptized Sept. 17, 1870, in Salt Lake City by Edward Stevenson and confirmed the same day by Orson Pratt. *Journal History,* Sept. 17, 1870.

Cowdery and Martin Harris came back humbly seeking membership in the Church and both died in full fellowship. David Whitmer remained out of the Church; however, all three of these men remained faithful to the testimony they gave to the world which is found in each copy of the *Book of Mormon*.

Their testimony is that they received a visitation of an angel from the presence of the Lord, who laid before them the golden record from whence the *Book of Mormon* was translated, and who also instructed them. They beheld the engravings upon the plates as the leaves were turned one by one before them, and the voice of God was heard by them declaring from the heavens that the translation was by the gift and power of God and commanding them to bear record of it to all the world.[9] These three witnesses, through adversity, persecution, and all the vicissitudes of life, always remained true to their testimony that they beheld the plates in the presence of an angel and heard the voice of God speaking to them from the heavens.

TOTAL OF TWELVE WITNESSES. There were eight other witnesses who also beheld the plates, handled them, and examined carefully the engravings upon them as they were shown them by Joseph Smith. Their testimony is also given to the world and appears in each issue of the *Book of Mormon*. All of these eight men remained true to this testimony until death.

These *twelve witnesses,* four of whom beheld angels and had heavenly visions, and eight who beheld the record as it was shown to them by Joseph Smith, are all, it appears, that the Lord deemed necessary to establish the truth of the *Book of Mormon,* as he promised through Nephi that he would do. "And wo be unto him that rejecteth the word of God!"[10] The testimonies of these men more than satisfy the law.[11]

---

[9]*History of the Church,* vol. 1, pp. 52-59.

[10]2 Ne. 27:14.

[11]Deut. 17:6; 19:15; Matt. 18:15-16; 2 Cor. 13:1.

ALL MEN MAY BECOME BOOK OF MORMON WIT-
NESSES. These are not all the witnesses who can speak
of the divine mission of Joseph Smith, or of the truth of
the *Book of Mormon.* The promise is made in the *Book
of Mormon* that *all* who desire to know whether it is true
and contains the word of the Lord may know that it is
true if they will ask with a sincere heart, with real intent,
having faith in Christ, for he will reveal it to them by
the power of the Holy Ghost.[12] There are hundreds of
thousands who have put this promise to the test and can
in all sincerity say that they have received that
knowledge.[13]

I am just as firmly convinced that this *Book of
Mormon* is the word of God and was revealed, as Joseph
Smith declared it was revealed, as I am that I stand here
looking into your faces. *Every soul on the face of the
earth who has intelligence enough to understand may
know that truth.* How can he know it? All he has to do
is to follow the formula that was given by the Lord himself when he declared to the Jews that they who would
do the will of his Father should know of the doctrine,
whether it was of God or whether he spoke of himself.[14]
My witness to all the world is that this book is true. I have
read it many, many times. I have not read it enough. It
still contains truths that I still may seek and find, for I
have not mastered it, but *I know it is true.*

I know that the testimony of these witnesses recorded in each copy of the *Book of Mormon* is true, that
they stood in the presence of an angel of God who declared unto them that the record as it was translated was
correct, that their testimony that God spoke to them from
the heavens calling upon them to bear witness of that
fact is true, and *there is not a soul who cannot receive
that testimony if he desires to receive it.* By reading this
book prayerfully and faithfully, with a desire to know

12Moro. 10:3-5.   14John 7:14-17.
13*Era,* vol. 30, pp. 952-953.

the truth as Moroni has declared by revelation, he shall
know the truth regarding the restoration of this scripture
given to the ancient inhabitants of this continent.[15]

WHERE IS THE HILL CUMORAH?

SPECULATION ABOUT BOOK OF MORMON GEOG-
RAPHY.   Within recent years there has arisen among
certain students of the *Book of Mormon* a *theory* to the
effect that within the period covered by the *Book of
Mormon*, the Nephites and Lamanites were confined almost entirely within the borders of the territory comprising Central America and the southern portion of Mexico
—the isthmus of Tehauntepec probably being the "narrow neck" of land spoken of in the *Book of Mormon*
rather than the isthmus of Panama.[16]

This *theory* is founded upon the assumption that it
was impossible for the colony of Lehi's to multiply and
fill the hemisphere within the limits of 1,000 years, or
from the coming of Lehi from Jerusalem to the time of the
destruction of the Nephites at the Hill Cumorah. Moreover, they claim that the story in the *Book of Mormon*
of the migrations, building of cities, and the wars and
contentions, preclude the possibility of the people spread-
ing over great distances such as we find within the
borders of North and South America.

EARTH POPULATED RAPIDLY.   If we are willing to
accept the *Bible* record, which is confirmed by the *Doctrine and Covenants*, the entire civilization of the earth
was destroyed in the flood except Noah and his family.[17]
Moreover, this destruction took place less than 5,000
years ago, and today the population of the earth, notwithstanding wars and destructions, is estimated at over
2,000,000,000 souls.

---

[15]Conf. Rep., Oct., 1949, p. 89; Moro.
10:3-5.
[16]Alma 50:34; 52:9; 63:5; Morm. 2:29;
3:5.

[17]Gen. 6; 7; 8; Moses 7:36-43, 51-52;
8:22-30; Alma 10:22; 3 Ne. 22:9;
Ether 6:7.

The population of Europe, based upon the best records available, is vastly increased over that at the time of the discovery of America; yet upon this hemisphere are to be found hundreds of millions of people, descendants of European and Asiatic ancestors who knew nothing of this land before the discovery by Columbus. The rapid increase of posterity is known to every genealogist who has traced the record of the early settlers in this western country.

LOCALE OF CUMORAH, RAMAH, AND RIPLIANCUM. This modernistic theory of necessity, in order to be consistent, must place the waters of Ripliancum and the Hill Cumorah some place within the restricted territory of Central America, notwithstanding the teachings of the Church to the contrary for upwards of 100 years. Because of this *theory* some members of the Church have become confused and greatly disturbed in their faith in the *Book of Mormon*. It is for this reason that evidence is here presented to show that it is not only possible that these places could be located as the Church has held during the past century, but that in very deed *such is the case*.

It is known that the *Hill Cumorah* where the Nephites were destroyed is the hill where the Jaredites were also destroyed. This hill was known to the Jaredites as *Ramah*. It was approximately near to the waters of Ripliancum, which the Book of Ether says, "by interpretation, is large, or to exceed all."[18] Mormon adds: "And it came to pass that we did march forth to the land of Cumorah, and we did pitch our tents round about the hill Cumorah; and it was in a land of many waters, rivers, and fountains; and here we had hope to gain advantage over the Lamanites."[19]

EARLY BRETHREN LOCATE CUMORAH IN WESTERN NEW YORK. It must be conceded that this description

---

[18]Ether 15:8-11.   [19]Morm. 6:4.

fits perfectly the land of Cumorah in New York, as it
has been known since the visitation of Moroni to the
Prophet Joseph Smith, for the hill is in the proximity of
the Great Lakes and also in the land of many rivers and
fountains. Moreover, *the Prophet Joseph Smith himself
is on record, definitely declaring the present hill called
Cumorah to be the exact hill spoken of in the Book of
Mormon.*[20]

Further, the fact that all of his associates from the
beginning down have spoken of it as the identical hill
where Mormon and Moroni hid the records, must carry
some weight. It is difficult for a reasonable person to
believe that such men as Oliver Cowdery, Brigham
Young, Parley P. Pratt, Orson Pratt, David Whitmer,
and many others, could speak frequently of the spot
where the Prophet Joseph Smith obtained the plates as
the Hill Cumorah, and not be corrected by the Prophet,
if that were not the fact. That they did speak of this hill
in the days of the Prophet in this definite manner is an
established record of history.

OLIVER COWDERY PLACES CUMORAH IN WESTERN
NEW YORK. The first reference of this kind is found
in the *Messenger and Advocate,* a paper published by
the Church in 1834-5. In a brief history of the rise of
the Church prepared by Oliver Cowdery, he makes
reference to this particular spot in the following words:

"By turning to the 529th and 530th pages of the
Book of Mormon you will read Mormon's account of the
*last great struggle as they were encamped round this
hill Cumorah.*[21] In this valley fell the remaining strength
and pride of a once powerful people, the Nephites—once
so highly favored of the Lord, but at that time in darkness, doomed to suffer extermination by the hand of their
barbarous and uncivilized brethren. From the top of this

---

[20]*History of the Church,* 1948 ed., vol.   [21]Morm. 5; 6.
2, pp. 79-80.

hill, Mormon, with a few others, after the battle, gazed
with horror upon the mangled remains of those who, the
day before, were filled with anxiety, hope, or doubt. A
few had fled to the south, who were hunted down by the
victorious party, and all who would not deny the Savior
and his religion, were put to death. Mormon himself,
according to the record of his son Moroni, was also slain.

"But a long time previous to this national disaster it
appears, from his own account, he foresaw approaching
destruction. In fact, if he perused the records of his
fathers, which were in his possession, he could have
learned that such would be the case. Alma, who lived
before the coming of the Messiah, prophesied this. He,
however, by divine appointment, abridged from those
records, in his own style and language, a short account
of the more important and prominent items, from the days
of Lehi to his own time, after which *he deposited,* as he
says, on the 529th page,[22] *all the records in this same hill,
Cumorah,* and after gave his small record to his son
Moroni, who, as appears from the same, finished, after
witnessing the extinction of his people as a nation. . . .

HILL RAMAH IN WESTERN NEW YORK. "This hill,
by the Jaredites, was called *Ramah;* by it, or around it,
pitched the famous army of Coriantumr their tents.
Coriantumr was the last king of the Jaredites. The
opposing army were to the west, and in this same valley,
and near by, from day to day, did that mighty race spill
their blood, in wrath, contending, as it were brother
against brother, and father against son. In this same
spot, in full view from the top of this same hill, one may
gaze with astonishment upon the ground which was *twice*
covered with the dead and dying of our fellowmen. . . .

"In this vale lie commingled, in one mass of ruin, the
ashes of thousands, and in this vale was destined to con-
sume the fair forms and vigorous systems of tens of

---

[22]Morm. 6:6.

thousands of the human race—blood mixed with blood, flesh with flesh, bones with bones, and dust with dust."[23]

PROPHET APPROVES OLIVER COWDERY'S VIEWS. The quibbler might say that this statement from Oliver Cowdery is merely the opinion of Oliver Cowdery and not the expression of the Prophet Joseph Smith. It should be remembered that these letters in which these statements are made were written at the Prophet's request and under his *personal supervision*. Surely, under these circumstances, he would not have permitted an error of this kind to creep into the record without correction.

At the commencement of these historical letters is found the following: "That our narrative may be correct, and particularly the introduction, it is proper to inform our patrons, that our Brother J. Smith Jr., has offered to assist us. Indeed, there are many items connected with the fore part of this subject that render his labor indispensable. With his labor and with authentic documents now in our possession, we hope to render this a pleasing and agreeable narrative, well worth the examination and perusal of the saints."[24]

Later, during the Nauvoo period of the Church, and *again under the direction of the Prophet Joseph Smith*, these same letters by Oliver Cowdery, were *published* in the *Times and Seasons*, without any thought of correction had this description of the Hill Cumorah been an error.[25]

TESTIMONY OF DAVID WHITMER TO HILL CU- MORAH. Another testimony of interest is that of David Whitmer given to Elders Orson Pratt and Joseph F. Smith in September 1878, when they paid him a visit at his home in Richmond. To these brethren he said: "When I was returning to Fayette, with Joseph and

[23]*Messenger and Advocate*, July, 1835, pp. 158-159.
[24]*Messenger and Advocate*, Oct., 1834, p. 13.
[25]*Times and Seasons*, Apr. 15, 1841, vol. 2, p. 379.

Oliver, all of us riding in the wagon, Oliver and I on an old-fashioned wooden spring seat and Joseph behind us —while traveling along in a clear open space, a very pleasant, nice-looking old man suddenly appeared by the side of our wagon and saluted us with, 'Good morning, it is very warm,' at the same time wiping his face or forehead with his hand. We returned the salutation, and, by a sign from Joseph, I invited him to ride if he was going our way; but he said very pleasantly, 'No, I am going to *Cumorah.*' This name was something new to me; I did not know what Cumorah meant. We all gazed at him and at each other, and as I looked around inquiringly of Joseph, *the old man instantly disappeared,* so that I did not see him again.''

Joseph F. Smith asked: "Did you notice his appearance?"

David Whitmer: "I should think I did. He was, I should think, about five feet eight or nine inches tall and heavy set. . . . His hair and beard were white, like Brother Pratt's, but his beard was not so heavy. I also remember that he had on his back a sort of knapsack with something in, shaped like a book.''[26]

"GLAD TIDINGS FROM CUMORAH." Who can read the words of Joseph Smith as recorded in section 128 of the *Doctrine and Covenants* and not feel that he had reference to the Hill Cumorah in western New York?

"And again, what do we hear? *Glad tidings from Cumorah!* Moroni, an angel from heaven, declaring the fulfilment of the prophets—the book to be revealed. A voice of the Lord in the wilderness of Fayette, Seneca county, declaring the three witnesses to bear record of the book!"[27]

While in this statement it is not positively declared that the Hill Cumorah is the place where the plates were obtained, yet the implication that such is the case is over-

[26]*Millennial Star,* vol. 40, p. 772.   [27]*D. & C.* 128:20.

whelming. Moroni declaring from Cumorah the book
to be revealed!

JOSEPH SMITH LOCATES CUMORAH IN WESTERN
NEW YORK. Perhaps this matter could rest at this point,
but the question of the territory now embraced within
the United States having been in possession of Nephites
and Lamanites before the death of Mormon, carries some
weight in the determining of this matter. *In the light of
revelation it is absurd for anyone to maintain that the
Nephites and Lamanites did not possess this northern
land.* While Zion's camp was marching on the way to
Jackson County, near the bank of the Illinois River they
came to a mound containing the skeleton of a man. The
history of this incident is as follows:

"The brethren procured a shovel and a hoe, and
removing the earth to the depth of about one foot, discovered the skeleton of a man, almost entire, and between
his ribs the *stone point of a Lamanitish arrow,* which
evidently produced his death. Elder Burr Riggs retained
the arrow. The contemplation of the scenery around us
produced peculiar sensations in our bosoms; and sub-
sequently *the visions of the past being opened to my understanding by the Spirit of the Almighty,* I discovered
that the person whose skeleton was before us was a *white
Lamanite,* a large, thickset man, and a man of God. His
name was *Zelph.* He was a warrior and chieftain under
the great prophet Onandagus, who was *known from the
Hill Cumorah, or eastern sea to the Rocky Mountains.*
The curse was taken from Zelph, or at least, in part—
one of his thigh bones was broken by a stone flung from
a sling, while in battle, years before his death. He was
killed in battle by the arrow found among his ribs, *during
the last great struggle of the Lamanites and Nephites.*"[28]

---

[28]*History of the Church,* 1948 ed., vol. 2, pp. 79-80. Through error the part
of this quotation *naming* the "Hill Cumorah" and specifying that Zelph died
in the *last* great struggle was omitted in editions prior to 1948. It was, however quoted correctly, as written by the Prophet and here given, in vol. 6
of the *Times and Seasons* of Jan. 1, 1846.

HEBER C. KIMBALL TELLS OF DEATH OF ZELPH.
Elder Heber C. Kimball who was present recorded the
following in his journal: "While on our way we felt
anxious to know who the person was who had been killed
by that arrow. It was made known to Joseph that he had
been an officer who *fell in battle, in the last destruction
among the Lamanites,* and his name was Zelph. This
caused us to rejoice much, to think that God was so
mindful of us as to show these things to his servant.
Brother Joseph had inquired of the Lord, and it was made
known in a vision."[29]

ANCIENT CITY OF MANTI IN MISSOURI. The fol-
lowing is also taken from the history of the travels of the
Kirtland Camp: "The camp passed through *Huntsville,*
in *Randolph County,* which has been appointed as one
of the stakes of Zion, and is the *ancient site of the City
of Manti,* and pitched tents at Dark Creek, Salt Licks,
seventeen miles. It was reported to the camp that one
hundred and ten men had volunteered from Randolph
and gone to Far West to settle difficulties."[30]

The following account of the same event is taken
from the daily journal of the Kirtland Camp, and was
written by Samuel D. Tyler: "September 25, 1838. We
passed through Huntsville, Co. seat of Randolph Co.
Pop. 450, and three miles further we bought 32 bu. of
corn off one of the brethren who resides in this place.
There are several of the brethren round about here and
this is the ancient site of the City of Manti, which is spoken of in the *Book of Mormon* and this is appointed one
of the Stakes of Zion, and it is in Randolph County,
Missouri, three miles west of the county seat."[31]

NEPHITE AND JAREDITE WARS IN WESTERN NEW
YORK. In the face of this evidence coming from the
Prophet Joseph Smith, Oliver Cowdery, and David

[29]*Times and Seasons,* vol. 6, p. 788.
[30]*Millennial Star,* vol. 16, p. 296.

[31]*Journal of Samuel D. Tyler,* Sept.
25, 1838, filed in Church Historian's
Office.

Whitmer, we cannot say that the Nephites and Lamanites did not possess the territory of the United States and that the Hill Cumorah is in Central America. Neither can we say that the great struggle which resulted in the destruction of the Nephites took place in Central America. If Zelph, a righteous man, was fighting under a great prophet-general in the *last battles* between the Nephites and Lamanites; if that great prophet-general was known from the Rocky Mountains to "the Hill Cumorah or eastern sea," then some of those battles, and evidently *the final battles did take place within the borders of what is now the United States.*

There were no righteous prophets, save the Three Nephites, after the death of Moroni, and we learn that Zelph was *slain during one of these battles during the great last struggle between the Nephites and Lamanites and was buried near the Illinois River.*

In the *Book of Mormon* story the Lamanites were constantly crowding the Nephites back towards the north and east. If the battles in which Zelph took part were fought in the country traversed by the Zion's Camp, then we have every reason to believe from what is written in the *Book of Mormon,* that the Nephites were forced farther and farther to the north and east until they found themselves in the land of Ripliancum, which both Ether and Mormon declare to us was the land of Ramah or Cumorah, a land of "many waters," which "by interpretation, is large, or to exceed all."[82]

This being true, *what would be more natural then that Moroni, like his father Mormon, would deposit the plates in the land where the battles came to an end and the Nephites were destroyed?* This Moroni says he did, and from all the evidence in the *Book of Mormon,* augmented by the testimony of the Prophet Joseph Smith, *these final battles took place in the territory known as the United States and in the neighborhood of the Great*

---

[82]Ether 15:8-11.

Lakes and hills of Western New York. And here Moroni found the resting place for the sacred instruments which had been committed to his care.[88]

IMPRESSIONS AT CUMORAH

LORD LED PROPHET'S FAMILY TO CUMORAH-LAND. As I stood upon these sacred places I had peculiar feelings which I cannot describe. I always do have such feelings; I have visited the Hill Cumorah and the Sacred Grove on other occasions. As I stood at the Smith home, I thought of the early struggles of the family, and wondered what means the Lord might have used to get them to move from Vermont or New Hampshire, if they had not been forced from these states by poverty. Their poverty was not the result of indolence, as the wicked have proclaimed, but the poverty and reverses of Providence, sent to give experience and to lead the family to a better land where the Lord could perform his work through the youthful Seer, yet to be raised up.

When the Smith family arrived in Palmyra they immediately bargained for the purchase of 100 acres of land. This is known today as the *Joseph Smith Farm* and is in the possession of the Church. In that day the land was covered with a heavy growth of timber. This had to be removed before the land could be planted and crops raised to pay for the farm. As I stood upon this ground, I thought of the struggles this entailed. My grandfather, Hyrum Smith, and his older brother, Alvin, were called upon to do much of this laborious task. The younger brother, Joseph, was too young at that time to give much help, being only about 10 years of age. Nevertheless he was called to assist, and a few years later—at the time of the vision—was under the necessity of performing labor required of a man.

The house which stands upon the farm was built

[88]*Church News*, Sept. 10, 1938, pp. 1, 6; reprinted, Feb. 27, 1954, pp. 2-3.

by these sons of Joseph Smith, Senior; but it is *not* the house, as many have been told, in which the Angel Moroni appeared to Joseph Smith. The older house has long since disappeared, and stood several rods to the north of the present home. After the proclamation of the Angel's visit persecution raged, and the family were not permitted long to enjoy the land which had cost them so much to prepare, because of others, who, through wickedness, for a season reaped the fruits thereof.

CUMORAH ONCE SITE OF CARNAGE AND DESTRUCTION. As I stood upon the summit of the Hill Cumorah, in the midst of a vast multitude, only a few of whom belonged to the Church, I tried to picture the scenes of former days. *Here were assembled vast armies filled with bitterness and bent on destruction.* I thought of the great promises the Lord had made through his prophets concerning those who should possess this choice land, and how those promises were not fulfilled because the people violated his commandments. *Here a people perished because of their extreme wickedness.*

There must be something in the destiny of things that would cause a repetition of this terrible scene on the same spot many centuries later. I reflected and wondered if this unhappy time would ever come when another still mightier people would incur the wrath of God because of wickedness and likewise perish. If so, would this same spot witness their destruction? I thought of the prophets, Ether, Mormon, Moroni, and tried to realize the sadness of their feelings as they witnessed the mad onrushing of their peoples to annihilation.

IMPORTANCE OF CUMORAH UNKNOWN TO WORLD. We sang the song, prepared for this celebration,[84] *Zionland,* and I entered heartily, sincerely, into the spirit of the song:

---

[84]President Joseph Fielding Smith was attending the first general conference of the Eastern States Mission, convened at the Joseph Smith Farm near Palmyra, New York, on Sept. 21 to 23, 1923—the one hundredth anniversary of the appearance of Moroni to Joseph Smith.

God bless our Zion-land,
Firm may she ever stand,
Through storm and night;
When the wild tempests rave,
Ruler of wind and wave,
Do Thou Thy Zion save
By thy great might!

For her our prayers shall rise
To God above the skies,
With Him we stand;
Thou who art ever nigh,
Guarding with watchful eye,
To Thee aloud we cry,
God save Thy land.

Here it was that Moroni, commanded by the Lord,
hid up the sacred records of his people. Here it was,
1,400 years later, that he, then a resurrected being, came
to Joseph Smith and committed these same records to
the young man's care. At the time of the Prophet's first
visit to the hill, it was covered with trees; today (1923)
it is stripped and bare, save for the grass which grows
abundantly. This former scene of strife and bloodshed,
where two nations perished, later the sacred repository
of ancient records, today is the abode of peaceful cattle,
reclining and chewing the cud. The many millions of
inhabitants of the land, who, because they love darkness
rather than light, will not believe, and although an angel
has declared it unto them, they appear to have no more
thought concerning the wonderful events that have taken
place near and on the Hill Cumorah, than have these
cattle.[35]

---

[35] *Rel. Soc. Mag.,* vol. 10, pp. 586-587.

CHAPTER 13

ISRAEL: GOD'S COVENANT PEOPLE

CHILDREN OF THE COVENANT

LORD'S COVENANT WITH ABRAHAM. *We are a covenant people*—that is we are subject to covenants and obligations as members of the Church. It has always been so.[1] The Lord established covenants with Adam in the beginning. You find that clearly stated in the Book of Genesis[2] and more clearly stated in the Book of Moses in the *Pearl of Great Price*.[3] He made covenants with Enoch that are also stated in those scriptures.[4] He made a covenant with Noah, which resulted in the saving of Noah's family and great promises being given to him in the flood.[5]

Then Abraham received covenants—very definite and important covenants that concern us very materially today. Let me say just a word about the covenant that was made with Abraham. In the Book of Abraham I read the following: "My name is Jehovah, and I know the end from the beginning; therefore, my hand shall be over thee." (That is what the Lord said to Abraham.)

"And I will make of thee a great nation, and I will bless thee above measure, and make thy name great among all nations, and thou shalt be a blessing unto thy seed after thee, that in their hands they shall bear this ministry and Priesthood unto all nations; And I will bless them through thy name; for *as many as receive this Gospel shall be called after thy name, and shall be accounted thy seed, and shall rise up and bless thee, as their father;* And I will bless them that bless thee, and curse

---

[1] 3 Ne. 20:25-27; Acts 3:23-26.
[2] Gen. 1; 2; 3; 4.
[3] Moses 2; 3; 4; 5; 6.
[4] Gen. 5:21-24 Moses 6; 7; 8.
[5] Gen. 6; 7; 8; 9; Moses 8.

them that curse thee; and in thee (that is, in thy Priesthood) and in thy seed (that is, thy Priesthood), for I give unto thee a promise that this right shall continue in thee, and in thy seed after thee (that is to say, the literal seed, or the seed of the body) shall all the families of the earth be blessed, *even with the blessings of the Gospel, which are the blessings of salvation, even of life eternal.*"[6] . . .

COVENANT WITH ABRAHAM FOR ALL HIS SEED. Of course the Lord established this covenant more particularly through Isaac and Jacob, and from Jacob through the 12 sons who stand at the head of the 12 tribes of Israel.[7] But I call your attention to this fact: According to the *Doctrine and Covenants,* Moses got his priesthood from Jethro, who was a descendant of Abraham but not a descendant in any way, as far as we know, of Jacob or Israel.[8] Jethro came through another branch of Abraham's family, that of Keturah.[9] He was a Midianite, and yet he held the priesthood.

We sometimes think, as the Jews in the days of Christ thought, that all the blessings of Israel pertain just to us. You know what a time the Lord had to convince the apostles in that early day that the gospel was for the Gentiles. You have read the story of Cornelius and how the Lord had to convince Peter that the gospel was for someone else besides the Jews.[10] We must not think that in those early days none except those who were descendants of Israel or Jacob were entitled to the blessings of the priesthood. That is shown clearly in this fact, as already pointed out, that the Midianites held the priesthood.[11]

PROCESS OF ADOPTION INTO HOUSE OF ISRAEL. Is it necessary that we be of the house of Israel in order

[6]Abra. 2:8-11; Gen. 12:1-3; 13:14-17;
    15:5-6; 17:1-27; 22:15-19.
[7]Gen. 26:1-5, 24; 28:1-22; 32:24-30;
    35:9-12; 48; 49.
[8]D. & C. 84:6-14.
[9]Gen. 25:1-4; 1 Chron. 1:32-34.
[10]Acts 10.
[11]*Church News,* May 6, 1939, p. 3.

to accept the gospel and all the blessings pertaining to it?
If so, how do we become of the house of Israel, by
adoption or by direct *lineage?*

*Every person who embraces the gospel becomes of
the house of Israel.* In other words, they become members
of the *chosen lineage,* or Abraham's children through
Isaac and Jacob unto whom the promises were made. The
great *majority* of those who become members of the
Church are *literal descendants* of Abraham through
Ephraim, son of Joseph. Those who are not literal
descendants of Abraham and Israel must *become* such,
and *when they are baptized and confirmed they are
grafted into the tree and are entitled to all the rights and
privileges as heirs.*[12] . . .

How All Nations Are Blessed Through Abraham. When the Lord called Abraham out of Ur, the
land of his fathers, he made certain covenants with him
because of his faithfulness. One promise was that
through him and his seed after him all nations of the earth
should be blessed.[13] This blessing is accomplished in
several ways.

1. Through Jesus Christ who came through the
lineage of Abraham;

2. Through the priesthood which was conferred
upon Abraham and his descendants;

3. Through the scattering of Israel among all nations by which the blood of Israel was sprinkled among
the nations, and thus the nations partake of the leaven
of righteousness, on condition of their repentance, and
are entitled to the promises made to the children of
Abraham; and

4. In the fact that the Lord covenanted with Abraham that after his time all who embraced the gospel
should be called by his name, or, should be numbered
among his seed, and should receive the Holy Ghost.

---

[12]Abra. 2:8-11; 3 Ne. 20:26-27; Joseph   [13]Gen. 12:1-3.
Fielding Smith, *Teachings of the
Prophet Joseph Smith,* pp. 149-150.

All of these promises were made to Abraham because of his faithfulness. *No person who is not of Israel can become a member of the Church without becoming of the house of Israel by adoption. . . .*

This doctrine of *adoption,* or *grafting in* of the wild olive branches into the tame olive tree, was understood by the prophets of Israel.[14] It was taught by John the Baptist[15] and by the Savior[16] and is expressed most emphatically and beautifully in the parable of the tame olive tree in the 5th chapter of Jacob, in the *Book of Mormon.*[17]

LINEAGE IN ISRAEL BY BLOOD RELATIONSHIP. Is the *lineage of Ephraim* traced through *blood relationship,* or is it traced by the *believing class?*

When a man who is of Israel joins the Church, his tribal relationship does not change. For instance, a descendant of Judah would be classed as of the tribe of Judah, a descendant of Benjamin as of the tribe of Benjamin, and so with those of other tribes. Ephraim was blessed with the *birthright* in Israel,[18] and in this dispensation he has been called to stand at the *head* to bless the other tribes of Israel.[19] This is the interpretation as discovered in the discourses of the leading brethren and in the blessings of the patriarchs of the Church from the beginning, as the following excerpts will show:

"There is the fact revealed through the Prophet Joseph Smith, who was of the lineage of Joseph through the loins of Ephraim, that the majority of the people who have been first to receive the gospel and priesthood of the latter-day dispensation, are descendants of some of the house of Ephraim scattered among the nations,[20] and therefore, the stick of Joseph—the *Book of Mormon*—is in their hands."[21]

"It is Ephraim that I have been searching for all

[14]Rom. 11.
[15]Matt. 3:9-10.
[16]Matt. 8:10-12.
[17]*Era,* vol. 26, pp. 1149-1150.
[18]Gen. 48:5-22; Jer. 31:9.

[19]*D. & C.* 133:30-34.
[20]Hos. 7:8; 9:16-17.
[21]Franklin D. Richards, quoted in *Contributor.* vol. 17, p. 428.

the days of my preaching, and that is the *blood* which ran in my veins when I embraced the gospel. If there are any of the other tribes of Israel mixed with the Gentiles, we are also searching for them. Though the Gentiles are cut off, do not suppose that we are not going to preach the gospel among the *Gentile nations,* for they are mingled with the house of Israel. . . . You understand who we are; we are of the house of Israel, of the royal seed, of the royal blood."[22]

President Brigham Young also said: "You have heard Joseph say the people did not know him; he had his eyes on the relation to blood-relations. . . . His descent from Joseph that was sold into Egypt was *direct,* and the blood was *pure* in him. This is why the Lord chose him, and we are pure when this blood-strain from Ephraim comes down pure. The decrees of the Almighty will be exalted—that blood which was in him was pure, and he had the sole right and lawful power, as he was the *legal heir* to the blood that has been on the earth and has come down through a *pure lineage."*[23]

PATRIARCHAL BLESSINGS REVEAL TRIBAL ANCESTRY. "If the patriarch who is here should lay his hands upon your head and declare your genealogy, he would tell you . . . that, almost without exception, you are the descendants of Ephraim."[24]

In the greater number of blessings given by our patriarchs similar expressions will be found to these:

"Brother Hyde:[25] I seal upon thee the blessings of Joseph, for thou art a pure descendant of Joseph through the loins of Ephraim." (Blessing by Joseph Smith, Sen.)

"Thou art of the lineage of Joseph, and a joint-heir of Abraham's blessings." (Blessing by Joseph Smith, Sen.)

Occasionally in patriarchal blessings the lineage is declared to be of *other* tribes. Here are examples:

---

[22]Brigham Young, quoted in *Journal of Discourses,* vol. 2, pp. 268-269.
[23]*D. & C.* 86:8-11.
[24]Anthony W. Ivins, quoted in *Gen. & Hist. Mag.,* vol. 23, p. 5.
[25]This is not Orson Hyde. J.F.S.

"Dear Brother: In the name of Jesus Christ I lay my hands on thy head and pray God the Eternal Father that the vision of my mind may be opened . . . Thou art of the tribe of *Dan,* yet if thou art faithful thou shalt attain to all the promised blessings." (Blessing by Joseph Smith, Sen.)

"Thou art *partly* of the *lineage of Judah.*" (Blessing by Joseph Smith, Sen.)

"Thou art of a slow and fearful spirit, but awake, arise, and be energetic, and thou shalt see within the veil, and the Lord will make known thy lineage to thee." (Blessing by Joseph Smith, Sen.)

"Thou art of the blood of Joseph and of the tribe of Manasseh." (Blessing by John Smith.)

"Thou art of the blood of Joseph and of the lineage of Manasseh." (Blessing by John Smith.)

It is clearly shown from these blessings and the interpretations given to the scriptures that the brethren from the beginning of the Church in these last days believed and taught that *lineage is a matter of blood relationship.* However, if a person should join the Church, and he is a pure Gentile, the Prophet has said the old blood would be purged out and he would be grafted into the house of Israel. In such a case the individual could be properly *assigned* to one of the tribes, probably to Ephraim.

ONLY THE RIGHTEOUS ARE HEIRS OF ABRAHAM. The terms *seed, heirs, sons,* and *daughters,* have a much deeper and greater meaning as used in the scriptures in reference to the becoming sons and daughters of Abraham, than to be literal descendants in the flesh. In the scriptural meaning there will be thousands of the literal descendants of Abraham, Isaac, Jacob, and Joseph, who will never be called by Abraham's name or be of the house of Israel.[26] This will be because they have rebelled against the truth and have not placed themselves

---

[26] Rom. 9:1-8.

in harmony with the covenants which are required in order that they may inherit as *sons* and *daughters*. In other words, to become a son or a daughter of Abraham, the individual must "do the works of Abraham." The Lord recognized the fact that the Jews were *descendants* of Abraham, but they could not be classed as the *children* of Abraham.[27]

We must remember that there are some blessings which come to us through *faithful membership in the Church*. Those who are obedient, and who keep the covenants which the Lord requires of those who obtain exaltation, are to be throughout all *eternity*, the children of Abraham, while those who rebel against the truth will be cut off, just as were the Jews in the days of our Savior.

I call your attention to the fact also that the Lord has said that those who receive the priesthood and are faithful also become the sons of Moses and of Aaron as well as the *seed* of Abraham, while the direct descendants of Moses and Aaron, as well as of Abraham, who are rebellious, will be disinherited and will not be called by their names.[28] We are taught that we are the offspring of God,[29] yet only those who *obey* will be called the sons of God and the children of God.[30]

MISSION OF EPHRAIM

EPHRAIM GAINED BIRTHRIGHT IN ISRAEL. Joseph, son of Jacob, because of his faithfulness and integrity to the purposes of the Lord, was rewarded with the birthright in Israel. It was the custom in early times to bestow upon the firstborn son special privileges and blessings, and these were looked upon as belonging to him by right of birth. Reuben, the first of Jacob's sons, lost the birthright through transgression, and it was bestowed upon Joseph, who was the most worthy of all the sons of Jacob.[31]

---

[27]John 8:33-59.
[28]D. & C. 84:33-41.
[29]Acts 17:29; Heb. 12:9.

[30]Rom. 8:14-17; Moses 6:68.
[31]1 Chron. 5:1-2.

When Jacob blessed Joseph, he gave him a double portion, or an inheritance among his brethren in Palestine and also the blessing of the land of Zion—"the utmost bound of the everlasting hills." He also blessed him with the blessings of heaven above, of the deep which lieth under, and of posterity.[32] Jacob also blessed the two sons of Joseph with the blessings of their father, which they inherited, and he placed Ephraim, the younger, before *Manasseh*, the elder, and by inspiration of the Lord conferred upon Ephraim the *birthright in Israel*.[33]

SCATTERING OF EPHRAIM AMONG THE NATIONS. After the death of Solomon his son Rehoboam was placed upon the throne of Israel, but the 10 northern tribes revolted and set up the *kingdom of Israel*, with Jeroboam, an Ephraimite, as their king. The southern kingdom, composed of the tribes of Judah and Benjamin, became known thereafter as the *kingdom of Judah*. The northern kingdom is frequently referred to in the chronicles and in prophecy as *Ephraim*. There are passages in the scriptures, however, which have direct reference to descendants of Ephraim and the blessings which were pronounced upon their heads. These blessings are to be realized in the latter-days.

While the Israelites possessed the land of Canaan, they were rebellious and failed to heed the commandments of the Lord. Among these tribes were none who were more guilty of this offense than Ephraim, and because of this rebellion the Lord punished him by mixing him among the nations. It is true that Israelites from the other tribes were also scattered among the nations, but particularly is this true of the Ephraimites. The words of Hosea have direct application to those of the tribe of Ephraim wherein he says: "*Ephraim, he hath mixed himself among the people;* Ephraim is a cake not turned."[34]

---

[32]Gen. 49:22-26.
[33]Gen. 48:5-22.

[34]Hos. 7:8.

In scattering Ephraim the Lord had two purposes in mind: 1. The scattering was to be a punishment to a rebellious people; 2. It was for the purpose of blessing the people of other nations with the blood of Israel among whom Ephraim "mixed" himself. The scattering of other Israelites answered the same purpose.

We have very good reason to believe, however, that it was the tribe of Ephraim, rebellious, proud, and headstrong, which was scattered *more* than any other among the people of other nations. The chief reason is that it is Ephraim who is now being gathered from among the nations. In these last days the Lord said that Ephraim should not be rebellious as he was formerly, and that now, the rebellious were not of Ephraim and should be "plucked out."[85]

EPHRAIM STANDS AT HEAD IN LATTER-DAYS. It is essential in this dispensation that Ephraim stand in his place at the head, exercising the birthright in Israel which was given to him by direct revelation. Therefore, *Ephraim must be gathered first to prepare the way,* through the gospel and the priesthood, for the rest of the tribes of Israel when the time comes for them to be gathered to Zion. The great majority of those who have come into the Church are Ephraimites. It is the exception to find one of any other tribe, unless it is of Manasseh.
. . .

It is Ephraim, today, who holds the priesthood. It is with Ephraim that the Lord has made covenant and has revealed the fulness of the everlasting gospel. It is Ephraim who is building temples and performing the ordinances in them for both the living and for the dead. When the "lost tribes" come—and it will be a most wonderful sight and a marvelous thing when they do come to Zion—in fulfilment of the promises made through Isaiah and Jeremiah,[86] they will have to receive the crown-

---

[85]D. & C. 64:35-36.

[86]Isa. 2:1-5; 5:26-30; 11:1-16; 18:1-3; 29:1-24; Jer. 3:12-18; 16:11-21; 31:6-14, 31-34.

*ing blessings from their brother Ephraim, the "firstborn"
in Israel.*

LATTER-DAY ISRAEL TO RECEIVE BLESSINGS FROM
EPHRAIM. The leaders of our people from the beginning
have looked forward to this great day when Ephraim
would be gathered and would stand in his place to *crown*
the tribes of Israel. In an epistle issued by the First
Presidency in October, 1852, the following appears:

"The invitation is to all, of every nation, kindred and
tongue, who will believe, repent, be baptized, and receive
the gift of the Holy Ghost, by the laying on of hands,
*Come home: come to the land of Joseph, to the valleys
of Ephraim.*"[37]

The Prophet Joseph Smith looked forward to the
great day when Israel would be gathered. He stated at
a conference held in June, 1831, "that John the Revelator
was then among the ten tribes of Israel who had been led
away by Shalmaneser, king of Assyria, to prepare them
for their return from their long dispersion."[38] President
Brigham Young had these same thoughts constantly in
mind and frequently spoke of them. "It is the house of
Israel, we are after," said he, "and it is the very lad on
whom Father Jacob laid his hands, that will save the
house of Israel. The *Book of Mormon* came to Ephraim,
for *Joseph Smith was a pure Ephraimite.*"[39]

"We are now gathering the children of Abraham
who have come through the loins of Joseph and his sons,
more especially through Ephraim, whose children are
mixed among all the nations of the earth. . . . I see a
congregation of them before me today."[40]

President Young declares that Joseph Smith was a
pure Ephraimite. This is true. Joseph Smith, father of
the Prophet, received the birthright in Israel which he

---

[37]*Journal History,* Oct. 13, 1852.
[38]*History of the Church,* vol. 1, p. 176.
[39]*Journal of Discourses,* vol. 2, pp. 268-269.
[40]*Discourses of Brigham Young,* 2nd ed., p. 670.

inherited through his fathers back to Ephraim and Joseph and Jacob to Abraham. For that reason the Patriarchal Priesthood was conferred upon him with the commandment that it should be handed down from father to son.[41]

GATHERING OF ISRAEL

PROPHETS PREDICTED GATHERING OF ISRAEL. Moses, by prophecy, declared to ancient Israel, even before they had the privilege of entering the land of their inheritance, that for their rebellion the tribes of Israel would be driven to the four corners of the earth, but in the last days, if they would humble themselves, the Lord would gather them again.[42] Such prophecies were constantly repeated by the prophets of Israel—Isaiah,[43] Jeremiah[44], Ezekiel,[45] Amos,[46] Hosea;[47] in fact, all of the prophets have spoken of this scattering and of the gathering of Israel.[48]

"And it shall come to pass in that day, that the Lord shall set his hand again the *second time* to recover the remnant of his people, which shall be left, from Assyria, and from Egypt, and from Pathros, and from Cush, and from Elam, and from Shinar, and from Hammath, and from the islands of the sea. And he shall set up *an ensign for the nations,* and shall assemble the outcasts of Israel, and gather together the dispersed of Judah from the four corners of the earth."[49]

CHURCH IS PROMISED ENSIGN TO WORLD. Over 125 years ago, in the little town of Fayette, Seneca County, New York, the Lord set up an ensign to the nations. It was in fulfilment of the prediction made by the Prophet Isaiah, which I have read. *That ensign was*

[41]*Gen. & Hist. Mag.,* vol. 21, pp. 1-4.
[42]Deut. 4:27-31; 28; 29; 30.
[43]Isa. 2:1-5; 5:26-30; 11:1-16; 14:1-2; 18:1-3; 29:1-24; 35:4-10; 43:5-7; 54:1-17; 61:4.
[44]Jer. 3:12-18; 12:14-17; 16:11-21; 23:2-8; 30:3; 31:6-14, 31-34; 32:37-40; 33:7-14; 50:4-8, 20.
[45]Ezek. 11:16-21; 20:33-44; 28:25-26; 34:11-31; 37:15-28.
[46]Amos 9:14-15.
[47]Hos. 1:10-11; 14:1-9.
[48]*Era,* vol. 55, p. 81; Neh. 1:8-9; Ps. 14:7; 107:1-7; Mic. 4:1-7; Zeph. 3:14-20.
[49]Isa. 11:11-12; Jos. Smith 2:36-41.

the Church of Jesus Christ of Latter-day Saints, which was established for the *last time,* never again to be destroyed or given to other people.[50] *It was the greatest event the world has seen since the day that the Redeemer was lifted upon the cross and worked out the infinite and eternal atonement.* It meant more to mankind than anything else that has occurred since that day.

No event should have been heralded among the people with greater effectiveness and received with greater evidence of joy and satisfaction. The nations should have rejoiced and welcomed it with gladness of heart, for with it came the establishment of divine truth in the earth—the gospel of Jesus Christ, which is the power of God unto salvation unto all who believe.[51] The world had been without this gospel for many hundreds of years, ever since the great apostasy and turning away from the truth which had been established by the primitive Church.

Following the raising of this *ensign,* the Lord sent forth his elders clothed with the priesthood and with power and authority, among the nations of the earth, bearing witness unto all peoples of the restoration of his Church, and calling upon the children of men to repent and receive the gospel; for now it was being preached in all the world as a witness before the end should come, that is, the end of the reign of wickedness and the establishment of the millennial reign of peace. The elders went forth as they were commanded, and are still preaching the gospel and gathering out from the nations the seed of Israel unto whom the promise was made.

ISRAEL GATHERS BY JOINING TRUE CHURCH. Thus our fathers were gathered and brought into the *true fold* in fulfilment of the prophecies made in ancient times by men inspired of the Lord, that he would recover a remnant of his people from the four corners of the earth. Scattered Israel is being gathered into the fold. Some

---

[50]Dan. 2:44.   [51]Rom. 1:16-17.

have rejected the testimony of the elders through ignorance and prejudice, not understanding the significance of the message delivered unto them. Others have rejected the truth wilfully because of the evil in their hearts and their subjection to unrighteousness.[52]

There are many nations represented in the membership of the Church, as we find them located in each stake of Zion, and they have come because the Spirit of the Lord rested upon them, and they could not stay themselves; but receiving the *spirit of gathering,* they left everything for the sake of the gospel and for the privilege of being numbered with, and obtaining an inheritance among, their fellow believers—the Latter-day Saints.

BLESSINGS OF GATHERING OF ISRAEL. Our ancestors were engaged in various pursuits in their native lands; some of them in the coal mines, some of them in the fisheries, some of them in the great factories; and thus they were employed in foreign countries, barely able to make a living. They heard the gospel, came to this land, became tillers of the soil, and stock raisers principally, and have been engaged of course, more or less, in the selling and buying of merchandise. They have been trained and educated in various professions: as lawyers, doctors, and in the arts and sciences, which never would have been their privilege had they remained in their native land, under the conditions which prevailed there.

And so the gospel has benefited them *temporally* as well as *spiritually,* and we all know that it has benefited them *morally,* that we are better by far in every particular than we could have been had we remained, or our parents remained, and we had been born to them in the countries from whence they came. The Church today numbers many many thousands and they are of the house of Israel, principally of the tribe of Ephraim—Ephraim having received the birthright in Israel and the mission

[52]Conf. Rep., Apr., 1911, p. 124.

to stand at the head, to perform a work for his fellow kinsmen of the other tribes in the dispensation of the fulness of times in which we live.

And so, we have seen the fulfilment of this promise that was made to the Prophet Joseph Smith, through the preaching of the gospel—the conversion of many souls from Europe, from Asia, and from the isles of the sea; and we are now witnessing the gathering of the *dispersed of Judah*. The Lord is now opening the way for the return of these outcasts who were scattered because of their disobedience and their rejection of the Son of God, and they have remained scattered among the nations until the time for their gathering, *which is now*.[53]

GATHERING OCCURS BECAUSE KEYS RESTORED. Moses received the *keys* of the gathering of Israel at Sinai, when he was called and sent to lead Israel from Egypt to the promised land which the Lord had given to their father Abraham.[54] He gathered Israel, and while he was not privileged to place them in possession of the land, nevertheless the keys were in his hands for the gathering. He came to Peter, James, and John on the mount at the transfiguration and there bestowed upon them the same keys for the gathering of Israel in the days in which they lived.[55] He was sent to the Prophet Joseph Smith and Oliver Cowdery to bestow the keys for the gathering of Israel in the dispensation of the fulness of times.[56]

It is by virtue of the restoration of those keys that you are here tonight. I take it for granted that I am looking into the faces of people who have come from all parts of Europe, from all parts of the United States, from Canada and other lands. *What brought you here?* The gospel of Jesus Christ, and *the power and the authority bestowed by Moses for your gathering* here.

The Jews today are gathering in Palestine in fulfil-

---

[53]*Gen. & Hist. Mag.*, vol. 14, pp. 2-3.   [55]Matt. 17:1-13; Smith, *op. cit.*, p. 158.
[54]Ex. 3:1-22.   [56]*D. & C.* 110:11.

ment of the predictions of the ancient prophets. Why are
they gathering to their homeland? Because of the restoration of the keys for the gathering of Israel. The Jews
are being restored to the land of their inheritance; and
there will yet come other gatherings, for we are informed
that there shall come the gathering of the lost tribes of
Israel, and all that by virtue of the restoration of the keys
of the priesthood held by Moses.[57]

FULNESS OF THE GENTILES

TIMES OF GENTILES DRAWING TO A CLOSE. Speaking of the overthrow of the Jews and the destruction of
Jerusalem, the Lord said to his disciples: "And they shall
fall by the edge of the sword, and shall be led away
captive into all nations: and *Jerusalem shall be trodden
down of the Gentiles, until the times of the Gentiles be
fulfilled.* And there shall be signs in the sun, and in the
moon, and in the stars; and upon the earth distress of
nations, with perplexity; the sea and the waves roaring;
Men's hearts failing them for fear, and for looking after
those things which are coming on the earth: for the
powers of heaven shall be shaken."[58]

This scripture was also referred to by Moroni when
he visited Joseph Smith in September, 1823, which scripture he said was soon to be fulfilled. He said that the
fulness of the Gentiles was soon to come in.[59] The words
of our Lord are very definite and explicit regarding the
time of the scattering of the Jews and the days of the
Gentiles. They give the key which unlocks the door to
the fulfilling of this prophecy.

We all know that from the time of the destruction
of Jerusalem in the year 70 A.D. until near the close of
World War I, Jerusalem was trodden down of the Gentiles, and during all of that time the Jews were scattered
and almost without privileges in the Holy Land. The

[57]*Gen. & Hist. Mag.*, vol. 27, pp. 99-
100.
[58]Luke 21:24-26.
[59]Jos. Smith 2:41.

Lord said they should remain scattered among the nations *until* the times of the Gentiles were fulfilled. Moroni said the times of the Gentiles were about to be fulfilled. Today we are living in the *transition* period; *the day of the Gentiles has come in, and the day of Judah and the remnant of downtrodden Israel is now at hand*. The sign for the fulfilment of this prophecy has been given.[60]

FIRST TO BE LAST AND LAST TO BE FIRST. In the former dispensation, the gospel was first preached to the Jews and then, after they had rejected it, it was taken to the Gentiles. In the dispensation in which we live, the gospel was first taken to the Gentile nations, and scattered Israel other than the Jews were gathered out; and after being preached among the Gentile nations, it shall go to the Jews, the first being last and the last being first, as the Savior promised.[61]

In section 45 of the *Doctrine and Covenants*, the Lord calls attention to the fact that when the fulness of the Gentiles should come in, a light should break forth among those that sat in darkness, and it should be the fulness of the everlasting gospel, but they would reject it. And in that generation shall the time of the Gentiles be fulfilled.[62] In the 133rd section of the *Doctrine and Covenants*, he warns all the tribes of Israel to flee to the mountains of Ephraim for safety, and for the Jews to flee to Jerusalem.[63]

From the time of the destruction of Jerusalem by Titus until the year 1917, Jerusalem was trodden down of the Gentiles. After General Allenby, at the head of the British forces, captured Palestine, that country became free from the tyranny and oppression of the Turkish empire, and after peace was declared, England sent to Palestine Dr. Herbert Samuel, a Jew, to be governor of the land, and that is the first time in all those years that a Jew has ruled in Palestine.

[60]*Church News*, Oct. 31, 1931, p. 6.   [62]*D. & C.* 45:28-30.
[61]1 Ne. 13:42; Luke 13:28-30.   [63]*D. & C.* 133:12-14.

BEGINNING OF RETURN OF JEWS TO PALESTINE.
Under his direction, and with the sanction of the British
government, which controls in that land, he is preparing
for the return of the scattered remnant—the dispersed of
Judah—to their own land, where they shall assemble in
fulfilment of these predictions made by Isaiah and other
prophets and quoted by Moroni to the Prophet Joseph
Smith, *where they too will have the privilege of hearing
the gospel and embracing it.*[64]

We see today a miracle being performed before our
eyes. Following the war, which we are pleased to call
the *first world war*, the British Premier issued a proclamation to the Jews telling them they could gather and
they could have in Palestine a *Jewish Home*, or state.
They began to gather in great numbers. At the beginning of this century things in Palestine were in a deplorable condition. They were using wooden plows, water
wheel irrigation; they had infested wells and streams.
They carried water in skins as of old. Sanitation was
deplorable.

LEBANON BECOMING A FRUITFUL FIELD.[65] The
British government changed all of this, when they obtained the *mandate*. You see, the mandate of Palestine
was given to Great Britain. That nation and other nations spent millions of pounds in rehabilitating that land.
The Sea of Galilee is now a great reservoir, and the flood
waters from the various streams are being diverted into it.

Canals have been built for irrigation, and the Jordan
has been changed from its natural channel into channels
or into canals on each side of the original stream. These
irrigate some seven million acres, which could not be
under cultivation otherwise. Hydroelectric stations have
been built on these streams. One power plant is located
about eight miles below the lake of Galilee, where there
is a similar dam to the Hoover Dam. This contains about
10 billion cubic feet of water for irrigation and power

[64]*Gen. & Hist. Mag.*, vol. 14, pp. 3-4.   [65]Isa. 29:17.

purposes. Passing through the turbines, most of the water is returned to the Jordan. The power plants are ample for a territory the size of Vermont. The Palestine Electric Corporation supplies electric power and light for all Palestine, except Jerusalem and its vicinity.

In 1929-30, the value of fruit exported from Jerusalem, oranges and grapefruit and lemon groves, was valued at 1.5 million dollars. In 1937 it was estimated to have increased to 20 million. During the same period the production of industrial enterprises of the Jewish people rose from 11 million to over 40 million.

From 1898 to 1940 the sum of 70 million dollars had been invested in Palestine through the national funds. These figures are for the years up to 1937. Since that time, there has been a great influx of Jews into Palestine, and of course, all that I have told you about money spent and what has been accomplished is only a fraction of what has been accomplished since. Tel Aviv, a Jewish city founded in 1910, is larger than Salt Lake City today. This is all in fulfilment of the prophecies. . . .

JERUSALEM NO LONGER TRODDEN DOWN OF GENTILES. England got tired of the mandate and wished to be relieved. On May 14, 1948, England withdrew and the Republic of Israel came into existence. This is a very significant event which we must not forget. It is a sign to us that the times of the Gentiles are drawing to their close and the day of the gathering of the Jews and the preaching of the gospel to them is at hand.

I will read to you some of the words of the Savior in regard to the scattering of the Jews and their gathering again, as recorded in the 21st chapter of Luke: "And when ye shall see Jerusalem compassed with armies, then know that the desolation thereof is nigh. Then let them which are in Judea flee to the mountains; and let them which are in the midst of it depart out; and let not them that are in the countries enter thereinto. For these be the days of vengeance, that all things which are written may be fulfilled. But woe unto them that are with child, and to them that give suck, in those days! for there shall be great distress in the land, and wrath upon this people. *And they shall fall by the edge of the sword, and shall be led away captive into all nations: and Jerusalem shall be trodden down of the Gentiles, until the times of the Gentiles be fulfilled.*"[66]

When Titus the Roman general laid siege to Jerusalem, he suddenly withdrew his forces for some unknown reason. This was the signal to the members of the Church to flee, and they took advantage of it. Titus returned and laid siege and it was at this time that the dreadful things occurred spoken of by Moses in the 28th chapter of Deuteronomy.

Today the Jews are building the waste places, building cities. They have their own government, have their own flag, and make their own laws. I wish you would obtain a copy of the *Voice of Warning*, by Elder Parley P. Pratt, which was written in 1837. He tells you all about these things and how they were to be fulfilled. Now, more than 100 years later, we see the Jews returning. We see their government established, and thus the foundation laid for the return of Israel, and yet, the blind leaders of the blind, can't see it.[67]

HOW LEHI'S DESCENDANTS WERE JEWS

LEHI A JEW BY CITIZENSHIP. In 1 Nephi 5:14, we are informed that Lehi was a descendant of Joseph, and in 2 Nephi 30:4, it states that the Nephites were descendants of the Jews. Since the Jews were descendants of Judah, how can these statements be harmonized?

It is true that Lehi and his family were descendants of Joseph through the lineage of Manasseh,[68] and Ishmael was a descendant of Ephraim, according to the statement of the Prophet Joseph Smith. That the Nephites were

---

[66]Luke 21:20-24.   [68]Alma 10:3.
[67]*Church News*, July 23, 1952. p. 14.

descendants of Joseph is in fulfilment of the blessings given to Joseph by his father Israel. The Nephites were of the Jews, not so much by descent as by *citizenship*, although in the long descent from Jacob, it could be possible of some mixing of the tribes by intermarriage.

It should be remembered that in the days of Rehoboam, son of Solomon, 10 of the 12 tribes of Israel revolted and were known as the kingdom of Israel from that time on until they were carried away into Assyria. The other two tribes of Judah and Benjamin remained loyal to Rehoboam and were known as the kingdom of Judah. *Lehi was a citizen of Jerusalem, in the kingdom of Judah.* Presumably his family had lived there for several generations, and *all of the inhabitants of the kingdom of Judah, no matter which tribe they had descended through, were known as Jews.*

The condition is comparable to conditions today, for example: Many members of the Church have been gathered out of England, Germany, the Scandinavian countries, and other foreign lands. Coming to this country they have taken out citizenship papers, and then they and their descendants are known as Americans, being citizens of this country.

How Paul Was a Jew. There is also a comparable example in the case of Paul the apostle. When he was arrested on complaint of the Jews, the chief captain mistook him for an Egyptian who had created a rebellion, and Paul said to the captain, "I am a man which am a Jew of Tarsus, a city in Cilicia, a citizen of no mean city: and, I beseech thee, suffer me to speak unto the people." When the privilege was granted, Paul spoke to the angry Jews and said: "I am verily a man which am a Jew, born in Tarsus, a city in Cilicia, yet brought up in this city at the feet of Gamaliel, and taught according to the perfect manner of the law of the fathers, and was zealous toward God, as ye all are this day."[69] In writing his

---

[69]Acts 21:37-39; 22:3.

epistles to the Roman saints Paul said: "For I also am an Israelite, of the seed of Abraham, of the tribe of Benjamin."[70] He made a similar statement in writing the saints at Philippi.[71]

Not only in the *Book of Mormon* are the descendants of Lehi called Jews, but also in the *Doctrine and Covenants*. In section 19, this is found: "Which is my word to the Gentile, that soon it may go to the Jew, of whom the Lamanites are a remnant, that they may believe the gospel, and look not for a Messiah to come who has already come."[72] Again, in giving instruction to the elders who had journeyed from Kirtland to Missouri, the Lord revealed the place for the building of the temple and gave instruction for the purchase of land "lying westward, even unto the line running directly between Jew and Gentile."[73] This line westward was the dividing line between the whites and Indians.[74]

---

[70]Rom. 11:1.
[71]Phil. 3:5.
[72]D. & C. 19:27.

[73]D. & C. 57:4.
[74]*Era*, vol. 58, p. 702.

Chapter 14

THE APOSTATE WORLD

APOSTASY FROM PRIMITIVE CHURCH

First Apostasy Began in Adam's Day. When the Lord formed the earth and its heaven, he pronounced them *very good*. He sanctified them, and when man was placed on the earth, this condition of goodness and sanctification prevailed.[1] We read in the words of Lehi to his son Jacob the following: "And now, behold, if Adam had not transgressed he would not have fallen, but he would have remained in the garden of Eden. And all things which were created must have remained in the same state in which they were after they were created; and they must have remained forever, and had no end."[2]

The charge given to Adam in the garden was that he was forbidden to eat the fruit of the tree of the knowledge of good and evil, for should he do so he would surely die. Through his transgression death came upon him, and the earth that was *very good* was *cursed* to bring forth thorns and thistles, which it did not bring forth before, and thus the earth and all creatures on its face partook of the fall. Through Satan's power many of the children of Adam and Eve rebelled, for *"they loved Satan more than God. And men began from that time forth to be carnal, sensual, and devilish."*[3]

Many Periods of Apostasy in Earth's History. The gospel, which had been given to Adam by the Lord, was changed; ordinances were broken; and *the perfect government revealed to him ceased to exist*. The bowing down to idols and the worship of imaginary gods soon prevailed. Violent and unrighteous men gained power

---

[1]Gen. 1; 2; Moses 2; 3.   [3]Moses 5:13.
[2]2 Ne. 2:22.

266

DOCTRINES OF SALVATION

and set themselves up as rulers, and man-made governments were formed in which the Divine Ruler was
ignored.

Then came the flood, and the earth was cleansed.
Once more the covenants and commandments were revealed to Noah for man's government, but before his
death corruption had again swept over the earth. It became necessary for the Lord to call Abraham from the
land of his birth and make covenants with him and his
seed after him which were to endure forever, and his
descendants, the children of Jacob, became the chosen
people of Israel.

In course of time, after Israel had been established
in their inheritances in Canaan, these covenants were
broken, and for the rebellion of the 10 tribes, then
known as the Kingdom of Israel, that kingdom came to
an end, the people were carried captive into Assyria, and
from that land they never returned. The remaining two
tribes about 130 years later were likewise punished and
carried away to Babylon. When they had suffered sufficiently and had repented, they were privileged to return
to their own land where they reconstructed the temple
and for a short season served the Lord.

Then once more came a departure from the Lord,
and when the time came for the appearance of the Son
of God, they rejected him and crucified him, but he again
established his Church with a few who were willing to
follow him and sent them forth into all the world to declare his gospel. Again, following the death of his
apostles, apostasy once more set in, and again the saving
principles and ordinances of the gospel were changed
to suit the conveniences and notions of the people. *Doctrines were corrupted, authority lost, and a false order of
religion took the place of the gospel of Jesus Christ, just
as it had been the case in former dispensations, and the
people were left in spiritual darkness.*[4]

APOSTASY FOLLOWING MERIDIAN OF TIME. It is within the power of every intelligent man to know that following the days of the ancient apostles there came a *falling away*, or an apostasy, from the doctrines and practices in the primitive Church. History shows that the priesthood which was organized by our Savior was corrupted, and offices were created that were unknown in the days of the apostles and which are foreign to the true Church of Jesus Christ.

Offices which were established by the Savior were discarded with the false assumption that they were no longer needed. Apostles and prophets, which officers Paul declares were to remain in the Church, "Till we all come in the unity of the faith, and of the knowledge of the Son of God, unto a perfect man, unto the measure of the stature of the fulness of Christ,"[5] were discarded.

Apostles and prophets ceased to exist, and therefore there was no more revelation or contact with the heavens, and it was proclaimed that the canon of scripture was full. The pure, understandable truths of the gospel became mixed with the pagan philosophies of that day, and the ordinances of the gospel no longer resembled those taught and practiced by the apostles of our Lord. Evidences of this are very apparent to every student of the history of the early centuries of the Christian era.

The Protestant rebellion did not correct these errors, for those who broke away from the *mother church* perpetuated these evils, and therefore the same corrupted doctrines and practices were perpetuated in these *protestant* organizations. The truth concerning the nature of God and the true relationship between the Father and the Son disappeared, and following the days of Constantine the incomprehensible doctrine of the Godhead was substituted in its place. Thus confusion regarding our Eternal Father and his Son Jesus Christ has persisted throughout all of Christendom to this day.[6]

---

[5]Eph. 4:11-14.   [6]*Church News*, Dec. 13, 1950, p. 15.

UNIVERSAL NATURE OF APOSTASY. All the men holding the priesthood should have a thorough understanding of the development of false doctrine and the gradual change which took place, after the death of the apostles, which transformed the Church of Jesus Christ into a system *as far removed from the primitive Church as are the poles of our hemispheres. Nothing by way of ordinance* and *very little by way of doctrine,* given by revelation in the days of our Savior and during the lives of the apostles, was left remaining. . . .

Many volumes could be written showing the departure from the original teachings and ministry of the Church. In fact impartial historians have pointed out down through the centuries how these changes came to pass. Moreover some historians who were adherents of the Catholic Church, perhaps unknowingly, have borne witnesses of these great changes.[7]

If we had access to all the documents dealing with the ecclesiastical changes of the first two or three centuries of the Christian era, there would come before the people some very startling discoveries. The information which is obtainable reveals deplorable conditions in the development of false doctrines, changes in ordinances, the order in the priesthood, and the government of the Church, that make it clear to all who earnestly consider them, that there came as predicted by the apostles of old, a *falling away* from the true Church of Jesus Christ. . . .

PETER AND PAUL FORETOLD GREAT APOSTASY. The apostasy did not come suddenly. It was a gradual development and commenced while some of the apostles were still living. Paul, at Miletus, when taking leave of the elders of Ephesus, said, "I know this, that after my departing shall grievous wolves enter in among you, not sparing the flock. Also of your own selves shall men

---

[7]Preface, James L. Barker, *The Divine Church,* vol. 2, p. 3.

arise, speaking perverse things, to draw away disciples after them."[8]

He warned the members of the Church in Thessalonica not to be deceived regarding the ushering in of the second advent of Jesus Christ. "For that day shall not come, except there come a *falling away* first, and that man of sin be revealed, the son of perdition; Who opposeth and exalteth himself above all that is called God, or that is worshipped; so that he as God sitteth in the temple of God, shewing himself that he is God."[9]

Peter also wrote saying: "But there were false prophets also among the people, even as there shall be false teachers among you, who privily shall bring in damnable heresies, even denying the Lord that bought them, and bring upon themselves swift destruction. And many shall follow their pernicious ways; by reason of whom the way of truth shall be evil spoken of."[10]

PAGANISM GRADUALLY OVERCAME GOSPEL TRUTH. It is very plain for all who seek to see that changes in the doctrines of the Church were introduced in the early centuries after the death of the apostles.

Then came gradually the ascendancy of the bishop of Rome over other bishops and officers in the Church, which led to the declaration that Peter had chosen that bishop to be his successor, notwithstanding the fact that John, and perhaps others of the apostles, were still living. There is evidence in the New Testament that it was the purpose in the beginning that the council of the apostles was to be perpetuated, for Paul was called to the apostleship and others such as Barnabas and James the brother of the Lord were so designated;[11] but this council gradually came to an end.[12]

As the Church grew and spread, especially after the death of the apostles, false doctrines crept in. *Pagan*

8Acts 20:29-30.
92 Thess. 2:3.
102 Pet. 2:1-2.

11Eph. 4:11-16; Acts 1:15-26; Rom. 16:7; 1 Cor. 12:28-29; 1 Tim. 2:7; Gal. 1:19.
12Barker, *op. cit.*, vol. 1, p. 3.

philosophy became mixed with the truth, and the simple, plain, principles and ceremonies of the gospel, so clear that the unlearned and common people could understand them, became so changed and mixed with error, mystery, and ostentation so foreign to the doctrines of Christ that the people were bewildered and confused. False teachers arose, and again the priesthood was withdrawn from among men to be restored at a better and more favorable day.[13]

JOHN SAW PRIESTHOOD TAKEN TO HEAVEN. John the apostle, when on the isle of Patmos, saw the time come when the Church was forced into the wilderness. The Church, in this vision, is represented by the figure of a woman, "clothed with the sun, and the moon under her feet, and upon her head a crown of twelve stars." "And there appeared another wonder in heaven, . . . a great red dragon" who drew one third of the stars of heaven and cast them to the earth. This dragon, when he was cast down to the earth, in great wrath persecuted the woman and the man child born of her.

The woman because of the persecution was given wings "that she might fly into the wilderness, into her place, where she is nourished for a time, and times, and half a time, from the face of the serpent." The man child representing the priesthood, who was chosen "to rule all nations with a rod of iron," was "caught up unto God, and to his throne," there to remain through the dark days of spiritual rebellion and satanic dominion, or until the earth could be prepared for his return to receive just and rightful power.[14]

This return of the Church and the priesthood had to be postponed until a day of religious freedom and to come in a land dedicated to religious liberty.[15]

NOTHING BUT RESTORATION COULD CURE APOSTASY. Joseph Smith was perfectly consistent in the

[13]*Millennial Star,* vol. 90, p. 307.   [15]*Church News,* Sept. 2, 1933, p. 4.
[14]Rev. 12

course he took. The fact that there was not found on
the earth in 1820 an organization which in any sense resembled the primitive Church, and which claimed to have
received authority, is almost beyond the possibility of
dispute. If the Church with its keys and priesthood was
to be restored, then it would have to be by the opening
of the heavens and the coming to earth of messengers
from the presence of the Lord. Man does not have
authority to make the Church for the Lord, and the Lord
is not bound to accept the organizations made by man
with their rules and regulations. His ways are not man's
ways, and when men endeavor to organize in a religious
way, their authority can extend only as far as man's
power extends, and therefore, all such organizations must
fail in the endeavor to give to men the blessings of
salvation.[16]

SOME TRUTH IN ALL CHURCHES. All churches
teach *some* truth, whether they profess belief in Con-
fucius, Buddha, the Greek and Roman gods, or anything
else; otherwise their churches would not endure a month.
*The fact that they teach some truth does not make them
the Church of God. There is but one Church of God.*[17]

MODERN APOSTATE CHRISTENDOM

MATERIAL PROGRESS WITHOUT SPIRITUAL ACCOM-
PANIMENT. Someone will say: "Are we not living in
the most enlightened age the world has ever seen? Is it
not true that great progress is being made to lessen the
burdens and increase the happiness of man?"

Yes, this is true in regard to many material things.
Great progress has been made in mechanics, chemistry,
physics, surgery, and other things. Men have built great
telescopes that have brought the hidden galaxies to view.
They have, by the aid of the microscope, discovered vast

---

[16]*Church News*, June 17, 1933, p. 11;   [17]Pers. Corresp.
    D. & C. 132:8-12.

worlds of microorganisms, some of which are as deadly as are men towards their fellow men.

They have discovered means to control disease; they have, by the aid of anesthesia, made men insensible to pain, thus permitting major and delicate operations which could not otherwise be performed. They have invented machines more sensitive than the human touch, more far-seeing than the human eye. They have controlled elements and made machinery that can move mountains, and many other things have they done too numerous to mention. Yes, this is a wonderful age.

However, all of these discoveries and inventions have not drawn men nearer to God! nor created in their hearts humility and the spirit of repentance. But to the contrary, to their condemnation, nearly everything, it seems, which has been given that should be a blessing to men, has been turned to evil.

Many of these discoveries and inventions are now being used to bring destruction to the human race. They are being used in the most cruel, most inhuman, godless wars this world has ever seen. They are employed by criminals to aid them in their crimes, by the ambitious in their efforts to destroy the agency of man, and by despots who are endeavoring to subjugate the world to an unholy, wicked rule.

MODERN AGE ONE OF APOSTASY AND CORRUPTION. Faith has not increased in the *world,* nor has righteousness, nor obedience to God. What the world needs today is to draw nearer to the Lord. We need more humble, abiding faith in our Redeemer, more love in our hearts for our Eternal Father and for our fellow men.[18]

We live in a wonderful age. The great inventions of our day exceed what was known in all former ages. Unfortunately these inventions have failed to bring men nearer to God. One might think that the revelations coming through radio, television and other things, would

18Conf. Rep., Apr., 1943, pp. 15-16.

draw men nearer to God; but it is not so. Men are more inclined to boast in their own strength, denying divine aid. Crime has increased. *The integrity of men has diminished.* From the writings of the press we may well believe that we are approaching the day predicted by Jesus Christ, when he said, "But as the days of Noe were, so shall also the coming of the Son of man be."[19]

Are the peoples of the earth approaching this same condition? World events indicate that they are; we have endured more grievous wars and bloodshed than in any other century. Nations have been, and are, arrayed against each other. Conflict, trouble, evil prevail. Governments with large populations have denied God. They have tried to make the state supreme and have taken from the people their agency.

RIGHTEOUSNESS DECREASING IN UNITED STATES. What of our own country? The Lord raised up honorable men to make it a land of freedom, and he declared: "It is not right that any man should be in bondage one to another. And for this purpose have I established the Constitution of this land, by the hands of wise men whom I raised up unto this very purpose, and redeemed the land by the shedding of blood."[20]

In those days men loved God. They walked humbly. They laid a firm foundation on which we were to build. Are we walking in their path? Are we maintaining the same standard, insuring a free government and a free people? Ours is a nation basically built on equity, virtue, and love. Have we lost our sense of justice? Our integrity? Our love of truth and our honor in the discharge of duty? Have we become victims of greed? Have we forgotten the path of virtue? Do we wink at and tolerate the violation of the marriage covenant and look upon marriage as a temporary contract to be broken at will? Is chastity forgotten?

When we learn of men chosen to represent the

---

[19]Matt. 24:37.   [20]D. & C. 101:79-80.

people violating their trust, when we read of robbery, murder, the reign of gangsters who brazenly defy the law, *we may wonder if we are not approaching the day of decadence like the ancient nations. . . .*

Let us return to individual and national integrity, love of God and country, be honest in our dealings with each other, virtuous in our lives. Here lies the only road to happiness and peace. Moreover, let us not forget that justice demands reparation for every wrong. Said Alma, a prophet of old: "What, do ye suppose that mercy can rob justice? I say unto you, Nay; not one whit. If so, God would cease to be God."[21]

WORLD GROWING WORSE, NOT BETTER. I am not one of those who believe that the world is growing better; I do not consider myself a pessimist either, but I do not believe that the world is becoming more righteous, that the inhabitants are drawing nearer unto God, that there is in the hearts of the people a greater desire today to serve him than in the year 1832; but, on the other hand, since that day the peoples of the nations of the earth have been drifting and drifting farther and farther from the truth.

When I make this statement, I am fully aware that there has been progression in certain directions. I am aware that in these latter-days there has been a movement among the nations and in our own land to overcome the evils of strong drink, and all these things will bring their results for good, but so far as their observance of the doctrines of the gospel is concerned, so far as their righteousness is concerned, I do not believe that they are any better, nay, I do not believe that the people are as good now as they were when this revelation was given.[22]

FALSE THEORIES AND PHILOSOPHIES PREVAIL IN WORLD. The world today is full of *vain philosophy*, full of doctrine that is not of the Lord, full of *false conclu-*

---

[21]*Church News,* Oct. 4, 1952, p. 12;   [22]*D. & C.* 84:44-53.
    Alma 42:25.

sions, ideas and *theories* that were not a part of the gospel in the days of the Son of God, and hence are not a part of it now, but on the contrary are in absolute contradiction of the truth. There are fewer, in my judgment, among the Christian peoples, who believe in the Son of God as the Redeemer of the world. The tendency has been, during all these years, to get farther away from the principles of the gospel as they are contained in the holy scriptures.

The worship of reason, of false philosophy, is greater now than it was then. Men are depending upon their own research to find out God, and that which they cannot discover and which they cannot demonstrate to their satisfaction through their own research and their *natural senses,* they reject. They are not seeking for the Spirit of the Lord; they are not striving to know God in the manner in which he has marked out by which he may be known; but they are walking in their own way, believing in their own man-made philosophies, teaching the doctrines of devils and not the doctrines of the Son of God.[23]

SOME EDUCATORS REBEL AGAINST GOD AND RELIGION. Some prominent educators have informed the world that we have no guide in religious thought beyond the power of man's wisdom, and therefore our individual reason is the best we have to lead us. For hundreds of years this babel of voices has been heard in the world of religion. Even at the present day there is little wonder that wise men[24]—that is, men wise in their own learning: editors, educators, doctors of the law, and of religion—should assemble, as was done in Chicago April 30th of this year 1933, to discuss what they deem the need of the present age in religion.

These wise men, if the press dispatches are to be accepted, met and declared, "The religious forms and

---

[23]Conf. Rep., Apr., 1917, pp. 59-60;   [24]D. & C. 1:17-23; 2 Ne. 9:42-43; Isa.
    D. & C. 112:23.   29:9-14.

ideas of our fathers are no longer adequate." As a substitute they offer "humanism," and give an explanation of their "faith" in 15 points. Their 15 points cannot be discussed here; let it suffice to say that they maintain that Christianity has failed, and that "religion must formulate its hopes and plans in the light of the scientific spirit and method." They say the distinction between the sacred and the secular cannot be maintained, that worship of the supreme ruler and religious prayer to him are futile. Men must find expression to their emotions in "a higher sense of personal life and in a cooperative effort to promote social well being." To these "worshipers" the universe is self-existing—it had no creator; Dr. Charles E. Schofield, in his book, *The Adventurous God*, says, "The major trend of unbelief today seems to be more and more towards the position that we very much need a religion, but it must be a religion without a God."[25]

LIQUOR AND TOBACCO FOSTER APOSTATE CONDITIONS. Sad to say, the world today is filled with evil, yes, the so-called Christian world. Mankind has turned from ways of righteousness to the wallowing in the filthiness of *unclean thinking*, degrading habits, soul destroying in their nature. In our country billions of dollars are spent annually for intoxicating liquors and tobacco. *Drunkenness* and the *filthiness* which these evils bring to the human family are undermining, not only the health, but the moral and spiritual bulwarks of humanity. It is deplorable that indulgence in liquor and tobacco are looked upon in such favor even in high places.

Moreover it is a crime that the manufacturers of these poisons can make an appeal to the public which receives a favorable response even from many well meaning persons, by declaring that we should furnish such things to the men in the service of our country. It is not because these interests have any regard for the welfare of these men, or desire to see them succeed in the stu-

---

[25]*Church News*, Aug. 26, 1933, p. 4.

pendous task before them, but because of their unholy greed to fill their iniquitous coffers to overflowing with ill-gotten gains. The weakening of the resistance and the impairment to the bodies of these men who should be physically strong and mentally alert means nothing to these soul destroying agencies.

How Men Bind Themselves with Chains of Hell. I am sure the Lord would incline his ear and hearken to our prayers and be more willing to help us in our battles if we would keep our bodies clean, our minds pure, and have respect for his divine laws. He has made the promise that if the inhabitants of this land, choice above all other lands, would humble themselves and give heed to his commandments, he would fortify this land and give us divine protection.[26]

Unfortunately the people of this land have not been willing to do this thing. They have turned from right-eous ways and the keeping of their bodies clean to ways of evil. Immorality rages, drunkenness prevails from sea to sea, the filthiness of tobacco has debased both men and women, and the stench thereof has ascended to high heaven. *By the practice of these evils humanity is binding itself by the chains of hell.*

Modern Nations Drunken with Iniquity and Abominations. In the very beginning, when the Lord gave the gospel to Adam, he commanded him to teach it to his children. We are told that Satan came among them saying: "Believe it not; and they believed it not, and they loved Satan more than God. And men began from that time forth to be carnal, sensual, and devilish."[27] These tendencies, through the aid of Satan, have pre-vailed in the world ever since. The Savior made this observation: "And this is the condemnation, that light is come into the world, and men loved darkness rather than light, because their deeds were evil."[28]

[26]2 Ne. 10:11-16.   [28]John 3:19.
[27]Moses 5:13.

Another prophet. who dwelt upon this hemisphere, predicted that in our day the wrath of the Almighty would be kindled against the inhabitants of the earth for their iniquities. "But, behold," said Nephi, *"in the last days,* or in the days of the Gentiles—yea, behold all the nations of the Gentiles and also the Jews, both those who shall come upon this land and those who shall be upon other lands, yea, even upon all the lands of the earth, behold, *they will be drunken with iniquity and all manner of abomination*—And when that day shall come they shall be visited of the Lord of Hosts, with thunder and with earthquake, and with a great noise, and with storm, and with tempest, and with the flame of devouring fire."[29]

Any man is very blind indeed if he cannot see and realize that this prophecy is being literally fulfilled. Why can we not turn from our evil ways? Why can we not remember that we are in very deed the children of God and through our obedience and the keeping of our bodies clean, be entitled to the fulness of the blessings of the kingdom of God?

ALL MEN JUDGED BY GOSPEL LAW. It appears that only a few of the human family realize that they were placed on this earth to be tried and proved, to see whether or not they will be obedient to divine commandments. All who prove themselves through their obedience are promised eternal life, which is exaltation in the celestial kingdom.[30] All who are unclean are to be cast out of that kingdom.[31]

John heard the voice of the Lord saying: "He that is unjust, let him be unjust still: and he which is filthy, let him be filthy still: and he that is righteous, let him be righteous still: and he that is holy, let him be holy still."[32]

In the resurrection every creature shall have his

---

[29]2 Ne. 27:1-2.
[30]Abra. 3:22-28; *D. & C.* 98:11-15.
[31]Alma 11:37; 3 Ne. 27:19:20; Moses 6:57.

[32]Rev. 22:11; 2 Ne. 9:16; Alma 41:13-15.

spirit and body restored to become immortal, that they can die no more. These same bodies which we possess here will be the bodies raised from the dead.

It has been written by one of old: "Therefore, all things shall be restored to their proper order, every thing to its natural frame—mortality raised to immortality, corruption to incorruption—raised to endless happiness to inherit the kingdom of God, or to endless misery to inherit the kingdom of the devil, the one on the one hand, the other on the other."[33]

So it will be in that great day of judgment. To the righteous who keep themselves clean, the Lord has said: "He that overcometh shall inherit all things; and I will be his God, and he shall be my son."[34]

NATIONS FALL FOR REJECTING CHRIST. It is true that a country cannot get ahead of its religion. The higher our ideals, the nearer we observe divine law and the stronger are our spiritual forces. *No Christian can forsake the divinity of Jesus Christ and not suffer.* In those lands in Europe where paganism has superseded the Christian ideals, there is bound to come decay and eventually, if there is no repentance, their former greatness will be forgotten. Jesus said, "And why call ye me, Lord, Lord, and do not the things which I say?"[35]

THE WORLD OF CARNALITY

DUTY OF SAINTS IN THIS WICKED WORLD. We are living in a *wicked world* where men's hearts have turned from truth to untruth, from righteousness to wickedness; we are living when men are unrighteously ambitious, seeking for power, when the liberties of the people are in danger. It behooves us as members of the Church to heed the counsels that are given by those who stand as our leaders under Jesus Christ. . . .

[33]Alma 41:4.
[34]*Church News*, Oct. 2, 1943, pp. 4, 12; Rev. 21:7.
[35]Conf. Rep., Apr., 1943, p. 15; Luke 6:46.

We are all aware that we are in imminent danger—danger because Satan rages in the hearts of the people. This has all been predicted, and the predictions are coming true.[36] Antichrist is gaining power, and Satan has put into the hearts of the people—the majority of them—*greed*, and the desire to dominate and take advantage of those who are weak.

Our duty is to keep the commandments of the Lord, to walk uprightly, to defend every principle of truth, to sustain and uphold the Constitution of this great country, to remember the Declaration of Independence, for upon these principles our country was based. They stand at the foundation, the cornerstones of the liberty that our fathers fought for, and which brought to pass, according to the word of the Lord, the redemption of this land by the shedding of blood.[37]

MANKIND CARNAL, SENSUAL, DEVILISH BY NATURE. There is no other course for us to take but the course of righteousness and truth. An ancient prophet on this continent said, *"The natural man is an enemy to God."*[38] The world today has become carnal, as much so now as in the beginning when Adam attempted to teach his children the principles of eternal truth, and Satan came among them and commanded them to believe it not. And we read, *"Men began from that time forth to be carnal, sensual, and devilish."*[39]

Surely we see these indications prevalent in our own land and in foreign lands. Men have become carnal. They have become enemies to God. They are seeking for their own advancement and not for the advancement of the kingdom of God. Let me call your attention to this fact which you, of course, all know, that we are living in the last days, the days of trouble, days of wickedness.

---

[36]2 Ne. 27; 28.
[37]*D. & C.* 101:77-80.

[38]Mosiah 3:19.
[39]Moses 5:13.

Seeming Prosperity in "Their World." If we are living the religion which the Lord has revealed and which we have received, *we do not belong to the world.*[40] We should have no part in all its foolishness. We should not partake of its sins and its errors—errors of philosophy and errors of doctrine, errors in regard to government, or whatever those errors may be—we have no part in it. The only part we have is the keeping of the commandments of God. That is all, being true to every covenant and every obligation that we have entered into and taken upon ourselves.

Brother Spencer W. Kimball in his remarks this morning spoke of a man who could not quite understand when he paid his tithing and kept the Word of Wisdom, was prayerful, and tried to be obedient to all the commandments the Lord had given him, and yet he had to struggle to make a living; while his neighbor violated the Sabbath day, I suppose he smoked and drank; he had what the world would call a *good time,* he paid no attention to the teachings of our Lord and Savior Jesus Christ, and yet he prospered.

You know, we have a great many members of the Church that ponder that over in their hearts and wonder why. Why this man seems to be blessed with all the good things of the earth—incidentally, many of the bad things that he thinks are good—and yet so many members of the Church are struggling, laboring diligently to try to make their way through the world.[41]

The answer is a simple thing. If I sometimes (and once in a while I do) go to a football game or a baseball game or some other place of amusement, invariably I will be surrounded by men and women who are puffing on cigarettes or cigars or dirty pipes. It gets very annoying, and I get a little disturbed. I will turn to Sister Smith, and I will say something to her, and she will say, "Well, now, you know what you have taught me. You are in

---

[40]John 17:14-16.   [41]Mal. 3:13-18.

their world. This is their world." And that sort of brings
me back to my senses. Yes, *we are in their world, but we
do not have to be of it.*

"THEIR WORLD" WILL SOON END.   So, as this is
their world we are living in, they prosper; but, my good
brethren and sisters, *their world is coming to its end.* It
will not be many years. I can say that. I do not know
how many years, but Elijah said when he bestowed his
keys, "By this ye may know that the great and dreadful
day of the Lord is near, even at the doors,"[42] and I am
sure that over a hundred years later I can say that the
end of this world is drawing to its end.

The day will come when we will not have *this* world.
It will be changed. We will get a better world. We will
get one that is righteous, because when Christ comes, he
will cleanse the earth.

Read what is written in our scriptures. Read what
he himself has said. *When he comes, he will cleanse this
earth from all its wickedness, and, speaking of the
Church, he has said that he would send his angels and
they would gather out of his kingdom—which is the
Church—all things that offend.*[43]   Then we are going to
have a new earth, a new heaven. The earth will be renewed for a thousand years, and there shall be peace;
and Christ, whose right it is, shall reign.[44]   Afterwards
will come the death of the earth, its resurrection, its glori-
fication, as the abode of the righteous or they who belong
to the celestial kingdom, and they only shall dwell upon
the face of it.[45]

HERESIES OF APOSTATE CHRISTENDOM

CHRISTENDOM WHOLLY APOSTATE IN 1820.   When
Joseph Smith went in the woods to pray, he received a
revelation of knowledge, truth, and power, which has

---

[42]*D. & C.* 110:16.
[43]*D. & C.* 101:24-25; Matt. 13:41-43.
[44]Tenth Article of Faith; *D. & C.*
     45:57-59; Rev. 5:10; 20:4-6.

[45]Conf. Rep., Apr., 1952, pp. 26-28;
     D. & C. 88:17-31.

been of inestimable value and blessing to the world. What was revealed to him there was given for the overthrow of false creeds and traditions of the ages and led ultimately to the restoration of the everlasting gospel as revealed by our Redeemer during his ministry.

For hundreds of years the world was wrapped *in a veil of spiritual darkness,* until *there was not one fundamental truth belonging to the plan of salvation that was not, in the year 1820, so obscured by false tradition and ceremonies, borrowed from paganism, as to make it unrecognizable; or else it was entirely denied.* By heavenly direction and command of our Lord Jesus Christ, Joseph Smith restored *all* these principles in their primitive beauty and power.

DOCTRINE OF APOSTASY PROVED BY FIRST VISION. Joseph Smith declared that in the year 1820 the Lord revealed to him that all the "Christian" churches were in error, teaching for commandments the doctrines of men.[46] The religious teachers taught that they were in the way of light and truth, notwithstanding their many conflicting creeds.

Amos said, speaking of the latter days: "Behold, the days come, saith the Lord God, that I will send a famine in the land, not a famine of bread, nor a thirst for water, but of hearing the words of the Lord."[47] Paul said: "For the time will come when *they will not endure sound doctrine;* but after their own lusts shall they heap to themselves teachers, having itching ears; And *they shall turn away their ears from the truth, and shall be turned unto fables.*"[48] "Let no man deceive you by any means: for that day [the Second Coming of Christ] shall not come, except there come a *falling away* first, and that man of sin be revealed, the son of perdition."[49] Again we find Joseph Smith in harmony with the *Bible* truth.[50]

---

[46]Jos. Smith 2:18-20.
[47]Amos 8:11.
[48]2 Tim. 4:3-4.

[49]2 Thess. 2:3.
[50]*Era,* vol. 23, pp. 496-498.

APOSTATE DOCTRINES PREVAILING AT TIME OF
FIRST VISION. What was the condition of the religious
world, which professed to believe in and practice the
doctrines of the Redeemer, when the Father and the Son
appeared to Joseph Smith and instructed him? The answer is found in the words of the Lord which are similar
to and a fulfilment of the prediction by Isaiah: "They
draw near to me with their lips, but their hearts are far
from me; they teach for doctrines the commandments of
men, having a form of godliness, but they deny the power
thereof."[51] Some of the leading teachings and practices
were as follows:

1. That God the Father, the Son, and the Holy
Ghost are not three personages, but one ethereal, imma-
terial God, unknown and unknowable to man, who fills
the immensity of space.

2. That the canon of scripture is full and complete,
and since the passing of the apostles there was to be no
more revelation, no opening of the heavens and communications by angels, but the people were left to rely on
what was written in the *Bible* or taught by their priests.

3. That baptism is to cleanse us from "original sin,"
and that all little children had to be "regenerated" by
baptism and if not baptized they will perish.

4. That baptism is an ordinance acceptable to the
Lord by sprinkling or pouring water on the heads of
unbaptized adults or infants.

5. That men may take upon themselves the authority to be ministers of the word of God, without a divine
appointment by one duly authorized by Jesus Christ.

6. That the organization of the Church as established in the days of Jesus Christ and his apostles is no
longer necessary; there were to be no more apostles,
prophets, and gifts of the spirit.

7. That man was not created in the image of God
in form, for God is not an anthropomorphic being.

---

[51]Jos. Smith 2:19; Isa 29:13.

8. Other doctrines, such as the necessity for keys for the restoration of Israel, the need of the coming of Elijah, as proclaimed in the scriptures, are not necessary.[52]

APOSTATE DOCTRINE DAMNING NON-CHRISTIANS. The Lord declared to Nicodemus, "Except a man be born of water and of the Spirit, he cannot enter into the kingdom of God."[53] It must be accepted by all who profess belief in our Savior that this edict is true and final. However, in the centuries which are passed, and even now in many so-called Christian communities, a wrong application of this doctrine has led to very serious errors and unwittingly to the committing of very grievous sins. I refer to the doctrine which proclaims that all who in the flesh have not professed belief in our Lord, or heard of him before death removed them from the earth, are forever damned and without means of escape from the torments of hell. This false conception and application of gospel truth has been a teaching of so-called Christianity from the earliest centuries of our era, but it never was a part of the gospel of Jesus Christ.

DANTE DEPICTS APOSTATE VIEW OF HELL. In his *Divine Comedy,* Dante depicts the doctrine of damnation for unfortunate souls who died without a knowledge of Christ, as that doctrine was taught in the 13th century. According to the story, Dante is lost in the woods where he is met by the Roman poet, Virgil, who promises to show him the punishment of hell and purgatory, and later, he is to have a view of paradise.

He follows the Roman poet through hell and later into Limbo, which (according to the story) is the *first circle of hell.* Here are confined the souls of those who lived virtuous and honorable lives, but because they were not baptized, these souls merit punishment and are denied *forever* the blessings of salvation. As Dante looks upon these miserable souls in the upper stratum of hell, and

---

[52]*Era,* vol. 55, p. 82.   [53]John 3:5.

sees, as the story says, "Many and vast, Of men, women
and infants," he marvels. His guide asks the question,
"Inquirest thou not what spirits Are those which thou
beholdest?"

Dante, showing a desire to know, the guide continues: "I would thou know, that these of sin Were
blameless; and if aught they merited, It profits not, since
baptism was not theirs, The portal of thy faith. If they
before The Gospel lived, they served not God aright;
And among them such am I. For these defects, And for
no other evil, we are lost; Only so far afflicted, that we
live Desiring without hope."

In answer to the earnest inquiry of his mortal guest,
who desires to know if any thus punished ever had the
privilege of coming forth from this sad condition of torment, the spirit-poet declares that the righteous, who
had known God from our first parents down to the time
of Christ, have been "to bliss exalted," but of these un-
fortunates who never heard of Christ, he says, "Be thou
assured, no spirit of human kind was ever saved."[54]

But Dante was not the author of this unfortunate
and erroneous doctrine. It had come from the earliest
days of apostasy from the true teachings of Jesus Christ.
. . . What a shame it is that this same awful doctrine has
come resounding down from that distant day of spiritual
darkness, and has been made to ring its terrible peal of
torment repeatedly in the ears of earnest souls who have
sought the salvation of loved ones who have gone before.

APOSTATE DOCTRINE OF PREDESTINATION. The
gospel of Christ is the gospel of *mercy*. It is also the
the gospel of *justice*. It must be so, for it comes from
a God of mercy, not from a cruel monster, who as some
religionists still believe and declare: "By the decree of
God, for the manifestation of his glory some men and
angels are predestined unto everlasting life, and others

---

[54]Dante, *The Divine Comedy*, English translator, Henry Francis Case,
pp. 14-15.

fore-ordained to everlasting death. These angels and men, thus predestined and fore-ordained, are particularly and unchangeably designed; and their number is so certain and definite that it cannot be either increased or diminished."[55]

Is it not horrible to contemplate that gospel truth has been perverted and defiled until it has become such an abomination? Justice, as well as mercy, pleads for the dead who have died without a knowledge of the gospel. How could justice be administered if all the untold multitudes who have died without a knowledge of Jesus Christ should be everlastingly consigned, without hope, to the damnation of hell, even if torment be in the first circle of the place of the damned? The scriptures say, "Justice and judgment are the habitation of thy throne: mercy and truth shall go before thy face."[56] The mercy and love of a just God are reaching out after all his children.[57]

FALSE EASTER WORSHIP. Today, April 8, 1917, throughout the world, the people of the various Christian denominations are assembling in their churches because it is Easter Sunday. They have not assembled there because they have faith in the literal resurrection of the Lord; they have not assembled there because they believe in the literal resurrection of all mankind through the atonement of our Lord, and they have not assembled because they accept him as the Son of God. (I want to make honorable exceptions, because there are some who have done so, but I speak generally.)

They have assembled there for a very different purpose—because it is the custom, because in many cases, among the sisters, they want to show their millinery and the styles of their clothing, their dress. They are there more in the nature of a *social function* and *fashion show* than to worship the Lord, and I say this notwithstanding

---

[55]*The New Schaff-Herzog Encyclopedia of Religious Knowledge,* pp. 191-198.
[56]Ps. 89:14.
[57]*Church News,* Apr. 22, 1933, p. 3.

the expression that appears in one of our morning papers to the effect that anybody who expressed this kind of an idea is cynical and expresses a perverted opinion.

The people of the various nations, who call themselves Christian, today do not worship the Lord Jesus Christ as the Redeemer of the world to the extent that they did in the day of the organization of the true Church. The doctrines today that prevail are in opposition to that truth, and ministers stand before their people denying the atonement of Christ, and hence showing their lack of faith in and understanding of the resurrection of the Son of God, and denying the universal resurrection which the scriptures promise shall come to all mankind.[58]

MODERNISTIC APOSTATE PHILOSOPHIES

EDUCATION, POLITICS, GOVERNMENT LINKED TO APOSTASY. Throughout the world today, as we have already been informed by a number of the speakers, there is commotion and a spirit of unrest; and the people, many of them, feel that it is something to their credit to hold *radical views,* to consider themselves to be *progressive,* and to make attack upon things that have stood and have endured throughout the ages. This tendency is not alone in the *political world.* It is found in the world of *education,* of *religion,* of *government,* of *business* and everywhere. Men are departing from the well worn paths, no matter how good they are, and feel that conservatism is a reproach; that it is the duty of man to do away with that which is old, or which has been established, and find something that is new.

We stand practically alone in the world, yes, absolutely alone in the world, representing the truth of the living God, declaring to all men the principles of eternal truth which do not change. The gospel of Jesus Christ is not new in the sense in which the world looks upon things as being new, for it has endured through the ages,

---

[58]Conf. Rep., Apr., 1917, p. 60.

not merely since the days of the advent of the Son of God, but from the beginning of the world, for the plan of salvation was prepared for the benefit of man, and declared unto him in the beginning. These principles do not change; they cannot change; they must endure immutably through all time.

The Christian world may be divided into two camps —one bitterly opposing the other, one calling itself the progressive or modernist division, the other calling itself the fundamentalist division. They may think they are founded upon the truth of the gospel as it has been established. But we stand for the revelations of God as they have been revealed in this dispensation (known as the dispensation of the fulness of times), unchangeable, immutable, enduring forever, because they are eternal.[59]

EVOLUTION, HIGHER CRITICISM PART OF APOSTASY. These modernists, who are instructing and leading astray the people of this and other lands, reject the doctrine of the atonement of Christ; they reject the resurrection of the Son of God and consequently the resurrection of all mankind. They have discarded entirely the miracles of the scriptures and make light of the saving ordinances of the gospel which the Lord declared to be so essential to our salvation; and in the stead thereof they have accepted the theories and notions advanced by modern scientists which are evidently false, and have taken to their hearts and hugged to their bosoms the falsehoods set forth in the theories of *evolution* and of *higher criticism* of the scriptures. And why have they done this thing? Because the simple truth, which is understood by the Spirit of God and not understood and comprehended by the spirit of man, does not appeal to their *reason*. . . .

REASON: FALSE GOD OF MODERNISTIC APOSTASY. All manner of *theory* and *error* they teach to the world, declaring that we cannot accept anything, only that which

---

[59]Conf. Rep., Oct., 1924, p. 100.

our *reason* teaches us. Therefore, if reason teaches me that baptism is not essential to salvation and it teaches you that it is, we are both right, which is a contradiction which cannot be true; and unless reason teaches us the same thing and we are agreed, both cannot have the truth and we are not in the narrow path, we are not in fellowship with God.

We must walk in holiness of life, in the light and in the truth, with proper understanding which comes through the gift and power of the Holy Ghost which is promised to all who will believe unto repentance and receive the words of eternal life. If we are in fellowship with this Spirit, then we walk in the light and have fellowship with God. He who is without the guiding light of the Spirit of God is in the midst of darkness and cannot with his reason, unaided and unenlightened, search and find out God.[60]

CHURCH TO TRIUMPH OVER MODERNISTIC APOSTATE VIEWS. President Rudger Clawson this afternoon read to us some views that are expressed today by certain ministers, religionists who call themselves *modernists,* and they appear to be in the ascendency; their doctrines are growing and are finding place in the hearts of the people, and the true doctrines of Christ and the testimony that Jesus is the Son of God is diminishing, is dying out in the world. It may be true, as one divine stated, that the Christian era is at an end, and the Church is in the course of dissolution, if he had reference to the so-called Christian churches of the day, because their doctrine is spurious; it is not the gospel of Jesus Christ, but a manmade system. But *Christianity, pure and undefiled, is not in the course of dissolution; it is not dying out, it is becoming more firmly rooted in the earth, and must do so, and shall continue until it shall fill the earth, for so it has been predicted.*[61]

---

[60]Conf. Rep., Apr., 1916, pp. 73-74;   [61]Dan. 2:44; *D. & C.* 65:1-6.
    1 Cor. 2.

However, true Christianity, so far as the latter-days are concerned, is very young, for it has only been since the year 1830 that the Church of Jesus Christ has been organized in the earth, and the gospel restored, containing the gifts and the blessings and the graces that existed in the Church in primitive days, and that Church with its doctrines of the gospel of Christ, shall grow.[62]

---

[62]Conf. Rep., Apr., 1924, p. 41.

CHAPTER 15

APOSTASY FROM LATTER-DAY KINGDOM

APOSTASY WITHIN THE CHURCH

CHURCH SURROUNDED BY APOSTATE INFLUENCES. Because of the love of the things of the world and the enticing influence of the powers of darkness, we (meaning Christian people generally) have departed from the strait path which leads to life and which our Lord has said few men find because they love darkness rather than light, their deeds being evil.[1] We have permitted the *philosophies of men,* which deny the divinity of Jesus Christ and mock at the sacred ordinances of the gospel, to enter into our *schools,* and *businesses,* and our *homes,* thus weakening our faith and our reverence for our Creator. We have forgotten that man was created in the image of God, that the scriptures declare that we are his offspring, and that we are commanded to seek first the kingdom of God and his righteousness.[2]

We Latter-day Saints have received the restored gospel and have made covenant with the Lord that we will serve him and accept him as the God of this land. Nevertheless, I want to call your attention to the fact that *the ways of the world have crept in among us* and are becoming established in the midst of the people of Zion. Right here in this city (Salt Lake City), which at one time was indeed a city of the saints, but is that no longer, can be found all manner of *abomination* and *iniquity.* The *ideas, theories,* the *fashions and ungodliness* of the world, their *sins* and *evil practices* are to be found within the borders of our cities.

---

[1]John 3:19. [2]Conf. Rep., Apr., 1943, p. 13; Matt. 6:33.

SAINTS MUST BE ON GUARD AGAINST WORLDLY INFLUENCES. Unless we are on our guard we are in constant danger. *This people who are under solemn covenants to keep the commandments of the Lord are threatened by the sins and worldly abominations of this generation,* and many among us are liable to be led astray, unless we keep a careful vigil and hedge them about by every means at our command. We have been called out from the world into the kingdom of God, and while we are yet in the world, we are not of the world in the sense that we are under any necessity to partake of their evil customs, and fashions, their follies, false doctrines and theories, which are in conflict with the spirit of truth.[3]

Today is the Sabbath day, and yet in this city the theatres, moving pictures, and places of amusement are running full blast as they are on every Sabbath day throughout the year, because of the selfishness of men and their disregard of the command of the Lord to obey his law and keep his day holy.[4] We are inflicted not only with these temptations, but they come to us in many other forms, and if we are not aware, there is danger of our losing the Spirit of the Lord and falling into transgression by yielding to temptations that may not appear to us as being of much consequence.

But little things lead to greater, and step by step we are carried away from that which is right and just, and gradually we become blind to the truth. The Lord has called upon us to be a sober-minded people, not given to much laughter, frivolity, and light mindedness, but to consider thoughtfully and thoroughly the things of his kingdom that we may be prepared in all things to understand the glorious truths of the gospel and be prepared for blessings to come.[5]

MODERN CONDITIONS ENCOURAGE UNRIGHTEOUSNESS. It seems to me as I reflect upon these things that it

---

[3]John 17:14-16.
[4]Ex. 20:8-11; D. & C. 59:9-20.
[5]Conf. Rep., Oct., 1916, pp. 69-70; D. & C. 88:67-69.

is perhaps a little more difficult for a man to be righteous today than it has been in some other periods of the world's history. I think this because of modern conditions with all the temptations and evils that now confront us at every turn. If this is the case, then Latter-day Saints should be just a little more prayerful, a little more diligent, and seek the Lord just a little more closely, that we might be kept free from all the evils that now prevail. The fact that we are baptized and have a standing in good fellowship in the Church will not insure for us our salvation. Evils may come upon *us*, for the Lord has said by way of warning, "Therefore let the church take heed and pray always, lest they fall into temptation."[6]

LORD FORGOTTEN IN DAY OF PROSPERITY. In the days of our prosperity, when we are at peace, when we have the luxuries as well as the necessities of life, there may be a tendency on our part to forget the Lord. This seems to be a failing of humanity. We are taught this lesson all down through the ages so far as the people of the Lord are concerned, as we read of them in the holy scriptures. In Palestine as well as upon this continent, when the people were prospered, they forgot the Lord. They turned from him and felt self-sufficient, rather than to feel the spirit of humility and to put faith in the Lord and to thank him for his blessings.[7]

The crime of ingratitude is one of the most prevalent and I might say at the same time one of the greatest with which mankind is afflicted. The more the Lord blesses us the less we love him. That is the way men show their gratitude unto the Lord for his mercies and his blessings towards them.[8]

FOLLOW CHURCH, NOT THE WORLD. A great many of the members of the Church evidently do not realize the importance of the blessings we receive in the temples of the Lord. I wish we all loved the gospel to

[6]Conf. Rep., Oct., 1927, pp. 142-143; [7]D. & C. 101:1-8.
   D. & C. 20:33.   [8]Conf. Rep., Apr., 1929, p. 54.

the extent that we would be willing to do anything the Lord asks of us irrespective of what the *world* thinks or does. Why can not the Latter-day Saints uphold the standards and the regulations of the Church with united effort notwithstanding what the world might do or think? With some of us it is the *custom* to do very much as the world does. We *dress* as the world does. We seek its *pleasures;* we follow its *customs;* and there is no question in my mind that these things do bring us somewhat in conflict with things the Lord has taught and commanded us to do.[9]

FOOLISH BELIEFS EVEN IN CHURCH. We should have some sympathy for people taught in the vagaries and foolish traditions of the world, when we discover how tenaciously members of the Church cling to foolish notions in spite of all that is written.[10]

APOSTASY BINDS WITH CHAINS OF SPIRITUAL DARKNESS. The man who receives the light of truth and then turns away, loses the light which he had, and if he continues in that course, eventually he will be bound by the *chains of spiritual darkness.* Darkness will take the place of truth, as the truth becomes gradually dimmed, until he has lost knowledge of spiritual things.[11] He who walks in the light of truth receives more truth until he is glorified in divine truth—the truth that saves.[12]

EVIL SPEAKING AGAINST LORD'S ANOINTED

UNGODLY MEN DEFAME AUTHORITIES OF CHURCH. It is a serious thing for any member of this Church to raise his voice against the priesthood, or to hold the priesthood in disrespect; for the Lord will not hold such guiltless; so he has promised, and he will fulfil. . . .

It seems to be the *heritage of the ungodly,* of the *bigoted,* and of those who *love iniquity,* to sit in judgment

[9]*Gen. & Hist. Mag.,* vol. 21, p. 97.
[10]Pers. Corresp.; 2 Ne. 28:14.
[11]Alma 12:9-11.
[12]*Church News,* Mar. 30, 1940, p. 5; D. & C. 50:23-29; 76:1-10.

and to place themselves as dictators, saying what shall be done and what shall be said by the authorities of the Church. They accuse the brethren of all manner of iniquity, dissimulation, falsehood, and try to cause a division between them and the people over whom they preside. They take unto themselves the prerogative of saying what shall and what shall not be the doctrine of the Church, what shall and what shall not be the government of the Church, when it concerns them not at all.

JUDGMENT AWAITS CHURCH MEMBERS WHO CRITICIZE BRETHREN. But it is not of this class particularly that I desire to refer, but to those members of the Church who have entered into the waters of baptism and have made covenants before the Lord that they will observe his laws and respect his priesthood, who have been persuaded, or who are in danger of being persuaded, by such characters.

Occasionally, when a man has himself committed sin and has lost the spirit of the gospel, he will raise his voice against the actions of the authorities who preside over the Church; he will call them in question, sit in judgment upon them and condemn them. I wish to raise a warning voice to all such who hold membership in the Church, and say unto them, that they had better repent and turn unto the Lord, lest his judgments come upon them, lest they lose the faith and be turned from the truth. . . .

It is a serious thing for a man holding membership in this Church to say in his heart, or openly, that these men holding the keys of the kingdom have sinned, when they have not sinned, and cause dissension, if it is in his power to do so among his brethren. *The judgments of the Lord will overtake him.* He will be brought in question before the Lord, and shall be cast out and find his place among the unbelievers; and those who flattered him and encouraged him to raise up his heel against his brethren will turn from him and leave him to his shame.[13]

WISE LEADERSHIP OF BRETHREN. I wish to testify that God has called these men, that he has appointed them, that he has given unto them the revelations of his mind and will, that they have the inspiration of his Spirit, that they are teaching and leading this people in truth. That is the conviction of every Latter-day Saint who has the gospel at heart.

What time, since the organization of the Church, have any of the brethren exercising the Spirit of the Lord, ever taught this people that which was false? When have they ever said unto you that you should do that which was not right; that which would not make you better citizens and better members of the kingdom of God?

You cannot, nor can any man, in righteousness, point to the time when any of them have wilfully stated anything that was contrary to the principles of righteousness, or that did not tend to make the people better in every way, that did not build them up in their salvation, temporally as well as spiritually. . . .

ABUSE AND EVIL CRITICISM NOT OF GOD. Do not be deceived by those falsifiers, those men whose hearts are filled with evil, and who say that the authorities have sinned when they have not sinned, who are themselves in the bondage of iniquity and are trying to destroy this work. So far as those men are concerned, who try to tear down and destroy, they do not preach that which they themselves believe. They do not teach the people that which is true or try to show them a better way, instead, they heap abuse upon the heads of the authorities of the Latter-day Saints.

Whenever you find a man who spends his time abusing his neighbors, trying to tear down other people, you put it down that that man is not possessed of the

[13]*D. & C.* 121:11-25.

Spirit of the Lord. But when a man tries to build up,
when he tries to show you a better way, even though
he be deceived, you may know that he is honest; but
never the man who tries to tear you to pieces, who tries
to destroy, without offering you something better in
return. Never is such a man honest.[14]

TEACH CHILDREN TO SUSTAIN AUTHORITIES. In
our homes do we talk before our children and criticize
the bishop of the ward, or the president of the stake, or
one of the General Authorities? Do we say things in
their presence which ought not to be said? Do we make
slighting remarks about the principles of the gospel? If
we do, we are not bringing up our children in light and
truth.[15] Are we guilty of these little slight offenses in
the home, and have we been trying to teach our children
to do something other than we do ourselves? If we do
we are making a failure of it.

In other words, to be frank, do you teach your children that they must not drink tea or coffee, and then you
do it yourselves? Do the fathers use tobacco, and then
try and train their boys not to use it? It does not work;
you cannot teach one thing and do another. Example
is the way we teach the gospel.[16]

EVIL OF BROAD-MINDEDNESS

BROAD-MINDEDNESS LEADS TO APOSTASY. I would
like for a few minutes to offer a few observations in
regard to the question of *tolerance* and *broad-mindedness.*
We hear so much in these days about being tolerant
and broad-minded. I suppose the world will never know
how many crimes have been committed through a mis-
interpretation and misunderstanding of these terms.
Satan is very broad-minded, extremely so as long
as he can get people to do evil and avoid the truth.
He will teach any kind of theory, or principle, or doctrine,

14Conf. Rep., Oct., 1910, pp. 39-41.   16*Rel. Soc. Mag.*, vol. 18, p. 687.
15*D. & C.* 93:40.

if it doesn't conform to the fundamental things of life—
the gospel of Jesus Christ. He is even willing to teach
some truth, if he can join that truth with error, and by
teaching the error with the truth lead men astray. This
is how broad-minded he is, and *that is how the apostasy,
came about in the primitive Church.* . . .

TOLERATING UNTRUTH LEADS TO APOSTASY. *Tolerance is not indulgence.* I think sometimes the terms
have been confused. *We must not get so broad-minded
that we would throw over the fundamental things of the
gospel of Jesus Christ.* I heard of one man—and I think
he filled a mission—who made the statement, as the report
comes to me, that in this enlightened age the Church of
Jesus Christ should get away from the narrow idea that
baptism for the remission of sins in water is essential to
salvation, that we should be *broader* than that.

Another man, with similar views, made the statement, so the report comes to me, that we shall have to
cease believing in the anthropomorphic God; we must quit
thinking of God as being in the form in which man is
made. He ridiculed the idea by saying, "Can we worship
a God who has to eat, who has to sleep, who has to take
a bath?"

Of course, in thinking of God as a person in whose
image we are created, we do not necessarily have to think
of him as having to conform to all the conditions of mortal
existence to which we, under present conditions, are
forced to subscribe. But is there anything wrong in
thinking of a God who eats? He did eat and has promised to eat again. What is wrong in it? He bathes, at
least in fire, so he tells us.[17] We are his offspring, and
he has given us commandments to serve him in the name
of his only Begotten Son.[18]

SALVATION AND BLESSINGS COME BY OBEDIENCE
TO LAW. Moreover, we know, because it has been re-

---

[17]*D. & C.* 29:12; 2 Thess. 1:8; Heb.   [18]*D. & C.* 59:5.
   12:29.

vealed, that all kingdoms have a law given, and that includes the kingdom of God. It is not something that stands apart from all other kingdoms in this regard, and he himself has said: "Unto every kingdom is given a law; and unto every law there are certain bounds also and conditions. All beings who abide not in those conditions are not justified."[19]

The Lord is very tolerant, yet he declares that we are bound by law, and if we violate the law we are not justified, and must remain filthy still.[20] You might just as well try to destroy the law of gravity, or say it is useless, that it has filled its purpose and is worn out, as to say that baptism is not essential to salvation. I believe in being tolerant, but I believe that tolerance will teach me to observe and keep the law and constantly abide in it, and not to make excuses for my wrong doing by saying I am *broad-minded*. . . .

I am satisfied, and I know that the kingdom of God is governed by a definite, fixed law, that cannot be controverted. We cannot change it because we perhaps become *modern* and say we are *broad-minded*, as some people understand broad-mindedness and tolerance to be. It does not change the fact in the least that if we would receive the kingdom of God and enter into its exaltation, we must comply with the fundamental truths, the laws upon which that kingdom is established. We have them; we are the advocates of these principles; they are in our keeping.

Why, bless your soul, the whole world ought to come to us with songs of everlasting joy, singing their hosannas to embrace the truth; but I wonder sometimes if we do not stress a little too much the fact that they today are receiving us in kindness. Let us not pat ourselves upon the back too much because we have little opposition. I see a danger in it; but let us go on keeping the commandments of the Lord in humility and truth, and

---

[19]D. & C. 88:38-39.   [20]D. & C. 88:32-35.

teaching the people the correct principles, drawing them
to us by our lives as well as by our precepts.[21]

AMUSEMENTS AND DANCING

DANGERS OF PUBLIC DANCE HALLS. I believe that
it is necessary for the saints to have amusements, but it
must be of the *proper kind*. I do not believe the Lord
intends and desires that we should pull a long face and
look sanctimonious and hypocritical. I think he expects
us to be happy and of cheerful countenance, but he does
not expect of us the indulgence in boisterous and unseem-
ly conduct and the seeking after the vain and foolish
things which amuse and entertain the *world*. He has
commanded us to the contrary for our own good and
eternal welfare.

I deplore the fact that these modern dances, some
of which had their origin in unsavory places, have come
among us. I regret beyond measure the *public dance*
which, in my judgment, in its baneful results—the destruction of good morals and virtue—is second only to
the saloon. This evil is growing and taking root in the
stakes of Zion, in the communities of Latter-day Saints.

There is today an excess in dancing—in some communities one or two dances each week, which is not good
no matter how innocent the dance may be. In these public
dance halls, which are run for the making of money, the
people in some localities, without regard to character or
standing of the individual, permit anyone to enter without
question, if he will pay the price of admission. This is
an abominable custom and should not be tolerated by
members of the Church in the settlements under their
control.

MODERN LIFE ENCOURAGES UNWHOLESOME REC-
REATION. The world is drifting. I do not believe, I
cannot feel, as I read the signs of the times, ponder over
things that come before me for consideration, that this

[21]Conf. Rep., Oct., 1936, pp. 60-62.

world is growing better; I do not believe it for a minute.
I believe that we are drifting. Many things are tolerated
today that would not have been tolerated for a moment
20 years ago. New problems have arisen with which
we must now contend that we never dreamed of even
in the days of my youth. We have evils in the world
now to combat that have been brought into existence
through modern invention and discovery, such as the
moving picture show, joy riding in automobiles and the
rapid means of transportation from place to place as a
means of seeking pleasure during the hours of both day
and night.

The moving picture should be of the greatest value
in the education and instruction of the people, and would
teach us history, geography and science, to the very best
advantage, if properly presented, but to the contrary, it
is largely controlled by unscrupulous men who give to
the public *a flood of miserable stuff that excites their
passions and appeals to the baser side of man.*

PARENTS TO SUPERVISE AMUSEMENTS OF CHIL-
DREN. I think the parents in Israel should protect their
children; they should have a little more watchcare over
them; they should pay a little more attention to them and
train them a little more carefully in the principles of the
gospel, both by precept and by example. Children should
not be permitted to go unprotected and without proper
escort to places of amusement, no matter where or how
harmless the amusement may be. . . .

Our children will have to be taught to discern between good and evil, otherwise in many respects they
will not be able to understand why they are not permitted
to indulge in practices that are common with their neighbors. Unless they are instructed in the doctrines of the
Church, they will not, perhaps, understand why there is
any harm in the Sunday concert, a Sunday theatre,
picture show, ball game, or something of that kind, when
their playmates, without restraint and with encourage-

ment, indulge in these things forbidden of the Lord on his holy day.

The parents are responsible for the proper teaching of their children; the Lord will condemn the parents if their children grow up outside of the influence of the principles of the gospel of our Lord Jesus Christ. I want to see righteousness prevail throughout Zion. I do not believe that it is necessary in the least for us to partake of all the notions and customs of the world. We should give our attention a little more seriously to the things of the kingdom of God. We are living in the latter-days when, it has been predicted, perilous times would come. These perilous times are here, which fact should cause us thoughtful reflection.[22]

GOSPEL PERMITS LAUGHTER AND MERRIMENT. We should not get the idea from this scripture[23] that the Lord is displeased with us when we laugh, when we have merriment, *if it is on the right occasions.* He has said, however, that *in our solemn assemblies such things as light-mindedness, laughter, and merriment are out of order.* We should cease from all light speeches, laughter, and wrongful thoughts and desires, from all things which will detract from the teachings and the influence of the Spirit of the Lord.[24]

EVILS OF CARD PLAYING

CHURCH OFFICIALLY CONDEMNS CARD PLAYING. We have been taught all the days of our lives that *card playing is not good and is contrary to the order and discipline of the Church.* The authorities have called upon the people, and it is published in our magazines, to refrain from this *evil indulgence.* Notwithstanding all this, we find among us some who look upon card playing as a very harmless pastime. It is not harmless, but very harmful. It shows a lack of obedience to the counsels

22Conf. Rep., Oct., 1916, pp. 70-72.   24Conf. Rep., Oct., 1929, p. 62.
23D. & C. 88:119-121.

of the Lord on the part of members who indulge in this evil, and if nothing more could be said of it, it is at least a most pernicious waste of time that could be employed in some better occupation.

I believe in physical sport, I believe in recreation and amusement of the kind that is beneficial to the body and the mind of man, and that play of the proper kind is good and ought to be indulged in at times, especially by those whose work is such that they do not get the necessary physical exercise required by their bodies. I do not believe in the waste of good time in practicing anything which is condemned by the authorities of the Church, as they give the counsel as it comes to them through the inspiration of the Spirit of the Lord. The Latter-day Saints should put their trust in their leaders and follow the teachings of the authorities of the Church, for they speak unto them with the voice of prophecy and inspiration.[25]

GAMBLING: AN EVIL DISEASE. Nothing good comes out of card games or games of chance. There are numerous ways in which we may obtain wholesome amusement and recreation which is beneficial to both body and mind. In games where cards are used, usually "stakes" are played for, and betting is done. Someone will obtain the "stakes," but no one really wins, for the one who obtains the "stakes" has lost part of his manhood which is difficult to regain.

There seems to be an urge in human nature which leads many men and women to seek to obtain something for nothing, and many have risked their hard earned sustenance on the altar of chance, hoping to win a fortune which they have not earned. There is a lure in all games of chance which Satan places before them, and in their greed or selfish desire for gain they take the uncertain bait far less innocently than does a fish which grabs the angler's hook.

The regular standard playing cards are used in gambling games. They are found in questionable resorts and gambling dens. Young people who have learned to play the games in their own homes or at card clubs with innocent intent too frequently are lured into questionable places where gambling prevails. Such games of chance are usually associated with cigarettes and beer, and those who indulge in cards acquire also the tobacco and drinking evils.

Card playing becomes a habit just as much as smoking and drinking. I remember a neighbor of mine who in his earlier days was addicted to gambling. Later in his life he repented and joined the Church. One day before a group of which I was a member, he emphatically impressed upon our minds the fact that *gambling is a disease which fastens itself so tenaciously upon those who indulge that they seldom quit.* Its influence upon character is just the same as the use of tobacco and strong drink. He advised all to shun all card playing and games of chance lest the habit would destroy them.

BRIGHAM YOUNG COUNSELS AGAINST CARD PLAYING. Card playing and all other games of chance should be avoided as the gate of destruction. All such practices have been discountenanced by the authorities of the Church from the beginning of our history. When the Mormon Battalion was called into the service of the country, President Brigham Young addressed the volunteers and said that he wished them to prove themselves to be the best soldiers in the service of the United States. He admonished the captains to be fathers to the men in their companies and to manage the officers and men by the power of the priesthood. They should keep themselves clean, teach chastity and gentility. There was to be no swearing, and no man was to be insulted. They were to avoid contention with Missourians—their enemies—and all other persons. They were to take their *Bibles* and copies of the *Book of*

Mormon with them and study them but not impose their beliefs on others. They were to avoid card playing, and if they had cards with them, they were to burn them. If they would follow this instruction, he promised them that they would not be called on to shed the blood of their fellow men.

JOSEPH F. SMITH CONDEMNS CARD PLAYING. President Joseph F. Smith has given this wholesome advice: "While a simple game of cards in itself may be harmless, it is a fact that by immoderate repetition it ends in an infatuation for chance schemes, in habits of excess, in waste of precious time, in dulling and stupor of the mind, and in the *complete destruction of religious feeling.* These are serious results, evils that should and must be avoided by the Latter-day Saints. Then again, there is a grave danger that lurks in persistent card playing, which begets the spirit of gambling, of speculation and that awakens the dangerous desire to get something for nothing."

Again: "Card playing is an excessive pleasure; it is intoxicating, and therefore in the nature of a vice. It is naturally the companion of the cigarette and the wine glass, and the latter leads to the poolroom and the gambling hall. Few men and women indulge in the dangerous pastime of the card table without compromising their business affairs and the higher responsibilities of life. Tell me what amusements you like best and whether your amusements have been a ruling passion in your life, and I will tell you what you are. Few indulge frequently in card playing in whose lives it does not become a ruling passion."[26]

MAN ACCOUNTABLE TO LORD FOR IDLE WORDS AND ACTS. The Lord said: "A good man out of the good treasure of the heart bringeth forth good things: and an evil man out of the evil treasure bringeth forth evil things.

---

[26]Joseph F. Smith, *Gospel Doctrine,*
   4th ed., pp. 412-413.

But I say unto you, That every idle word that men shall speak, they shall give account thereof in the day of judgment. For by thy words thou shalt be justified, and by thy words thou shalt be condemned."[27] *This being true of words that are idle, may we not say that idle acts spent in evil practices will merit the same reward?*

This does not mean that the Lord frowns on innocent amusement and the time spent in wholesome games. The human body needs relaxation, and this can be obtained in a legitimate way. For this purpose, in part, the Mutual Improvement Associations have been organized where proper forms of amusement and entertainment may be taught, and thereby the body strengthened and the mind quickened and developed.

PROPER AND WHOLESOME RECREATION ENCOURAGED. In one of the darkest hours in the history of the Church, when the weary members were crossing the plains having been driven from their homes, the Lord through President Brigham Young said to them: "If thou art merry, praise the Lord with singing, with music, with dancing, and with a prayer of praise and thanksgiving. If thou art sorrowful, call on the Lord thy God with supplication, that your souls may be joyful."[28]

The Prophet Joseph Smith engaged in manly sports on the few occasions that came to him. President Brigham Young and his brethren built the Salt Lake Theatre and the Social Hall. The drama, the dance, and other entertainments were given to the members of the Church, and by this means they were edified and strengthened; all such entertainments were opened and closed with prayer. The auxiliary organizations encourage athletic contests and sports under proper supervision and regulations. *Our people are encouraged, not curtailed, in every kind of needful recreation and amusement; but all things which the world seeks, leading to evil, such as card playing, raffling, and indulging in playing machines*

---

[27]Matt. 12:35-37.   [28]D. & C. 136:28-29.

*of chance, are frowned upon as destructive of morals and
abiding faith in that which is just and true.*[29]

FATE OF APOSTATES

MANY DEGREES OF CONVERSION AND FAITHFUL-
NESS. If a member of the Church should apostatize, or
fall away, and should reject his covenants, to which
degree of glory will he be relegated?

It is impossible to state the degree of reward or punishment which shall be measured out in each individual
case of transgression or apostasy. All do not receive the
same light and knowledge when they come into the
Church, because some are more diligent and faithful than
others in observing the commandments. Our Savior has
given us an excellent illustration of this in the parable
of the sower.[30] Some men receive a thorough knowledge
and testimony of the truth through faithful diligence and
obedience to the gospel. The Spirit of the Lord rests
upon them and they can truthfully say that they know
that Jesus is the Christ and Redeemer of the world.
Others do not receive such great light and testimony,
because they are less diligent. They believe that Jesus
is the Son of God and accept the truth, but do not have
a perfect understanding.

It is possible also that some have come into the
Church because the doctrines appeal to them as being
logical and consistent, but they never exert themselves
to get the Spirit of the Lord. Others have come into the
Church because of ulterior motives, and such never do
comprehend the light and seldom remain, for disappoint-
ment is bound to come when their objective is not attained,
and they fall away again.

The Lord declares in one of the revelations: "To
some it is given by the Holy Ghost to know that Jesus
Christ is the Son of God, and that he was crucified for
the sins of the world. To others it is given to believe on

---

[29]*Era,* vol. 58, pp. 302-303.   [30]Matt. 13:1-9, 18-23.

their words, that they also might have eternal life if they continue faithful."[31]

UNREPENTED SIN ALWAYS CAUSES SPIRIT TO WITHDRAW. Almost without exception when a person leaves the Church, it is due to *transgression*. The Spirit of the Lord will not dwell in unclean tabernacles, and *when the Spirit is withdrawn, darkness supersedes the light, and apostasy will follow. This is one of the greatest evidences of the divinity of this latter-day work. In other organizations men may commit all manner of sin and still retain their membership, because they have no companionship with the Holy Ghost to lose; but in the Church when a man sins and continues without repentance, the Spirit is withdrawn, and when he is left to himself the adversary takes possession of his mind and he denies the faith.*

It is possible for a man who has received a perfect understanding of the truth and has walked in the light of the Holy Spirit to fall away through transgression. But *when he turns away, he still knows that he once had the light.* The Lord has said of such: "All those who know my power, and have been made partakers thereof, and suffered themselves through the power of the devil to be overcome, and to deny the truth and defy my power —They are they who are the sons of perdition, of whom I say that it had been better for them never to have been born."[32]

TRANSGRESSORS JUDGED ACCORDING TO THEIR WORKS. We should hardly expect the Lord to measure out this same punishment to the man who departs from the Church because of some supposed grievance or misunderstanding, when that man never did have a testimony of the gospel and was never led by the spirit of truth. Yet, such a man bars himself, unless he repents, from the celestial kingdom, according to the word of the Lord.

[31]D. & C. 46:13-14.   [32]D. & C. 76:31-32.

He had his opportunity and rejected the gift that was
presented to him, therefore the reward of the faithful
shall not be his portion. "He who is not able to abide the
law of a celestial kingdom cannot abide a celestial glory.
And he who cannot abide the law of a terrestrial kingdom
cannot abide a terrestrial glory. And he who cannot
abide the law of a telestial kingdom cannot abide a telestial glory; therefore he is not meet for a kingdom of
glory. Therefore he must abide a kingdom which is not
a kingdom of glory."[33] All things are governed by law,
and whosoever is unable or unwilling to abide by the law
of any one of these kingdoms, cannot be sanctified by the
law governing therein, "neither by mercy, justice, nor
judgment."[34]

SEVERITY OF JUDGMENT UPON APOSTATES. The
Lord will judge each individual case and will assign
transgressor to that degree to which each is entitled
according to his works. If a man only merits a place in
the telestial, that will be his reward; if it should be the
terrestrial, then he shall be admitted to that kingdom. In
order to enter the celestial a man must be true and faithful to the end, observing all things which the Lord has
commanded, otherwise he shall be assigned to some other
kingdom, or to outer darkness if his sins so merit.

Let it be remembered, however, that the punishment
of the apostate, no matter who he is or what degree of
knowledge he may have attained, shall be most severe.
"Hearken and hear, O ye my people, saith the Lord and
your God, ye whom I delight to bless with the greatest
of all blessings, ye that hear me; and ye that hear me
not will I curse, *that have professed my name*, with the
heaviest of all cursings."[35]

It would be well to read in connection with this subject the following: Luke 12:9-10; 2 Peter 2:19-22;
Hebrews 6:4-8; Mosiah 3:24-27; Alma 34:32-35.[36]

[33]D. & C. 88:22-24.   [35]D. & C. 41:1.
[34]D. & C. 88:35.   [36]*Era*, vol. 22, pp. 621-623.

GENEALOGIES OF APOSTATES NOT TO BE KEPT. In November, 1832, the Lord said: "It is the duty of the Lord's clerk, whom he has appointed, to keep a history, and a general church record of all things that transpire in Zion, and of all those who consecrate properties, and receive inheritances legally from the bishop; And also their manner of life, their faith, and works; and also of the apostates who apostatize after receiving their inheritances.

"It is contrary to the will and commandment of God that those who receive not their inheritance by consecration, agreeable to his law, which he has given, that he may tithe his people, to prepare them against the day of vengeance and burning, should have their names enrolled with the people of God. *Neither is their genealogy to be kept*, or to be had where it may be found on any of the records or history of the church. Their names shall not be found, neither the names of the fathers, nor the names of the children written in the book of the law of God, saith the Lord of Hosts."[37]

Those who have received the truth and turned away from it and have rejected it and denied it shall be sorry. But I mention this in passing because people are coming constantly to have work done in the temples for people of this kind, in spite of all the Lord has said. This is worthy of your consideration.[38]

EXCOMMUNICATED PERSONS LOSE ALL BLESSINGS. What will be the status of a person born under the covenant if excommunicated from the Church?

When a person is excommunicated from the Church, every blessing is withdrawn and lost, and such a person stands just the same as if no ordinances had ever been performed. Should such a person later repent and be found worthy to return to the Church then all blessings may be restored by and with the approval and authorization of the man who holds the keys—the President of

---

[37]*D. & C.* 85:1-5.   [38]*Gen. & Hist. Mag.*, vol. 16, p. 56.

CHAPTER 16

KINGDOMS OF THIS WORLD

GOVERNMENTS OF MEN

FIRST EARTHLY GOVERNMENT A THEOCRACY. I think it stands to reason without any argument that he who created all things, including this earth, has the best *right to rule and reign upon it.* But for some 6,000 years, according to our chronology, with few exceptions among a minority of the people, the Son of God, who performed this great labor and who had this honor and whose right it is to reign, has not done so among the peoples of the earth. On the contrary men have turned from him and have set up their *own rulers,* have organized their *own governments* and have enacted very largely their *own laws,* ignoring both the Creator as the rightful ruler and the commandments which he originally gave to the children of men.

The first government upon this earth was a theocracy. It was a government in which God ruled by giving his commandments and his laws to the children of men. He directed by revelation, in some instances by messengers direct from his presence, in others by speaking from time to time through his servants who held the priesthood; he directed them not only in regard to matters of a spiritual nature but also pertaining to their *civil welfare.* It was the intention of the Lord that this should continue. If man had been willing to hearken to the voice of the Lord and walk according to his commandments, as those commandments were given in the beginning even unto this day, this world would have seen peace, and righteousness would have prevailed upon its face.

When Adam was driven out of the Garden of Eden, he was not left without direction, but the Lord sent messengers to him and even spoke to him by his own voice. Although Adam had been driven from his presence and he could not behold him, yet he received commandments and revelation for his guidance.[1]

GOVERNMENT OF GOD LOST TO MEN. Now if their sons and daughters had been obedient as Adam and Eve were obedient, if their posterity after them had continued in obedience, then I say peace and righteousness, which are the natural result of obedience, would have continued in the earth until this time. But there were other influences at work.

The influence of Satan has been felt in this world for 6,000 years. It is being felt today. As a result of Adam's children hearkening to the voice of Lucifer and following him, *governments were established in the earth which were not under the direction of revelation.* Nor did they hearken to the commandments of the Lord. Men arose and *usurped* the right to rule and reign. They ignored the mandates and the rights and privileges of him whose right it is to rule and reign, and as men spread upon the face of the earth they forgot God.

The result has been wickedness, strife, unrest, and contention, with all their attendant evils. And so we find the world today. *The world is sick* and has been sick during its mortal history, but today we are living in very troublous times. The hearts of men are failing them. Selfishness, unrighteousness, the desire to possess, to take advantage, and withal the fear that accompanies evil are found in the hearts of men.[2]

POWER OF SATAN IN GOVERNMENTS OF WORLD. The United States is not the kingdom of God, neither is England, Germany, or France. Take all of the nations put together, they do not constitute the kingdom of God, but are only *man-made worldly governments.* Notwithstanding the Father raised up righteous men and directed

---

[1] Moses 5:4-12.   [2] *Church News*, Feb. 6, 1932, p. 5; Moses 5:13-14.

them in the framing of this government and in giving
the people the Constitution of the United States, it is not
the government of God.[3] Like all the rest, it is a man-
made government,[4] and *we will not have the government
of God until Christ comes to reign,* and when he comes
he is going to be King of kings. He is going to take his
rightful place.[5]

Satan has control now. No matter where you look,
he is in control, even in our own land. *He is guiding the
governments as far as the Lord will permit him.* That is
why there is so much strife, turmoil, and confusion all
over the earth. One master mind is governing the nations.
It is not the President of the United States; it is not
Hitler; it is not Mussolini; it is not the king or government
of England or any other land; it is Satan himself.

WORLD TURMOIL SPAWNED BY SATAN. What does
the Lord say in the 1st section of the *Doctrine and Covenants*: "The hour is not yet [this was over 100 years
ago], but is nigh at hand, when peace shall be taken from
the earth, and *the devil shall have power over his own
dominion.*"[6]

Well, Satan certainly has dominion over his own,
for *his is the power of confusion, strife, bitterness, and
class distinction.* His is the power of *delusion* and not
one of peace and righteousness. Where can righteousness be found in the world? In Europe, in Asia, in the
United States? I say unto you, *you are not going to have
peace in the United States or anywhere in the world until
the Prince of Peace comes to bring it.*

Men have taken the law in their own hands, have
defied law and order. *When strikes are settled in one
place, they will break out in another.* Why? Because
Satan has power over his own dominions, and even
among our legislators and the men sworn to preserve the
Constitution, we find those who encourage this lawless-

---

[3]*D. & C.* 101:77-80.
[4]*D. & C.* 87:6.

[5]Rev. 11:15; 12:10; Dan. 7:9-10, 13-
14, 18, 22, 27.
[6]*D. & C.* 1:35.

ness and lend to it their support. This condition does not come out of the kingdom of God. These things will *increase* until the prophecies will all be fulfilled, and eventually the earth will be cleansed, and Christ will come as King of kings.[7]

LACK OF CHRISTIANITY AMONG NATIONS. It seems a shame that billions in money have to be spent and extra burdens be placed upon the backs of the people in order that nations may protect themselves, fearing attack of other nations, and that men cannot live together in this world in peace. The United States is considered to be, or has been in the past, a Christian nation. So likewise are the nations of Europe. Yet we find this condition prevailing: fear in the hearts of the people, nation preparing against nation; struggles have arisen.

We have seen the distress in years gone by that has come out of disagreements and selfishness and greed and determination of nations unrighteously to succeed in unrighteous desires. If they were really Christian nations, if they were truly worshiping the Lord Jesus Christ, if they believed in his doctrines, if they were applying them, these conditions would not prevail.[8]

ANARCHY AND TROUBLE AHEAD. Notwithstanding all the warnings the Lord has given us, we are rushing madly, headstrong, to destruction, preparing ourselves if you please for the burning. Do not think that the Lord does not mean what he says, for that which was predicted by ancient prophets, and which has been repeated in latter-day revelations shall be fulfilled.[9]

The Lord said through Isaiah that, "The earth mourneth and fadeth away," and because of the wickedness of the world it should be "burned, and few men left."[10] This prediction was repeated by the Prophet Malachi, as you read it in the last chapter of that book.[11]

---

[7]Pers. Corresp.
[8]*Church News*, Aug. 5, 1939, p. 1.
[9]*D. & C.* 63:32-34; 64:23-25; 101:23-25; 133:45-51.
[10]Isa. 24:1-6.
[11]Mal. 4:1.

So I say I am troubled; I am concerned over this nation; I am concerned over the nations, because of the wickedness of the people. I can see evil in the trend of the times. *I can see anarchy ahead of us.* If we are going to permit men, in organized form, to desecrate the sacredness of the laws of this country and the Constitution of this country; if we are going to permit them, in the spirit of anarchy, to take possession of that which does not belong to them, without protest, we are going to reap the whirlwind, just as surely as we live.

GOVERNMENT IS BASED ON RELIGION. I have here something that is just as good as scripture, written by President Calvin Coolidge; I am going to read it to you: *"Our government rests upon religion.* It is from that source that we derive our reverence for truth and justice, for equality and liberality, and for the rights of mankind. Unless the people believe in these principles they cannot believe in our government. There are only two main theories of government in the world. One rests on righteousness and the other on force. One appeals to reason, and the other appeals to the sword. One is exemplified in the republic, the other is represented by a despotism.

"The government of a country never gets ahead of the religion of a country. There is no way by which we can substitute the authority of law for the virtue of man. Of course we endeavor to restrain the vicious, and furnish a fair degree of security and protection by legislation and police control, but the real reform which society in these days is seeking will come as a result of our religious convictions, or they will not come at all. Peace, justice, humanity, charity—these cannot be legislated into being. They are the result of divine grace."

Well, words like that, I believe, are spoken by inspiration. This is a warning to the people of this nation, coming from a former president of the United States. It is in full harmony with the word of the Lord in the Book of Ether in the *Book of Mormon,* in regard to this land.[12] We cannot get away from the God of this land, without dire consequences following.[13]

LORD CONTROLS EARTHLY GOVERNMENTS

GOVERNMENTS ACCOUNTABLE TO GOD. Governments are like individuals in this: they will have to give an accounting unto the Lord. The Lord requires of every man that he will answer for his sins. Every man must stand to be judged according to his works, and *the Lord will also judge the nations according to their works.* While it is a fact that men have turned from the Lord and have established their own governments, yet the Lord has never surrendered his rights, has never wholly withdrawn and relinquished his rule and given over to the government of men the ruling of his earth without an accounting. He controls and directs, and he lets men go just as far as in his wisdom he desires they shall, and then he checks them.

MAN WITHOUT GOD INCAPABLE TO GOVERN PROPERLY. Men, without the aid of the Spirit of God and the direct communication from him and direction which he is willing to give if they are repentant, have always proved themselves incompetent to rule. That is true today. *If we had righteous government, we would have peace.* One righteous man cannot make a people righteous. In order that righteousness may come, there must be obedience to righteous laws on the part of the people.

In our own land wickedness, murder, all kinds of abominations prevail today among the people. And as it is here so it is in other lands everywhere upon the face of the earth, and that government which the Lord set up in the beginning is ignored. In fact, in a very large

---

[12]Ether 2:8-12.   [13]*Church News,* May 8, 1937, p. 5.

part of the history of the world it has not been found among the children of men.

The Lord has been under the necessity from time to time of withdrawing his priesthood from the earth, from among the children of men. He has been under the necessity of taking away his prophets and his righteous servants and leaving the people to themselves because of their wickedness, and they have groped in darkness, wandering without the guidance which they so greatly needed to bring them into paths of righteousness.[14]

PERFECT GOVERNMENT BASED ON LOVE OF GOD. So it has been in the history of this world with few exceptions. There have been times when certain peoples of the earth have been willing to listen to the voice of God, when they have had among them prophets to teach them, when they have been directed by constant revelation, when their hearts have been set upon righteousness, and one condition of that kind we read of very briefly in the *Bible*. But there are very few sentences recorded regarding it. It was during the time of Enoch. So righteous did his people become that the Lord took them from the earth.[15]

Upon this continent there was another time of peace and righteousness that prevailed when people were willing to listen to the voice of the Lord. We do not know just how far this influence and this righteousness has prevailed among other peoples from the beginning, because our history is so brief. But upon this continent, for 200 years following the crucifixion of our Redeemer, the people lived in this state of righteousness.

I wish to read to you what the prophet who wrote the history of that people has to say regarding those conditions: "And it came to pass that there was no contention in the land, *because of the love of God which did dwell in the hearts of the people*. And there were no envyings,

---

[14]Rev. 12.

[15]Gen. 5:22-24; Heb. 11:5; Moses 6: 7; 8.

nor strifes, nor tumults, nor whoredoms, nor lyings, nor
murders, nor any manner of lasciviousness; and surely
there could not be a happier people among all the people
who had been created by the hand of God. There were
no robbers, nor murderers, neither were there Lamanites,
nor any manner of -ites; but they were in one, the children
of Christ, and heirs to the kingdom of God."[16]

What a glorious time that must have been when
everybody was happy, when everybody was at peace,
when everyone loved his neighbor as himself, and above
all he loved God, because we are informed here that the
thing which brought about this condition of happiness
was the fact that the love of God was in the hearts of
the people. There never will be a time of peace, happiness, justice tempered by mercy, when all men will receive that which is their right and privilege to receive,
until they get in their hearts the love of God.

LORD DESTROYS NATIONS WHEN THEY TURN TO
WICKEDNESS. So far as this land is concerned, the Lord
has said that no people can dwell upon it without destruction coming to them if they permit themselves to
turn from the living God, and this destruction will come
when their hearts are filled with wickedness and their
cup of iniquity is overflowing.[17] They must serve him;
they will have to keep his commandments; at least they
will have to have some semblance of righteousness or
when the fulness of wickedness comes, he certainly will
remove them. That has been done in the past. It occurred,
as recorded, in the *Book of Mormon,* with two nations
that were swept off the face of this land;[18] and according
to the revelations given through the Prophet Joseph
Smith with one other nation, or perhaps more than one
nation before that time, for the Lord swept the people
from the face of the earth by the flood.[19]

Then this land was reinhabited. The Lord brought

---

[16] Ne. 15-17.
[17] Ether 2:8-12.

[18] Ether 15; Morm. 6.
[19] Moses 8; *D. & C.* 107:53-57; 116.

people here and gave them this precious land, a land that he said was choice above all other lands, and he said they could have it for their inheritance on conditions that they would serve him, but, when they turned from him and became wicked, they were destroyed. Another nation came with like instructions, and when their cup of iniquity was full, they too were destroyed.

This warning has gone out to the people dwelling in this land today that unless they keep the commandments of the Lord like destruction will eventually overtake them.[20] And what the Lord says of this land is also true in a large measure of other lands. History records the rise and the downfall of nations. We have before us the history of Babylon, of Assyria, of Egypt, of Rome, and other nations. *Why were they destroyed? Because they refused to hearken to the spirit of truth, to the voice of righteousness, and to walk in that spirit before the Lord.* In the days of their iniquity trouble came upon them, and the Lord's anger was kindled against them, and they fell from their high and exalted positions.[21]

AMERICA: CHOICE ABOVE ALL LANDS

WICKEDNESS WILL BRING JUDGMENTS UPON AMERICA. These passages of scripture from the *Book of Mormon* are true;[22] this nation is not exempt, and the people, if they continue to pursue the course of evil and ungodliness that they are now treading, shall eventually be punished. If they continue to disregard the warning voice of the Lord, deny their Redeemer, turn from his gospel unto fables and false theories, and rebel against all that he has through his servants in this day declared for the salvation of man; and if they increase in the practice of iniquity, I want to say to you, that if they do these things, *the judgments of the Lord will come upon this land, and this nation will not be saved;* we will not be

---

[20]Ether 2:11-12; *D. & C.* 97:21-28.   [22]Ether 2:7-12.
[21]*Church News*, Feb. 6, 1932, p. 5.

spared from war, from famine, from pestilence and finally from destruction, as a nation.

Therefore, I call upon the people not only Latter-day Saints, but to all throughout the whole land to repent of their sins and to accept the Lord Jesus Christ, who is our Redeemer and the God of this land. Turn from your evil ways, repent of your sins and receive the fulness of the gospel through the waters of baptism and obedience, that the judgments which shall be poured out upon the ungodly may pass you by.[23]

AMERICA: A LAND OF PROMISE AND REFUGE. America is not only a *land of promise* reserved for a righteous people, but it is also a *land of refuge* for the downtrodden and oppressed. The Puritans came here seeking religious freedom when oppression raged in the old world. The same is true of earlier colonies. The Jaredites came seeking a land of freedom. The Nephites came out of Jerusalem because the Lord had called them from a land of sin and bondage whose people were about to go into captivity as a punishment.

There was also another colony which came to this land of promise from Jerusalem at the time Nebuchad-nezzar was waging war on the Jews. This colony was also led by the hand of the Lord. We know very little of their journeyings, how they came and the number in their company, for they had no records. We have learned, however, that they brought with them the youngest son of Zedekiah, king Judah.

The *Bible* states that the sons of Zedekiah were slain before his eyes, and then the Babylonians put out his eyes and carried him in fetters into Babylon.[24] Mulek, son of Zedekiah, was spared by the power of the Lord and with other fugitives was directed across the "great waters" to this land. Here they multiplied, but without religious teachings. It was this people who discovered Coriantumr, the Jaredite, who lived with them for nine

---

[23]Conf. Rep., Oct., 1916, p. 72.   [24]2 Kings 25:7.

months before his death.[25] These Mulekites were later discovered by the Nephites and the two people became one, the Mulekites being known henceforth as Nephites, sharing with them in the blessings of their faith.

In brief, such is the story told in the *Book of Mormon* of the ancient inhabitants of America. They were highly civilized. They worshiped the true and living God, in a land which is dedicated to his worship and held in reserve for a righteous people, until they became confirmed transgressors. Let the Gentiles upon this land heed the warning and serve Jesus Christ, lest destruction also come upon them, for it has been prophesied that the present inhabitants if they turn from the worship of the true and living God shall bring down upon them the same destruction, "as the inhabitants of the land have hitherto done."[26]

JAREDITES: COVENANT PEOPLE OF THE LORD. On this land the Jaredites multiplied and prospered, sinned and were punished, repented and were forgiven—during a long period of years. They had among them men holding the priesthood and a Church organization. The Lord established his covenants with them as he did with Abraham and Israel. They built cities and became skilful and cunning workmen in gold and silver, in weaving textiles and in the cultivation of the soil. They spread over the whole face of the land and were an intelligent people with a written language and a thorough knowledge of the coming of Jesus Christ.

Eventually through sin their civilization crumbled. They killed their prophets. Plague and constant warfare decimated them until eventually they were entirely destroyed. Their last king, Coriantumr, lived to see another people come to possess the land which he and his people had lost through transgression, in fulfilment of the prediction of their first prophet, Mahonri Moriancumer:

---

[25]Omni 21.   [26]*Church News*, July 18, 1931, p. 2; Ether 2:11.

"Whatsoever nation shall possess it [this land] shall serve God, or they shall be swept off when the fulness of his wrath shall come upon them."[27]

LORD SETTLED MODERN AMERICA. In looking over the early history of the United States, one cannot help but see the truth of the words of the Apostle Paul that, "the powers that be are ordained of God."[28] I firmly believe that through the inspiration of the Lord the first settlers of America were moved upon to take up their journey from the old world and make their homes in this land of freedom. Generally they were of humble birth, yet honest, industrious and brave; men, such as the Lord would choose to cope with the many problems which are always to be met and overcome in the settlement of a new country or in th framing of a new nation.[29]

AMERICA AND HER CONSTITUTION

LORD ESTABLISHED CONSTITUTION OF UNITED STATES. No nation has been more greatly blessed than has the United States. We live in a land which has been called choice above all other lands by divine pronouncement. The Lord has watched over it with a jealous care and has commanded its people to serve him lest his wrath be kindled against them and his blessings be withdrawn.

Our government came into existence through divine guidance. The inspiration of the Lord rested upon the patriots who established it, inspired them through the dark days of their struggle for independence, and through the critical period which followed that struggle when they framed our glorious Constitution which guarantees to all the self-evident truth proclaimed in the Declaration of Independence, "that all men are created equal; that they are endowed by their Creator with cer-

---

27*Church News,* July 4, 1931, p. 2;
   Ether 2:9.
28Rom. 13:1.

29*Topsfield Historical Collection,* vol.
   8, p. 87.

tain inalienable rights; that among these are life, liberty, and the pursuit of happiness."

That is to say, it is the right of every soul to have equal and unrestricted justice before the law, equal rights to worship according to the dictates of conscience and to labor according to his individual inclinations, independently of coercion or compulsion. That this might be, the Lord has said, "I established the Constitution of this land, by the hands of wise men whom I raised up unto this very purpose, and redeemed the land by the shedding of blood."[30]

UNITED STATES FOUNDED AS A CHRISTIAN NATION. The founders of this nation were men of humble faith. Many of them saw in vision a glorious destiny for our government, provided we would faithfully continue in the path of justice and right with contrite spirits and humble hearts, accepting the divine truths which are found in the holy scriptures. The appeal of these men has echoed down the passing years with prophetic warning to the succeeding generations, pleading with them to be true to all these standards which lay at the foundation of our government.

This country was founded as a Christian nation, with the acceptance of Jesus Christ as the Redeemer of the world. It was predicted by a prophet of old that this land would be a land of liberty and it would be fortified against all other nations as long as its inhabitants would serve Jesus Christ; but should they stray from the Son of God, it would cease to be a land of liberty and his anger be kindled against them.[31]

It is a sad reflection, but one that cannot be successfully refuted, that we have forgotten the admonition which has come down to us, just as Israel forgot the commandments which would have blessed that nation in the land of Canaan forever had they been observed.[32] In

---

[30]D. & C. 101:80.   [32]Deut. 28; 29; 30.
[31]2 Ne. 10:10-16; Ether 2:8-12.

forsaking these laws we stand in danger of punishment as the people of Israel stood in danger of punishment because they forsook the Lord and failed to repent and accept the warnings of their prophets.[33]

CONSTITUTION TO HANG BY A THREAD.   The statement has been made that the Prophet said the time would come when this Constitution would hang as by a thread, and this is true.   There has been some confusion, however, as to just what he said following this.   I think that Elder Orson Hyde has given us a correct interpretation wherein he says that the Prophet said the Constitution would be in danger.

Said Orson Hyde: "I believe he said something like this—that the time would come when the Constitution and the country would be in danger of an overthrow; and said he: *If the Constitution be saved at all, it will be by the elders of this Church.*' I believe this is about the language, as nearly as I can recollect it."[34]

Now I tell you it is time the people of the United States were waking up with the understanding that if they don't save the Constitution from the dangers that threaten it, we will have a change of government.[35]

[33]Conf. Rep., Apr., 1943, pp. 11-12.   [35]Conf. Rep., Apr., 1950, p. 159.
[34]*Journal of Discourses*, vol. 6, p. 152.

CHAPTER 17

EXODUS OF MODERN ISRAEL[1]

PERSECUTIONS OF LATTER-DAY SAINTS

PERSECUTION ENDURED FOR GOSPEL'S SAKE.   I have visited most of the scenes of early Church history. I have gone over a good part of the trail which the saints followed when they came to these valleys. I have reflected a good deal upon these scenes, the travels, the hardships, the travails, and suffering and persecutions of these early days; and as I have stood in these hallowed spots and have traversed some of the territory which they passed over, my heart has been touched, but I have realized that it is beyond my power to understand and perhaps to feel all that these good faithful souls endured —*and all for the sake of the gospel of Jesus Christ.*

PERSECUTIONS IN NEW YORK, OHIO, MISSOURI, AND ILLINOIS. The Church had its beginning in New York. Persecution came upon the saints from the beginning, and they were driven out. The Lord gave them a commandment to assemble in Ohio.[2] They established their headquarters at Kirtland in that state. No doubt they had no intention of leaving when they first went there, but the Lord revealed to them that there was another place, the place which he called *Zion,* on the borders of the Lamanites,[3] and so their hearts were turned to that place; however, they never had intended to forsake altogether their headquarters in Kirtland, but persecution came upon them, and they were forced out.

With rejoicing they assembled in large measure in Jackson County where it had been made known to them

[1]Joseph Fielding Smith, *Essentials in Church History,* pp. 91-461.
[2]*D. & C.* 37.
[3]*D. & C.* 54:7-10.

that the great city, the new Jerusalem or Zion would be built,[4] and they rejoiced over it, but they were not privileged to remain there. Their enemies came upon them with hatred and bitterness in their hearts and drove them out.

They moved to another part of the state of Missouri and there again intended and tried to establish themselves, but persecution still followed them, and the hatred of the officials in that state resulted in their banishment and an edict coming from the governor of that state that they would have to leave or be exterminated. They went back eastward, crossed the great river, and made their settlement at Nauvoo, in the state of Illinois. For a season they prospered but not without persecution, not without hatred, and finally that hatred reached its peak, and their Prophet and his brother, my grandfather, were martyred.[5]

HARDSHIPS OF THE WESTWARD TREK. Their enemies thought that would be the end of the Church. The papers so declared it. Their enemies rejoiced, but it did not bring the end. Still the Church grew. So also grew the animosity and the hatred of their enemies, and finally the saints were driven from their homes, robbed of practically all that they possessed and thus set upon their journey to this western land, destitute, in poverty, and the world said they had gone to their destruction, and rejoiced.

I tell you, my brethren and sisters, we do not realize all that they went through—their hardships, their sufferings, the persecutions, the murders, the drivings that came upon them before they started on their westward journey—and they arrived in this valley rejoicing.[6] It was President George A. Smith who was responsible for the statement that they came here of their own free will and choice—because they had to; and that is true.

---

[4] *D. & C.* 45:64-67; 84:4-5.   [6] *D. & C.* 136.
[5] *D. & C.* 135.

They crossed the plains, many of them pushing handcarts, containing the meager possessions which they had. They traveled the weary miles with sore and bleeding feet, through hardships and suffering which we do not understand, and arrived in this valley of the Salt Lake, and were grateful to the Lord that he had preserved their lives and brought them to a place of peace where they could worship; and all this, if you please, *because they loved the truth.* . . .

ARE WE WORTHY OF OUR PIONEER HERITAGE? Now I have been thinking, as I have thought many times in the past, of this great legacy which is ours, the great blessings which have come to us, built upon the foundation of persecution, death, hardships, men and women laying down their lives that we might dwell in this land in peace and safety; and how do we feel today about it? Do we keep the Sabbath day holy? Do we pray? Are we grateful in our souls for all that has been done for us by these sturdy people who loved the truth and came here that they might worship God according to the dictates of their consciences? How do we feel?

When I see reports of conditions in this state and surrounding states where Latter-day Saints dwell, the amount of liquor that is consumed, and tobacco that is consumed, and tea and coffee and other things destructive of health, and contrary to the commandments of the Lord, when I see the people violating the Sabbath day and committing all other kinds of sins contrary to that which they have been taught, I wonder if the Lord is pleased with us.[7]

EXODUS FOREKNOWN

ZION TO FLOURISH UPON THE HILLS. The foreshadowing of this exodus is seen in a revelation to the Church as early as December, 1830, wherein we read: "Keep all the commandments and covenants by which

[7]Conf. Rep., Apr., 1947, pp. 58-60.

ye are bound; and I will cause the heavens to shake for
your good, and Satan shall tremble and *Zion shall rejoice
upon the hills and flourish.*"[8]

Again in March, 1831, in a revelation it is written:
"But before the great day of the Lord shall come, *Jacob
shall flourish in the wilderness,* and the Lamanites shall
blossom as the rose. *Zion shall flourish upon the hills
and rejoice upon the mountains,* and shall be assembled
together unto the place which I have appointed."[9]

PROPHET FORETOLD COMING OF SAINTS TO ROCKY
MOUNTAINS. The significance of these sayings did not
penetrate the minds of the members of the Church at that
time, but in 1842, when Nauvoo was only about three
years old, the Prophet Joseph Smith recorded in the history, under date of August 6th, the following: "I prophesied that the saints would continue to suffer much
affliction, and would be driven to the *Rocky Mountains,
many would* apostatize, others would be put to death by
persecutors, or lose their lives in consequence of exposure
or disease, and *some of you will live to go and assist in
making settlements and build cities, and see the saints
become a mighty people in the midst of the Rocky
Mountains.*"[10]

Without question this exodus was constantly in the
mind of Joseph Smith, although the members of the
Church failed to comprehend the significance of his words
in the midst of their surroundings. Perhaps many of them
shared the thought expressed by Senator George H.
McDuffie of South Carolina, who as late as 1843 when
speaking of the occupancy of the western slope said on
the floor of the United States Senate:

"Who are to go there, along the line of military
posts, and take possession of the only part of the territory
fit to occupy—that part upon the sea coast, a strip less

[8]*D. & C.* 35:24; 39:13.
[9]*D. & C.* 49:24-25; 64:37; 117:7-8;
  Isa. 40:9.

[10]Joseph Fielding Smith, *Teachings of
  the Prophet Joseph Smith.* p. 255.

than 100 miles in width? Why, sir, of what use will this
be for agricultural purposes? I would not for that purpose give a pinch of snuff for the whole territory. I wish
to God we did not own it.''[11]

PROPHET'S PLANS FOR WESTERN COLONIZATION.
A few months later, when persecution raged against the
saints, a meeting was called by Joseph Smith to consider
the exploration of the west. He records in his journal
under date of February 20, 1844, the following:

"At 10 a.m. went to my office, where the Twelve
Apostles and some others met in council with Brothers
Mitchell Curtis and Stephen Curtis, who left the pinery
on Black River, 1st January. They were sent by Lyman
Wight and Bishop Miller to know whether Lyman should
preach to the Indians, the Menominees and the
Chippewas having requested it. . . .

"I instructed the Twelve Apostles to send out a
delegation and *investigate the locations of California and
Oregon,* and *hunt out a good location, where we can
remove to after the Temple is completed, and where we
can build a city in a day, and have a government of our
own*—get up into the mountains where the devil cannot
dig us out, and live in a healthful climate where we can
live as long as we have a mind to."[12]

Then under date of Wednesday, February 21, 1844,
the Prophet records: "Council of the Twelve met in my
office. I insert the minutes: 'At a meeting of the Twelve
at the Mayor's office, Nauvoo, February 21, 1844, 7
o'clock p.m., Brigham Young, Parley P. Pratt, Orson
Pratt, Wilford Woodruff, John Taylor, George A.
Smith, Willard Richards and four others being present,
called by previous notice by instruction of President
Joseph Smith on the 20th instant, *for the purpose of se-
lecting a company to explore Oregon and California,* and
select a site for a new city for the saints. Jonathan Dun-

[11]Cited in, Smith, *Essentials in Church*   [12]*History of the Church.* vol. 6, p. 222.
    History, p. 446.

ham, Phineas H. Young, David D. Yearsley, and David
Fullmer volunteered to go; and Alphonso Young, James
Emmett, George D. Watt, and Daniel Spencer were requested to go. Voted, the above persons to be notified
to meet with the council on Friday evening next at the
assembly room.—Willard Richards, clerk.' ''[13]

PROPHET'S INSTRUCTIONS TO EXPLORING PARTY.
Friday, February 23, the minutes say: "Met with the
Twelve in the assembly room concerning the Oregon and
California exploring expedition; Hyrum and Sidney
present. I told them *I wanted an exploration of all that
mountain country*. Perhaps it would be best to go direct
to Santa Fe. 'Send twenty-five men; let them preach the
gospel wherever they go. Let that man go that can raise
$500, a good horse and mule, a double barrel gun, one
barrel rifle and the other smoothbore, a saddle and a
bridle, a pair of revolving pistols, bowie knife, and a good
sabre. Appoint a leader and let them beat up for volunteers. I want every one that goes to be a king and a
priest. When he gets to the mountains he may want to
talk with his God; when with the savage nations have
power to govern, etc. If we don't get volunteers, wait
till after the election.' George D. Watt said: 'Gentle-
men, I shall go.' Samuel Bent, Joseph A. Kelting, David
Fullmer, James Emmett, Daniel Spencer, Samuel Rolf,
Daniel Avery, and Samuel W. Richards, volunteered to
go."[14]

It should be understood that California and Oregon
as comprehended at that time embraced *all of this country
where we now are in the western part of the Rocky
Mountains*. It was not the Prophet's intention that they
should go down to the coast, and his remarks clearly so
indicate, for these explorers were to *explore the Rocky
Mountains* and there *seek a site for the building of a city*.
At that time Santa Fe was the logical point from which
to make such a start in this exploration of the west.

---

[13]*History of the Church*, vol. 6, p. 223.   [14]*History of the Church*, vol. 6, p. 224.

JOSEPH SMITH PROPHESIES TRIUMPH OF SAINTS. Saturday, February 24, several brethren called at the home of Joseph Smith and volunteered to join this expedition, and the following day he preached at the temple block where he prophesied that *"Within five years we should be out of the power of our old enemies,* whether they were apostates or of the world, and told the brethren to record it, and when it comes to pass they need not say they had forgotten the saying."[15]

During the week following, Ira S. Miles, Almon L. Fuller, Hosea Stout, Thomas S. Edwards, Moses Smith, Rufus Beach and others volunteered to go on this expedition. Monday, March 4, 1844, Joseph Smith wrote a letter to James Arlington Bennett of New York in which he said: "All is right at Nauvoo. *We are now fitting out a noble company to explore Oregon and California,* and progressing rapidly with the great temple which we expect to roof this season."[16]

PROPHET PETITIONS CONGRESS FOR RIGHT TO OPEN WESTERN AMERICA. One week later, March 11, the Prophet spent the day in council with the Twelve and others, principally the volunteers of this exploration company, where matters concerning the expedition were considered; and on the 26th of that same month, Joseph Smith addressed a memorial to the Congress of the United States, asking for authority to raise a company of 100,000 men in the United States, to proceed to the west in the neighborhood of Oregon and California, for the purpose of opening "The vast regions of the unpeopled West and South to our enlightened and enterprising yeomanry; to protect them in their researches; to secure them in their locations, and thus strengthen the government and enlarge her border; to extend her influence; to inspire the nations with the spirit of freedom, and win them to her standard; ... to supersede the necessity of a standing army on our western and southern

---

[15]*History of the Church,* vol. 6, p. 225.   [16]*History of the Church,* vol. 6, p. 232.

frontiers; to create and maintain the principles of peace and suppress mobs, insurrections, and opposition in Oregon and all lands bordering upon the United States and not incorporated into any acknowledged national government; to explore the unexplored regions of our continent; to open new fields for enterprise for our citizens and protect them therein, . . . and exalt the standard of universal peace."[17]

Orson Hyde was appointed to carry the memorial to Washington. This appointment appeared on the record of the city council minutes, with the seal of the corporation, signed by Joseph Smith, mayor, and Willard Richards, recorder. April 25, 1844, Orson Hyde made a lengthy report of his labors in Washington. Orson Pratt was with him, and they drafted a bill to be presented to Congress in which they said their general course would be westward, through Iowa to the Missouri River, thence up the "North Fork of the Platte into the mouth of the Sweetwater River in longitude 107 degrees, 45 minutes west, and thence up said Sweetwater River to the south pass of the Rocky Mountains about 1100 miles from Nauvoo; and from said south pass, in latitude 42 degrees, 28 minutes, north to the Umpaqua and Klamet Valleys in Oregon bordering on California."[18]

JOSEPH'S PLAN TO PRECEDE EXPLORING PARTY TO WEST. While this expedition was preparing for the journey to the west, the difficulties arose in Nauvoo which culminated in the seizure of the Prophet and his brother Hyrum, and their imprisonment in Carthage, Illinois, in June. Before the Prophet surrendered and yielded to the demands of his accusers and the leaders of what later became the mob which took his life, he crossed the Mississippi River at Nauvoo, with his brother Hyrum, Porter Rockwell, and Willard Richards, with the intention of *preceding the exploring company to the west.* This action was taken on the grounds that it was Joseph

---

[17]*History of the Church,* vol. 6, p. 276.   [18]*History of the Church,* vol. 6, p. 374.

Smith whose blood the mob desired, and if he were out of the way, peace would be restored.

The minutes of these trying scenes are as follows: "Saturday, June 22, 1844.—About 9 p.m. Hyrum came out of the Mansion and gave his hand to Reynolds Cahoon, at the same time saying, 'A company of men are seeking to kill my brother Joseph, and the Lord has warned him to flee to the Rocky Mountain to save his life. Good-bye. Brother Cahoon, we shall see you again.' In a few minutes afterwards Joseph came from his family. His tears were flowing fast. He held a handkerchief to his face and followed after Brother Hyrum without uttering a word.

"Between 9 and 10 p.m. Joseph, Hyrum, and Willard while waiting on the bank of the river for the skiff, sent for William W. Phelps, and instructed him to take their families to Cincinnati by the second steamboat arriving at Nauvoo; and when he arrived there commence petitioning the President of the United States and Congress for redress of grievances, and see if they would grant the Church liberty and equal rights. . . .

"About midnight, Joseph, Hyrum, and Dr. Richards called for Orrin P. Rockwell at his lodgings, and all went up the river bank until they found Aaron Johnson's boat, which they got into and started about 2 a.m. to cross the Mississippi River. Orrin P. Rockwell rowed the skiff, which was very leaky, so that it kept Joseph, Hyrum, and the doctor busy bailing out the water with their boots and shoes to prevent it from sinking.

MARTYRDOM ENDED PLANS FOR WESTWARD EXPLORATION. "Sunday 23rd—At daybreak arrived on the Iowa side of the river. Sent Orrin P. Rockwell back to Nauvoo with instructions to return next night with horses for Joseph and Hyrum, pass them over the river in the night secretly, and be ready to start for the Great Basin in the Rocky Mountains. . . .

"At 1 p.m. (Sunday 23rd) Orrin P. Rockwell returned from Nauvoo with a petition from some of the citizens requesting him to come back. It was said that these were saying that it was like the fable, when the wolves come the shepherd ran from the flock and left the sheep to be devoured."

To this accusation the Prophet replied: "If my life is of no value to my friends, it is of none to myself."[19] This accusation, without doubt, hurt him even more than the assassins' bullets a few days later at Carthage, Illinois. He and his brother Hyrum had been preparing provisions in anticipation of their journey to the west, but this was all changed when this accusation came, and so Joseph Smith and his brother, who so dearly loved him, returned and were taken to their martyrdom. This, of course, put an end to the proposed expedition of exploration, and some months later when the Latter-day Saints were forced by cannon and musket to abandon their homes and take up their journey towards the west, the experience and information which it was hoped would be available from the exploration party obviously was not obtained.[20]

SAINTS AT WINTER QUARTERS

PERSECUTION NOT ALLAYED BY DEATH OF PROPHET. When the enemies of the Church accomplished their wicked purpose in the martyrdom of the Prophet Joseph Smith and his brother Hyrum, they were confident that they had brought the Church of Jesus Christ of Latter-day Saints to its end. They were sure that it could not survive and that its members would be scattered to the four winds. They gloated over their murderous accomplishment, but this gloating was of short duration.

To their amazement the members of the Church rallied and continued to build and pursue their daily voca-

---

[19]*History of the Church,* vol. 6, pp. 548-549.   [20]*Church News,* July 21, 1934, p. 7.

tions. In the eyes of the mob this would not do, and so the persecutions continued with renewed determination. Mob conventions were held, and demands were made that the Latter-day Saints should leave the state of Illinois. It is regrettable to say that these enemies had the sympathy and treacherous aid of Governor Thomas Ford. The saints asked for time to dispose of their property and in their petition to their enemies said:

"That we will use all lawful means, in connection with others, to preserve the public peace while we tarry; and shall expect, decidedly, that we be no more molested with house-burning, or any other depredations, to waste our property and time, and hinder our business.

"That it is a mistaken idea, that we have proposed to remove in six months, for that would be so early in the spring that grass might not grow nor water run; both of which would be necessary for our removal. But we propose to use our influence to have no more seed time and harvest among our people in this country after gathering our present crops; and that all communications to us be made in writing."[21]

PERILS OF EXODUS FROM NAUVOO. The request of President Brigham Young and his brethren was granted, but within a week was broken, and the fury of the mob increased as the mob issued an ultimatum that the saints make an immediate removal. Wednesday, February 4, 1846, the first of the saints left Nauvoo and crossed the Mississippi on their way to the West. Others followed as rapidly as they could. It was an extreme winter. They were without sufficient food, clothing, and provender for their teams. Their covered wagons would not successfully shed the snow and rain, and many wagons were without covers. On Sugar Creek a temporary camp was made. On the first night of the encampment, nine infants were born.

President Young spent February 16, 1846, in or-

[21]Smith, op. cit., p. 396.

ganizing the camp. March 1st the camp was broken and
the journey resumed in cold, stormy weather. Several
members of the camp died from exposure. Some 400
wagons, without sufficient teams, had been assembled to
transport these miserable exiles. By April the great body
of the saints was on its way. Near the Chariton River
the exiles were organized into companies with captains
over tens, fifties, and hundreds. The apostles were
appointed to take charge of divisions.

TEMPORARY CAMPS AT GARDEN GROVE AND MOUNT
PISGAH. April 24, 1846, a settlement was selected on
Grand River, Iowa, and named *Garden Grove*. Here a
council meeting was held, and 359 laboring men were
reported in the camp. From these, 100 were appointed to
cut trees and make rails, 10 to build fences, 48 to build
houses, 12 to dig wells, and 10 to build bridges. The
remaining number were to prepare land for cultivation.
A temporary organization to look after the spiritual as
well as the temporal needs of this settlement was also
appointed.

May 18, 1846, some 27 miles farther west, Parley
P. Pratt with his company had camped. It was decided
here to make another temporary settlement, and it was
named *Mount Pisgah*. As in Garden Grove, arrangements were made for the convenience of those appointed
to remain. These *temporary camps* were essential to the
welfare of the exiles and were organized for the purpose
of raising grain and provisions to help the members on
their westward journey.

SAINTS LOCATE AT WINTER QUARTERS. On June
14, President Brigham Young, Heber C. Kimball, Parley
P. Pratt, and others with the advanced companies, arrived on the banks of the Missouri River, not far from
Council Bluffs. The next day a council meeting was
held, and it was decided to move back onto the bluffs
where spring water could be obtained and there would
be protection from the Indians. The brethren found that

the Pottawattami Indians were very friendly and their chief showed the saints some favors. The Omaha Indians across the river were not so friendly.

June 29, 1846, a ferryboat was finished on the east bank of the Missouri. The building of this boat was under the supervision of Frederick Kesler, who for many years was the bishop of the Sixteenth Ward, Salt Lake City, and incidentally the bishop of President Joseph F. Smith's family. The next day President Young and others crossed the river seeking a site for the location of the camps of Israel. In early September such a site was chosen and named *Winter Quarters*. This place was to be the outfitting point for those who were to continue their journey to the Great Basin.

A regular city was laid out according to the plans which were adopted for the settlements of the Latter-day Saints. Several years later, after the abandonment by the saints, the place was named *Florence* and today is a suburb of the city of Omaha. Winter Quarters, under the direction of 12 men appointed for the purpose, was organized into wards over each of which was a bishop. These bishops so appointed at this early period were Levi W. Riter, William Fossett, Benjamin Brown, John Vance, Edward Hunter, David Fairbanks, Daniel Spencer, Joseph Matthews, Abraham Hoagland, David D. Yearsley, and Joseph B. Noble.

INDIAN OPPOSITION AT WINTER QUARTERS. In a very short period of time, for the settlers labored diligently, Winter Quarters took on the appearance of a city. The houses were chiefly built of logs gathered from the surrounding forest, but some of the saints made their dwellings by making caves. Some trouble arose through the stealing of cattle and horses by the Indians, and this loss the members of this settlement could not afford. Their number of horses, mules, and cattle was too meager and was sorely needed for the ploughing of the land and for the anticipated journey to their promised land in the

Rocky Mountains. Most members of the Church are familiar with the story told by President Joseph F. Smith of his encounter with the Indians when he was a herd boy of only eight years, and how through his ingenuity and the blessing of the Lord he saved the cattle but lost his horse and was himself miraculously saved from death. This occurred just out of Winter Quarters.[22]

The Indians felt that the members of the Church who were dwelling on their lands were intruders; no doubt they felt justified in their marauding, done in part at least, in the spirit of retaliation, for the settlers were killing and eating the wild game and cutting the trees to build houses and corrals on these Indian lands. Chief Big Elk tried to restrain his people, but they would not be controlled. President Brigham Young counseled the members of the Church to treat the Indians kindly but was forced to build a stockade around Winter Quarters as a protection against Indian raids.

COUNCIL HOUSE AND GRISTMILL BUILT AT WINTER QUARTERS. Knowing the need of keeping the people busy, President Young assigned duties to all, keeping the minds of the saints occupied and thus more contented than if they had idle time on their hands. Of course there were cattle and horses to feed and fields to be cultivated preparatory to a harvest in the rapidly approaching fall.

A gristmill was built, as much to furnish employment as to be of need in the preparation of flour and other grains. President Young said if the saints did not continue to use it, the Indians could. According to Latter-day Saint custom, this mill was built with a condition of permanency although it was known that in a short time Winter Quarters would be abandoned. In addition to the building of houses and a gristmill, a council house was constructed suitable to these primitive conditions, where council meetings, sacrament, and other meetings

[22]Joseph Fielding Smith, *Life of President Joseph F. Smith*, ch. 10.

for the benefit of the settlers at Winter Quarters could be held.

We think today that we have difficulties in housing two and sometimes three wards in one meetinghouse, but these bishops in Winter Quarters had no separate buildings or even houses where two wards could meet with staggered time. Such meetings as were held had to be in this council house or in the open. The duty of the bishops was largely in caring for the members who were under their jurisdiction, temporally and spiritually, without the convenience of separate places of worship. A condition of this kind had prevailed in Nauvoo where many wards were created, but houses of worship were not provided. Notwithstanding this inconvenience, regular meetings were held where the members partook of the sacrament and were instructed.

BRIGHAM YOUNG RECEIVED REVELATION AT WINTER QUARTERS. This council house was used for all general purposes. Dances and other entertainments were held in it. All amusements were opened and closed by prayer. It was at Winter Quarters where President Brigham Young, January 14, 1847, received a revelation of encouragement and direction for the members of the Church, to govern them while on their journeys and encampments preparatory to the settlement in the Salt Lake Valley.[23]

In this word of the Lord, directions were given as to the travels of the saints, their deportment on the way and in their camps. They were taught to be unselfish and helpful to those who were less fortunate, the widows and fatherless, and were given a promise of blessings if they would remain faithful. The original pioneer company was ordered to go in advance with its captains over hundreds, fifties, and tens. The members were instructed and encouraged to "praise the Lord with singing, with

[23]D. & C. 136.

music, with dancing, and with a prayer of praise and thanksgiving," and if sorrowful, to "call on the Lord" with supplication, that their souls might be joyful.[24]

Some thoughtless persons have condemned the pioneers for their dancing and merriment while on the plains, but all of this was done by commandment of the Lord and in the spirit of prayer and thanksgiving. Truly it was, as with David of old, "dancing before the Lord"[25] and done in the spirit of true humility. Would that all of our dancing and amusement entertainments today could be conducted in like spirit. How much better the saints would be, how much happier than when many of these things are conducted in the spirit of the world.

The saints were told not to fear their enemies, for they were in the hands of the Lord. They were not to harbor feelings of revenge or hatred towards their enemies. The saints were to be tried in all things, and if they would bear chastisement, they would be worthy of the kingdom of God. It was made known to them why the Prophet and Patriarch had to meet a violent death and have their blood shed. The Lord said, "Many have marveled because of his [Joseph Smith's] death; but it was needful that he should seal his testimony with his blood, that he might be honored and the wicked might be condemned." The conclusion of this counsel was: "Be diligent in keeping all my commandments, lest judgments come upon you, and your faith fail you, and your enemies triumph over you. So no more at present. Amen and Amen."[26]

LIFE AND LABORS OF SAINTS AT WINTER QUARTERS. The principal diet of the people at Winter Quarters in the winter of 1846-47 was corn and pork. These articles could be secured more readily and were brought to Winter Quarters from what was called *Upper Missouri,* along the western borders of that state. There were very few

---

[24]*D. & C.* 136:28-29.
[25]2 Sam. 6:16.

[26]*D. & C.* 136:39-42.

gristmills in that part of Missouri at that time where the
grain was bought.

Some of the brethren found work during these trying months and by that means were able to purchase their
meager supplies preparatory to the journey to the Rocky
Mountains. Wheat, boiled whole, and corn, such as
could be obtained, was ground into meal in hand mills,
a few of them being in the camps. In the fall of 1846, in
Upper Missouri, wheat sold for 19 to 25 cents and corn
for 10 to 12 cents a bushel, but these prices were advanced to twice the price as the saints continued their
purchases. While these prices were low, yet they placed
a strain upon the pocketbooks of the poor exiles, for their
means were woefully deficient. Besides the feeding of
the people, cattle and horses had to be fed, and this required grain. Without the abundant mercy and assistance from the Lord these impoverished saints would have
perished.

Notwithstanding all their hardships and the poverty
of the saints, they were usually happy, for they had the
Spirit of the Lord to guide them and they had leaders
with indomitable wills and wonderful resourcefulness
aided by the help of the Lord. There were a few among
them who lacked the faith to continue the journey and
fell by the wayside, among them Bishop George Miller
and Alpheus Cutler.

After the encampment was made at Winter Quarters, November 1, 1846, Major H. M. Harvey, Superin-
tendent of Indian Affairs, called on President Young at
Winter Quarters and stated that he wished the camp to
remove from the Indian lands, that the members of the
camp were burning the Indians' wood, and he had received letters from Washington from the Department
of Indian Affairs giving instructions that no white settlers
were to be permitted on the Omaha Indian lands without
the authority of the government. President Young told
Major Harvey that the government had called into the

service of the United States Army the most efficient men from the camps of the pioneers, thus weakening and placing extra burdens upon those who remained. This had caused delay. It was later learned that such drastic demands had not come from Washington.

SAINTS SETTLE KANESVILLE. Winter Quarters was not completely abandoned until 1848, and it continued to be the place for fitting out companies for the journey across the plains and mountains to the Salt Lake Valley. Many of the members of the Church had located at Council Bluffs, and those not prepared to cross the plains moved to the eastern side of the Missouri. This new settlement was named *Kanesville,* in honor of General Thomas L. Kane who had befriended the Latter-day Saints on several occasions. Kanesville became a thriving town before the members of the Church were called to abandon it. During its most prosperous days there were more members of the Church there than in the Salt Lake Valley. A newspaper called the *Frontier Guardian* was published, with Elder Orson Hyde of the Council of the Twelve as editor. It was at Kanesville that Oliver Cowdery came in October 1848 to plead for admission back into the Church; his request was granted.

CALL OF MORMON BATTALION. Twelve days after the arrival of President Brigham Young on the bank of the Missouri River, Captain James Allen of the United States Army arrived at Mount Pisgah with a call from the government for four or five companies of volunteers to serve in the Mexican War. He was advised to go to Council Bluffs to see President Brigham Young. He arrived there on the 30th day of June and the following day met with President Young and the brethren.

President Young informed him that the volunteers would be furnished. It was moved by Heber C. Kimball and seconded by Willard Richards that a battalion of 500 men be raised, which was carried unanimously at a meeting of the brethren who were called together for this occasion. This necessitated the return of President Young to Mount Pisgah and the sending of letters to Garden Grove and Nauvoo notifying the members of the Church in these places of this action. The calling of this Mormon Battalion and its wonderful march and achievements are well known among the Latter-day Saints, but the true spirit and significance of their march has never received the proper honor and place which it should have been accorded throughout the nation.[27]

---

[27]*Era*, vol. 55, pp. 224-226, 281-282.

CHAPTER 18

MORMON PIONEERS AND COLONIZATION

SETTLING OF UTAH

SAINTS MADE DESERT BLOSSOM AS THE ROSE. A traveler passing through the fertile Utah valleys in a luxurious Pullman car, on his way to the Golden State, volunteered to say as he looked out over the cultivated fields and blooming orchards: "No wonder Brigham Young chose these well watered and beautiful valleys as a permanent home for your people."

It was the spring of the year; the fields were green with the grain of the summer's harvest; the fruit trees along the way were in full bloom, and everywhere, in a land of great fertility, appeared the glorious prospect of an abundant yield. Such remarks are often made by those who hurriedly pass through our State and see conditions as they are today. How very little do they know of the early history of our State, and the almost superhuman struggle of the pioneers to make "the wilderness and the solitary place . . . glad for them," and "the desert . . . rejoice, and blossom as the rose."[1]

It was a very different aspect that confronted the small but determined band of pioneers as they entered the Valley of the Great Salt Lake, July 24th, 1847, and took possession as the first permanent settlers of the great intermountain region. The soil, they found, was hard and sunbaked. There was little vegetation save the stubby growth of saltgrass, greasewood, and sage that covered the Valley, and the few willows and cottonwood trees that stood on the banks of the canyon streams. The scene was most desolate and uninviting.

---

[1] Isa. 35:1.

SAINTS SETTLED A BARREN DESERT LAND. The
pioneers attempted to plough, but the ground, uncon-
quered for so many ages, refused to yield to the plow-
man's share. By diverting the waters of a canyon stream
and thoroughly soaking the soil, they were able to turn
the earth and prepare it for the limited but extremely
valuable supply of seed which they had brought with
them. And thus commenced a determined battle with the
elements under adverse conditions which was to result
in the conquering of the desert and the beginning of our
modern system of successful cultivation by irrigation.

It must be remembered that the great Rocky Mountain region and much of the plains to the east, at that
time, formed a desert that was unknown save to the trapper and hunter, and to them, little was known of the great
possibilities of the intermountain country. The few emigrants who traversed the country, prior to that time,
hurried on to the great Pacific coast. None thought of
occupying the barren and apparently unproductive region
of the Rocky Mountains. Bridger, the trapper and scout,
was so sure that the Salt Lake Valley would not produce,
that he declared he would gladly give one thousand dollars if he knew an ear of corn would ripen in that valley.
His view was shared by others who were acquainted with
the region.[2]

MORMON PIONEERS DESTINED TO COME WEST.
It might be thought by the casual reader of the history
of the Latter-day Saints, that their coming into these
valleys when and as they did was merely a matter of
necessity, without design so far as the purposes of the
Lord were concerned. President George A. Smith, one
of these pioneers, very frequently stated—speaking of
Latter-day Saints—"that we came here of our own free
will and choice, because we had to."

However, it was the design of the Lord that the

[2]*Gen. & Hist. Mag.*, vol. 7, pp. 11-12.

Latter-day Saints should possess these valleys of the mountains. It took persecution and the extreme opposition and hate on the part of their enemies to accomplish this end and bring to pass the driving of the members of the Church from their homes in Illinois.

It seems to me that if the Latter-day Saints had been left in peace, without opposition, and the Lord had commanded them to leave their comfortable homes and make the journey across the barren plains and mountains to these valleys that many of them would have refused to come. They were content and comfortable so far as their homes were concerned. They were happy. They had been prospering. They had found the first years of peace in the history of the Church while they sojourned at Nauvoo, even though these years were few.

PROPHETS FORETOLD SETTLING OF SAINTS IN ROCKY MOUNTAINS. During the last two years and more that they dwelt there the hatred of their neighbors became intense. Nevertheless they had built up a city, the largest city in the state of Illinois, a city of power and influence. They had comfortable homes. They were building a magnificent temple in which to worship God, and naturally they desired to stay there, but the Lord had other designs; so also had their enemies.

But it was *not* this hatred and persecution, and the driving of the saints from the City of Nauvoo and from the State of Illinois, that constituted the greatest factor in their removal and the commencing of their trek across the boundless plains and the seeking of new homes in the valleys of the Rocky Mountains. While persecution and hate were the *immediate causes* for this removal, yet back in the early days of the Church, as early as the year 1830, and again in the year 1831, the Lord had indicated by revelation that the time would come when they would be established in the mountains.[3]

---
[3]*D. & C.* 35:24; 39:13.

Isaiah, some 700 years before the birth of Christ, had made that prediction.[4] My own grandfather, in the year 1834, while administering to a brother of President Brigham Young, Elder Lorenzo D. Young, predicted upon his head that he would come with the body of the saints to these valleys of the mountains.[5]

FAITHFUL SAINTS FOLLOWED BRIGHAM YOUNG. There were some who feared the hardships of a journey across the plains to a region practically unknown which, Washington Irving said, would never become the habitation of civilization.

These fearful ones sought refuge in their flight from the stricken city of Nauvoo among the settlements of Illinois, Wisconsin and surrounding territory where they were received in peace and without danger of molestation. The *great majority* of the members of the Church, however, had faith enough to follow President Brigham Young and the Twelve, implicitly believing that the Lord would prepare the way and lead them on the journey to the west. It was the *fair weather* members, said General Thomas L. Kane, who deserted the Church in its hour of trial and sought refuge among the peaceful communities where anti-Mormon mobs did not control. The staunch and proved members of the Church did not falter, but endured the hardships which they realized were before them in leaving all behind in Nauvoo.[6]

SAINTS CAME WEST TO SERVE GOD. We came into these valleys for one purpose. What was it? The primary purpose was *to serve the Lord, to keep his commandments, to worship him in spirit and truth* without interference, according to the dictates of our conscience. That was the object which President Young taught the people; the elders taught it, and they were filled with the spirit of faith, and they guided the people.

---

[4]Isa. 2:1-5   [6]*Church News*, July 21, 1934, pp. 1, 7.
[5]*Church News*, Aug. 7, 1937, p. 5.

But as time went on other elements were developed; others came among us, other influences, and see what is the condition today. We are outnumbered by people who love money, who are not a God-fearing people; they are people who love this world, the things of this world, the pleasures of this world, the wealth of this world; and their minds are set upon getting it, and we are following very largely in their footsteps to the displeasure of our Father in Heaven.[7]

ASSEMBLING ISRAEL'S PIONEERS

GEOGRAPHICAL ORIGINS OF PIONEERS OF 1847. It was July 24th, 1847, when the pioneers entered the Salt Lake Valley. They had made the journey from Winter Quarters on the banks of the Missouri River, to the Valley in about 102 days, building roads, fording streams and cutting a passage through mountain gorges, blazing the way for the companies which were preparing to follow.

The original company was composed of 143 men, three women and two children. Of this number, as far as we can determine, 21 were natives of New York, 14 were natives of Vermont, 11 of Ohio, 10 of Massachusetts, four of Pennsylvania, four of Connecticut, three of North Carolina, two of Illinois, two of Virginia, two of Maine, three of New Hampshire, two of Mississippi, two of New Jersey, three of Tennessee, and one each of Alabama, Indiana, South Carolina, Kentucky and Rhode Island—19 states of the Union, a large majority at that time. Five were natives of Canada, four of England and one each of Ireland, Scotland, Denmark, Norway, and Germany.

It is remarkable that without premeditation these pioneers should have been gathered from nearly every state in the Union and the various countries of Europe

[7]Rel. Soc. Mag., vol. 18, pp. 684-685.

from whence most of our stable immigration has come.
It is reasonable to believe that the others, whose places
of birth we do not know, were from just as wide a range
of territory.

Five days after the arrival of the pioneers they were
joined by a detachment of about 150 men from the Mormon Battalion, which served in the Mexican war, and
about 50 immigrants from Mississippi. The first few days
in the Valley were spent in exploring, surveying and
laying out a city; in ploughing and planting, with the
hope, although the season was far advanced, of raising
a crop before the autumn frosts set in. They ploughed
84 acres and planted them in corn, potatoes, beans and
other products of the soil.

ESTABLISHMENT OF SETTLEMENT IN SALT LAKE
VALLEY. Monday, August 2nd, the survey of Salt Lake
City was commenced, also on the 10th the building of
the *Old Fort,* or stockade, which was erected on the 10
acres now known as Pioneer Park, as a protection against
hostile Indians. They also erected 27 log cabins and were
engaged in various other pursuits towards the establishment of a permanent home for themselves and the people
who were to follow.

Wednesday, August 18th, nearly one-half of the
pioneer company commenced to retrace their steps
towards Winter Quarters, to assist their families and the
exiled immigrants who were on the way to the Valley.
These were followed by another detachment from the
little band on the 26th. That fall between 600 and 700
wagons and about 2,000 persons arrived in Salt Lake
Valley, coming principally with ox-teams.

While crossing the plains the immigrants were organized in companies of tens, fifties and hundreds, with
a captain over each. Thus they traveled in organized
form and with correct discipline governing all their move-
ments. Each morning at bugle call they assembled for

prayer, and in the evening likewise; and notwithstanding the hardships of the journey, they were buoyed up in their hopes of obtaining a haven of rest in the new Zion, where, at least, they would be free from persecution.

A total of 1,891 persons with 623 wagons left Winter Quarters on the Missouri River, May 31, 1848, and arrived in the Valley September 20, following. These were principally from the exiled Latter-day Saints from Nauvoo, with a sprinkling from European countries. At this time there were 450 buildings in the Fort, three saw mills had been erected, a flour mill was in operation and various necessary industries were under way.

NATIONALITIES OF EARLY MORMON CONVERTS. In 1840-50 increased efforts were put forth in proselyting throughout the world; missionary work was vigorously carried on in the British Isles, Germany, Scandinavia, France, Italy, Switzerland, Australia and many other lands, including the islands of the sea, and many converts were made.

In 1849 the Perpetual Emigration Fund Company was organized, the object being to make a systematic effort to assist all who desired help to emigrate from foreign lands to the body of the people in Utah. This movement was not inaugurated for speculation, but as a means of helping the poor and the needy to better their conditions in the *promised land*. Those aided by this fund were expected to repay the amount they borrowed that others might also obtain assistance, thus making the fund perpetual in its working.

Between the years 1847 and 1856, there were 59 companies of emigrants, comprising in all 16,911 souls that sailed from European shores bound for Utah. Five thousand more had previously emigrated, making a total of 21,911. They were principally from the British Isles, Scandinavia, Germany, and Switzerland, with a sprinkling from France, Italy and other nations.

VOCATIONS OF EARLY MORMON CONVERTS. They came from the factories and the mines of Great Britain, the fisheries and the dairy farms of Scandinavia, the workshops of Germany, the vineyards of France and Italy—from various pursuits and occupations wherein they were unable in the old world, from the scanty pittance they received as wages, to save enough to buy a passage across the sea.

Of the emigration between 1850 and 1860 it has been estimated that 28 per cent were common laborers, 14 per cent miners, and about 27 per cent mechanics. There were also found in these ranks, the merchant, the doctor, the professor, the skilled engineer and artisan, the financier, and the artist. Occasionally there was one possessed of abundance of this world's goods and big enough to share with his less fortunate neighbor, for they were not confined solely to the poor and the needy, the unlearned or the ignorant.

They were gathered from all nations, but they were not the scum of the earth and the moral outcasts of society; *they were the very bones and sinews of the nations from whence they came*—the life's blood, the brawn without which nations would perish from the earth. This class, despised and trodden under foot from time immemorial by the haughty, the proud, the titled nobility, but upon whom, nevertheless, the aristocratic population depend for their very existence, are in very deed *the salt of the earth*. Remember, the scriptures say it was the poor that had the gospel preached to them, and it was the common people who heard it gladly.[a]

EXTENSIVE SCOPE OF PIONEER IMMIGRATION. These pioneer immigrants, who established the State of Utah, belonged to the great industrial class, honest though generally poor, that laid the foundation of our glorious nation. Among them were men of renown who fought

[a]Matt. 11:5-6; Mark 12:37; Luke 7:22-
    23.

in freedom's cause and stood in the defense of liberty. For in Utah a very large percentage of the inhabitants are descendants of the early Colonial families of New England and the border Atlantic states.

Thus Mormonism took hold of the dependent thousands of poor from all parts of the earth who had embraced the faith and made them virtually independent by placing them on farms and otherwise furnishing them with remunerative employment by which they became financially free. In 1880—30 years after the organization of Utah Territory—the population was 143,963. Of this number 43,944 were of *foreign birth*. There were 14,550 persons engaged in agriculture, 4,149 employed in various trades and 10,212 in mining, mechanics, and factory activities.

According to the State's report in 1896, the year Utah was admitted into the Union, there were 19,816 farms and of that number 17,584 were free from incumbrance of mortgage and debt, and while conditions have not improved since the advent of the automobile and modern methods of extravagance, even today the great majority of the Latter-day Saints dwell in their homes with clear titles.

EARLY MORMON COLONIZATION

ORDERLY NATURE OF MORMON COLONIZATION. Within two years after Salt Lake City was founded, the immigration had become so great that the population could not be supported. Many parties were sent out, principally to the north and south, to form new settlements—not merely in the vicinity of Salt Lake City, but to the remote parts of the territory, which at that time extended from the borders of Nebraska and Kansas to California, east and west, and from Oregon to New Mexico, north and south. Exploring parties were sent in advance and when a site was selected a large company of volunteers followed to make the permanent settlement.

In these companies care was taken that there should be a proper representation of craftsmen, that the needs of the new colony might be met; there were skilled carpenters, masons, millwrights, blacksmiths, cobblers, etc., in each company, and each individual was given some specific work to do. All performed their portion of the labor in harmony with the plan arranged. Every man was supplied with all necessary tools, a gun and other portable necessities, for individual protection and labor; ploughs, seeds and the required number of animals for ploughing, ditch building and other purposes were also provided.

This labor was performed on the co-operative plan and all shared alike according to their respective needs. They were happy notwithstanding the rigorous toil required to subdue the desert places, and, as it has been written of them, they "made more progress and suffered less privation in reclaiming the waste lands of the wilderness than did the Spaniards in the garden spots of Mexico and Central America, or the English in the most favored region near the Atlantic seaboard." But let it be understood this was not accomplished without severe suffering.

WHY MORMON COLONIZATION PROSPERED. The reason they were able to obtain such excellent results is that they had a perfect organization and were loyal and obedient to the authority over them, which naturally resulted in complete operation and unity of purpose. Then, again, their ideas and desires were one—*they were united*. They had not come into this promised land for worldly aggrandizement; they were not like the Spaniards, seeking for gold, but to build and establish permanent homes where they could dwell in peace and unmolested worship God according to the dictates of their conscience.

As immigrants arrived in Salt Lake City, from the several states or from foreign shores, they were sent out to colonize and blaze the way for others to follow. Men taken from the looms of England, the shops of Germany and from various other dependent occupations in the cities and towns of Europe, were under the necessity of practically changing the nature of their lives. They were sent out to reclaim the desert wastes and to till the soil and were thus transformed into successful and independent farmers, stockraisers, blacksmiths, and were made free landholders in a land of liberty.

It mattered not if these settlers came from the four corners of the earth, speaking various languages and with trades and occupations as far apart as the two poles, new conditions coupled with the same religious views soon welded them together into one race and people. They learned to think and to speak alike; their aims were the same, their desires mutual; and each was brought by common interest to understand the viewpoint of the rest. Thus they lived in harmony, and each was interested in the progress and welfare of the whole community. Such conditions caused them to forget their nationality, for they became absorbed by their environment, truly becoming a part of the very soil on which they dwelt. They were and are loyal to their adopted country. *Hyphenated Americans* are practically unknown in the Mormon settlements of the Rocky Mountains.

BEST BLOOD OF MANY NATIONS ASSEMBLED IN UTAH. As England was made the great world power that she is by conquest and mingling of Norman, Saxon, and Dane with the native tribes of the British Isles, so also our country has partaken of the *best life blood of many nations,* which has, through intermarriage made her strong.

Likewise in Utah the amalgamation of the races has been even more complete than in the nation at large; for Utah has drawn on nearly every nation under heaven, sifting and gathering from them of their best, and, due to the peculiar circumstances that prevail and unity of purpose, is moulding out of the mixture of blood a *new race* typically American. Her people are strong, mentally, spiritually, and physically. Battling with the elements and contending with many difficulties have made them so.

In patriotism they are the peers of any. They believe this is the land of Zion, a land preserved by the great I Am as an abiding place for the pure in heart. It is to them a land of refuge and liberty to the oppressed of the nations, who have come to a "land choice above all other lands," and to a nation raised up, directed and preserved by Divine Providence.[9] To this land they have come from all parts of the earth, with gladness and with "songs of everlasting joy," to obtain an inheritance for themselves and children that shall endure forever.[10]

PIONEER CO-OPERATIVES AND HOME INDUSTRY

HOME INDUSTRY FLOURISHED AMONG PIONEERS. In the early days of the Church in these valleys, great stress was placed upon industry by President Brigham Young and the other brethren, and it was necessary because our forefathers came here with nothing. They had to work. They had to be industrious. It was essential that they produce the things they needed, and therefore counsel to that extent and in that direction was given to them constantly that they should be *industrious*. They were taught not to be proud in their hearts. They came out here where they could worship the Lord their God and keep his commandments. They were told to be humble as well as to be diligent. They were to make their own garments, and they were to be plain.[11] Oh, I wish we could remember that. I am sorry that we have forgotten.

And President Brigham Young, Heber C. Kimball, and others of the brethren in those early days taught the

---

[9]Ether 2:7-12; D. & C. 98:4-10;   [11]D. & C. 42:40-42.
   101:77-80.
[10]Gen. & Hist. Mag., vol. 7, pp. 14-19;
   D. & C. 133:26-33; Isa. 35; 51:11;
   Jer. 31:12.

people and prevailed upon them to start industries throughout this country; to raise sheep, to gather the wool, to make their own clothes out of that wool; to plant cotton that they might have cotton also to make clothing; to plant flax that they might get linen; to build tanneries that they might tan the hides and make themselves leather, and a thousand other things. We used to have some of these industries here among us, and would still have them if we had been willing to adhere to these counsels that had been given to us in those early days by the authorities of the Church, which we do not do.[12]

HOME INDUSTRY: BULWARK OF STABLE ECONOMY. The early settlers were taught by their leaders to produce, as far as possible, all that they consumed, to be *frugal* and not wasteful of their substance. The establishing of home industries was the text of many a sermon, and following the advice of President Brigham Young to draw from the native elements the necessities of life, to permit no vitiated taste to lead them into expensive indulgence, and "to let home industry produce every article of home consumption"—they engaged in the establishment of many useful and necessary industries. Woolen mills, tanneries, ironworks, sawmills, gristmills, potteries and other industries were established. The people learned to manufacture the articles they used and to raise the provisions they consumed. Their clothing, though plain, was durable and the workmanship of their own hands, and of it they were not ashamed.

We are told that "necessity is the mother of invention." The fact that the people of Utah were at that early day isolated by more than 1,000 miles from the borders of civilization made it necessary for them to be producers of most that they consumed. Alas, in this one particular, in later years after the advent of the continental railroad, this condition was somewhat changed,

[12]Conf. Rep., Apr., 1945, pp. 48-49.

and not for the betterment of the people. Not that the railroad was not a great boon, but it was so much easier to buy articles from the east than it was to manufacture them, and therefore, instead of raising that which they consumed and manufacturing their own apparel, they commenced to receive supplies, in many instances inferior, from abroad.

CO-OPERATIVE MORMON ENTERPRISES. From the time of laying Utah's foundation to the present, co-operation has been a strong feature in every Mormon community, and while this condition has been marred by the closer communication with the outside world and the influx of people of divergent views, yet to a large degree it continues. In pioneer days *houses* were built, *ditches* were dug, *fields* planted, *reservoirs* constructed, and various other community interests cared for on the cooperative plan, *without the aid of money*. There was no money to be had, and such was the interest of the individual in the welfare of all that his time was given gratis in such necessary labor, for he realized that he was bound to reap his portion of the benefits of his toil.

Today it is largely the case that a man who gives his time, even though it be in some labor from which he will receive his portion of the reward, feels that he must be given some monetary consideration for the time he spends. And, thus, due to labor agitation and closer contact with the outside world, with its customs, theories, and established institutions, this excellent and neighborly co-operative system, to a great degree, is changed.

These modern conditions tend to destroy the *unity of spirit* and *common interest* of the individual in the well being of the community and to narrow down the *liberal spirit* in which each member showed his love for his fellow man. *Self aggrandization has increased; community interest and neighborly love have correspondingly diminished.*

Yet, under prevailing conditions, it is hard to see how things can be different in our larger cities where the people are of all religious views and have few interests in common. Co-operation cannot dwell where there is no union—where the people are not one in thought, one in purpose and desire, and where each refuses to labor unselfishly in the common interest of all, or, where the love of money and worldly gain is paramount. In the distant settlements, however, of the Latter-day Saints, and even with exclusive organizations in Salt Lake City, co-operation still exists.[18]

PATRIOTISM AND LOYALTY OF SAINTS

MORMON BATTALION AND PATRIOTISM OF SAINTS. There is not a more patriotic people in the United States than the Latter-day Saints, for they have been weighed in the balance and not found wanting. One of the first things the pioneers did, on entering the Valley of the Great Salt Lake, was to unfurl the Stars and Stripes from Ensign Peak and take possession of the land in the name of the United States, this country at the time being at war with Mexico. Even while the exiled Saints, who had been forced from their homes without one protecting word or action from the government in their behalf, were on their westward march, in the depths of poverty, they raised a battalion to serve in the Mexican War. These troops loyally and cheerfully volunteered and performed their labors faithfully and well.[14]

Thomas H. Benton, principally, and others associated with him—Thomas H. Benton was from the State of Missouri and a very bitter enemy of the Latter-day Saints—prevailed upon the President of the United States to make this trial of the Mormon people who were in the wilderness, asking for a battalion of 500 men. Mr. Benton felt, I am sure, positive in his own mind that under

---

[18]*Gen. & Hist. Mag.*, vol. 7, pp. 19-20.   [14]*Era*, vol. 10, p. 102.

the conditions President Brigham Young would refuse, and with that refusal he would place himself apparently as an enemy of the United States, and further persecution could be heaped upon the Latter-day Saints resulting in their destruction.

But the battalion was raised. There was no opposition. President Young said if he could not raise men enough, he would arm the women, but the government should have its battalion. And so it was furnished, and made its march to the Pacific coast.[15]

BE SUBJECT TO THE POWERS THAT BE. Any member of this Church who will not sustain the established laws of the land is not only disloyal as a citizen of the government, but he is disloyal to his Church and disloyal to God. We should understand it, and above all else we should be law-abiding and live in righteousness with each other, with our neighbors, and worship the living God in the spirit of truth and righteousness and at the same time have loyal hearts to the nations which bear rule and will bear rule until he comes whose right it is to reign.[16]

EARLY DAY ANTI-MORMONS IN UTAH. There was in Utah a class of individuals who spent the greater part of their time in circulating wicked and malicious reports about the saints, threatening their lives, committing crimes and attempting to make the saints their scapegoats.

The officers of the law were general government officials appointed by the President of the United States, and I am sorry to say, some of these were among the chief villifiers of the people. The most damnable and bloodthirsty falsehoods were concocted and served up to the people of the United States to stir them up to anger against the despised Mormons.

Almost every crime that was committed within 1,000 miles of Salt Lake City was charged to the leaders

---

[15]*Church News*, Aug. 7, 1937, p. 7.   [16]*Church News*, Feb. 6, 1932, p. 8; D. & C. 58:20-22.

of the Mormon people and became the foundation of a multitude of anti-Mormon publications that still flood the world. Because of these false and highly colored tales, in 1857 the government of the United States sent an army to suppress in Utah *a rebellion that never existed,* and forced the saints to defend themselves. When the government found out how it had blundered, it was humiliated.[17]

---

[17]*Blood Atonement and the Origin of Plural Marriage,* p. 38.

[END OF VOLUME III]

INDEX

A

Aaron: See Sons of Aaron.

Aaron, Aaronic Priesthood conferred upon, 85-86.

Aaronic Order: See Aaronic Priesthood.

Aaronic Priesthood: See Priesthood.

Aaronic Priesthood, administration restrictions of, 176; ancient Israel possessor of, 85-86; baptism followed receipt of, 90; continuation of, to Christ's coming, 86; duties of holders of, 111-114; future continuance of, 91-92; Israel retained powers of, 83-84; John's part in restoration of, 88-92; Law of Moses administered by, 83-84; Melchizedek Priesthood holders also possessors of, 103-104; no oath and covenant incident to, 141; Oliver Cowdery's testimony of restoration of, 99-100; presiding bishop holds keys of, 92-93; reconferral of, 91; restoration of, 87-92; temporal affairs governed by, 92; temporal matters concern of, 103.

Abominations, nations drunken with, 277-278.

Abraham, all nations blessed through, 246-247; blessings of seed of, 244-264; covenant that extends to seed of, 245; Lord's covenant with, 244-245; patriarchal status of, 160; plea of, for Sodom and Gomorrah, 39; priesthood continues in lineage of, 87; priesthood held by, 82; righteous become heirs of, 249-250; Urim and Thummim had by, 222-223.

Adam, baptism of, 82; coming of Christ to, at Adam-ondi-Ahman, 13-14; first apostasy began in days of, 265; keys and priesthood held by, 81-82; Patriarchal Order began with, 160; theocratic government had by, 313-314.

Adam-ondi-Ahman, Adam bestows blessings at, 163-164; coming of Lord to, 13-14; Zion and Eden same as, 74.

Administering to Sick: See Administrations.

Administering to Sick, instructions relative to, 172-180, 183.

Administrations, ancient performance of, 172-174; forgiveness of sins through, 177-178; instructions relative to, 174-180; participation of women in, 176-178; proper procedures in, 176; repeated anointings not needed in, 178-179; restoration of, 174-175; sick not dedicated to Lord in, 179-180.

Adoption, becoming of Israel by, 245-247.

Affliction, disobedience cause of, 28-29.

Allegory, *Bible* abounds in, 189-190.

Allen, Capt. James, Mormon Battalion requested by, 344-345.

Allenby, General, capture of Jerusalem by 258-259.

America, choice status of, 321-324; constitutional guarantees of, 324-326; Lord governed settling of, 324; petition for exploration of, 333-334; refuge provided by, 322-323; wickedness will bring judgments upon, 321-322.

Amorites, Lord's destruction of, 39-40.

Amusements, encouragement of, if proper, 307-308; proper and improper use of, 301-303.

Anarchy, prediction of, 316-317.

Ancestry, patriarchal blessings reveal identity of, 248-249.

Ancient of Days, status of Adam as, 13-14.

Angels, Aaronic Priesthood holds keys of administering of, 84; reaping of earth by, 15-18.

Animals, future sacrifice of, 94; millennial and paradisiacal status of, 57-58.

Anointing: See Administrations.

Anointing, instructions on, 174-176; repetitions of, not proper, 178-179.

Anointing Oil: See Consecrated Oil.

Anointing Oil, meridian of time use of, 182-183; rebellious Israel denied use of, 182.

Anthon, Professor, Isaiah prophecy fulfilled by, 213-214.

Anti-Mormons, early day bitterness of, 361-362.

Apostasy, Adam's day saw beginning of, 265; *Bible* printing resisted because of, 184-188; broad-mindedness leads to, 298-299; chains of darkness result from, 295; christendom in state of, 271-279, 282-288; Church loses

Original Sin, apostate doctrine of, 284.
Other Sheep, *Book of Mormon* fulfils prophecy of, 214-215.

P

Pagan Churches, some truth in, 271.
Paganism, gospel overcome by, 269-270.
Page, Hiram, false revelations of, 75-76.
Palestine, Dr. Herbert Samuel, governor of, 259; Jewish home status of, 260; return of Jews to, 258-262.
Palmyra, arrival of Smith family in, 241-242.
Papal Inquisition, *Bible* reading curtailed by, 186-187.
Paradisiacal Earth: See Millennium.
Paradisiacal Earth, nature of life on, 55-60.
Paradisiacal Glory, millennial nature of, 56-58.
Parents, providing of libraries duty of, 204-205; recreation of children supervised by, 302-303.
Parliament, possession of scriptures forbidden by, 185-186.
Pastors, nature of office of, 108-109.
Patriarchal Blessings, conditional nature of promises in, 171; fathers pronouncement of, 172; nature and purpose of, 170; Negroes recipients of, 172; preparation for giving of, 171; sacred nature of, 172; samples of lineage revealed by, 248-249; tribal ancestry revealed by, 248-249.
Patriarchal Keys, Joseph Smith Sr., holder of, 162-164.
Patriarchal Lineage, latter-day designation of, 162-169; law of, 160-169.
Patriarchal Office, hereditary nature of, 160-169; nature and service of, 169-172; William Smith never sustained in, 166-168.
Patriarchal Order: See Melchizedek Priesthood; Priesthood.
Patriarchal Order, ancient descent of, 160-162; ancient Israel lost system of, 161-162; ancient nature of, 104; historical development of, 83.
Patriarchal Promises, conditional nature of, 171.
Patriarchs, Joseph Smith Sr., first chosen among, 162-164; lineage declared by, 171-172; nature of office of, 104-106; position of evangelists as, 108.
Patriarch to Church, Asael Smith did not serve as, 168; hereditary nature of office of, 160; latter-day lineage of, 162-169; position of, as father to Israel, 169; William Smith did not serve as, 166-168; worthiness and lineage prerequisites to office of, 169-170.
Patriotism, response of Mormon Battalion evidence of, 360-361; saints excel in, 360-362.
Patten, David W., apostolic call of, 150; quoted—nature and number of dispensations, 96-97.
Paul, apostasy foretold by, 268-269; apostasy teachings of, 283; Jewish status of, 263-264.
Peace, earth bereft of, 48-52; elders insure existence of, 7-8; fear basis of modern search for, 50-51; futility of insincere prayers for, 51; gospel rejection brings loss of, 50-51; olive oil an emblem of, 180-181; second coming will be beginning of, 43; wickedness prevents gaining of, 49-51.
Penalty, breaking priesthood covenant leads to, 141-142.
Perils, escape of saints from, 43-44.
Perpetual Emigration Fund, establishment of, 352.
Persecution, gospel cause of, 327; martyrdom of Prophet did not bring end to, 336-337.
Persecutions, saints subjected to, 327-329.
Pestilence, latter-day existence of, 19-21.
Peter, apostasy foretold by, 268-269.
Peter, James, and John, Elijah gave sealing keys to, 128-129; First Presidency consisted of, 152-153; keys of kingdom restored by, 98-102; Melchizedek Priesthood keys restored by, 125; Melchizedek Priesthood restored by, 139.
Peterson, Ziba, Lamanite mission of, 76.
Phelps, W. W., exploration participation of, 335; printing operations of, 192-193.
Philosophies, apostate status of, 288-291.
Philosophies (false), prevalence of, 274-275.
Plagues, disobedience, cause of, 27-28; repentance enables escape from, 44.
Plates: See Gold Plates.
Plural Marriage, time of first revelation of, 197-198.
Pioneer Heritage, greatness of, 329.
Pioneer Immigration, scope of, 353-354.